# BIG BOOK OF Bible Story Fun

# HOW TO MAKE CLEAN COPIES FROM THIS BOOK

**You may make copies of portions of this book with a clean conscience if**

- you (or someone in your organization) are the original purchaser;
- you are using the copies you make for a noncommercial purpose (such as teaching or promoting your ministry) within your church or organization;
- you follow the instructions provided in this book.

**However, it is ILLEGAL for you to make copies if**

- you are using the material to promote, advertise or sell a product or service other than for ministry fund-raising;
- you are using the material in or on a product for sale; or
- you or your organization are not the original purchaser of this book.

By following these guidelines you help us keep our products affordable.

Thank you,

*Gospel Light*



Editorial Staff
**Founder,** Henrietta Mears • **Publisher Emeritus,** William T. Greig • **Publisher, Children's Curriculum and Resources,** Lynnette Pennings, M.A. • **Senior Consulting Publisher,** Dr. Elmer L. Towns • **Managing Editor,** Sheryl Haystead • **Senior Consulting Editor,** Wesley Haystead, M.S.Ed. • **Senior Editor, Biblical and Theological Issues,** Bayard Taylor, M.Div. • **Editorial Team,** Mandy Abbas, Mary Gross, Karen McGraw • **Designers,** Zelle Olson, Carolyn Thomas

# Contents

# Picture This!

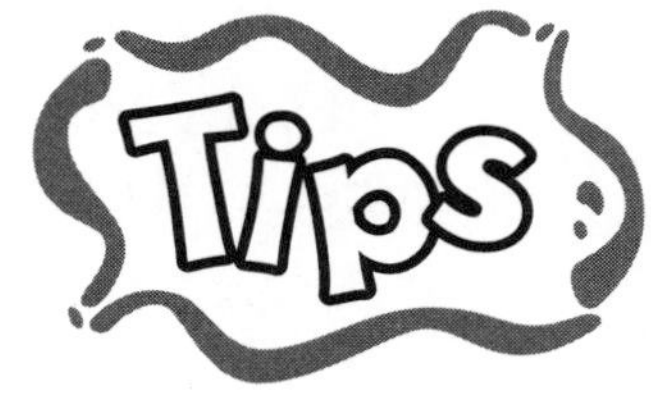


Children will learn and understand Bible stories in a fresh way as they become personally involved in "drawing through" the stories. You'll find it easy to keep your students' interest!

## Draw It!

You can do it! Even if you don't have an artistic bone in your body, the sketches that illustrate each story are designed to be user-friendly for easy drawing.

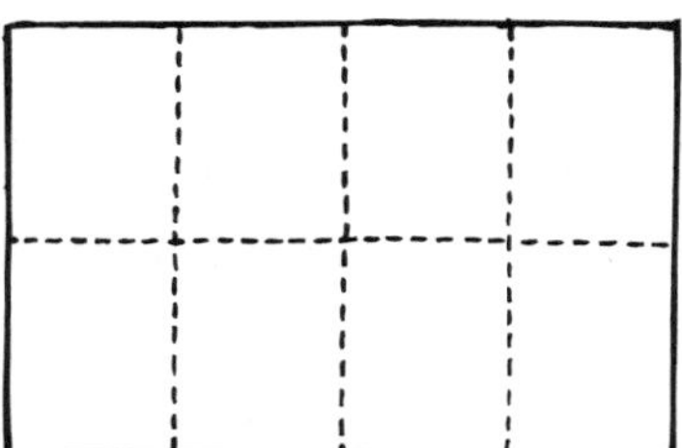

Before telling the story, ask students to divide their drawing paper into eight (or more, if needed) sections either by drawing lines on their papers or by folding their papers in half three times.

It's best to draw these sketches as you talk. However, if students have difficulty drawing along with you or if you have difficulty sketching while you talk, sketch before each paragraph and then encourage children to copy your sketch and to listen to find out what that sketch is about.

A variety of drawing materials and equipment will work for you as a teacher. Consider these options: butcher paper taped to wall, large pad on an easel, chalkboard, white board or overhead projector. Whatever option you choose, make sure that all students can clearly see your sketches. Varying the drawing materials from week to week will help to keep student interest high.

### What drawing materials does the student need?

Provide a commercially produced sketch pad for each child or make individual sketch pads by stapling sheets of newsprint to poster board (see sketch). Students will enjoy personalizing their sketch-pad covers. Make sketchbooks for every 13-week quarter or one large sketchbook for the entire year.

If sketch pads are not possible, choose from these ideas: paper on clipboards (with extras for visitors), butcher paper taped to tabletops, sheets of paper taped to wall, sheets of paper that are collected weekly and compiled into a book (teacher makes copies of her drawings for absentees) or rolls of adding-machine tape (child draws every week to make a personal "big picture" mural).

### What are some tips and alternatives to drawing the sketches as I talk?

- Another teacher or an older child can draw each sketch as you tell the story.
- You may lightly sketch the illustrations ahead of time and then copy over them with a felt marker as you tell the story.
- Draw the sketches ahead of time on large sheets of paper. Flip to the picture of each new sketch as you tell the story.

## How can I help younger students draw?

• If your group is mainly younger students, reduce the number of sketches you make.

• Draw a bit more slowly.

• Lead students to complete their drawings before you tell each paragraph, encouraging children to listen to find out why they drew the sketch.

• Pair older students with younger ones.

• Remember that the point of sketching is not to produce great art; it's to involve children in remembering the Bible story. If a child seems to doodle, don't worry. What he or she is drawing will still aid the child's memory!

## What are some options for older students?

• If your group is mainly older students, encourage them to expand and personalize their sketches.

• If the story is a familiar one, invite students to tell the story action as you draw sketches. Supplement story details as needed.

• Some students might enjoy making a dictionary of sketches to supplement the ones given in the lesson.

• Invite an older student to photocopy his or her page to send to an absentee.

## What are some enrichment tips?

• If a child says "Wait! I'm not finished!" remind everyone that there will be time to copy sketches in greater detail when the story is over. Remind children, too, that their sketches are their own art. There is no wrong way to do them!

• Encourage children who finish early or seem bored to add more details to their sketches. **You might add more people to the crowd, Jana. I see Ron has added another tree.** As children personalize and expand their sketches, they will increase their enjoyment and understanding.

## How can I use the drawing technique with other Bible stories?

• Look in each section of the story for one object, keyword, action or person that could be depicted in a simple sketch.

• Make use of letters, shapes and numbers to create your simple sketches.

• Make a sketch that can be added to throughout the whole or part of the story (for example see "Solomon Builds the Temple," p. 76).

• Look through other drawing stories in *The Big Book of Bible Story Fun* for ideas—you may even find a simple way to make the exact sketch you need.

# Let Your Hands Do the Talking

Children will learn and understand Bible stories in a fresh way as they become personally involved in "signing their way through" the stories. Even during this sitting time, you will find it easy to keep your students' interest! Some children in your group may already know some sign language, and throughout the course all children will become familiar with specific signs which are frequently repeated ("God," "Jesus," "pray," etc.).

## Sign It!

You can do it! Even if you have never tried to use sign language before, the illustrations are designed for easy use.

• Before telling the story, practice the signs yourself until you feel confident demonstrating them.

• The task of demonstrating and leading signs may also be given to a helper, an older student or even a group of interested students in your class. Signs for the next week's story may be given out ahead of time, so helpers may practice.

• Before you begin the story with the question in the upper right-hand box, ask students to briefly practice each sign with you. Encourage children to listen carefully, so they know when to make the appropriate sign.

• Make flash cards or write the signed words on the chalkboard. Hold up cards or point to words on board to cue students.

• Teach one sign to a small group of students. Those students practice that sign and then stand and demonstrate the sign whenever they hear that word.

### How can I help younger students accurately learn signs?

• If your group consists mainly of younger students, practice each sign several times before the story is told. Pause during the story to sign a bit more slowly. Another option with younger students is to choose fewer signs to use.

• Lead students to make the sign; then encourage them to listen for the word they signed.

• Pair older students with younger ones so that younger ones may more easily see how signs are made.

• Help children understand that it is acceptable for a student to sit and watch until he or she feels comfortable doing the signs.

• If the process becomes too distracting, don't deliberately teach the signs to students. Simply make each sign as you tell the story, without pausing or commenting.

• Remember that the point of signing is not necessarily to produce ASL experts, although this may well be a side benefit. The purpose is to involve children in remembering the Bible story. If a child's signing seems less than perfect, don't worry. What he or she is doing will still aid the child's memory!

## What are some options for older students?

• If your group consists mainly of older students, encourage them to expand the number of words signed in a paragraph (based on other signs they have learned).

• If the story is a familiar one, invite students to tell the story action as you or a helper signs. Supplement both signs and story details as needed.

• Some students might enjoy making or referring to a dictionary of signs to supplement the ones given in the lesson.

• For a fresh review idea, after telling the story, make the sign for the first segment of the story. Students retell the part of the story represented by the sign. Continue until story has been reviewed.

## How can I use the signing technique with other Bible stories?

• Look in each section of the Bible story for a keyword. Find the sign for that word in a sign-language book or on the Internet.

• Look in each Bible story section for action words that you could depict with a simple motion, instead of using an actual sign-language sign.

• Look through other sign-language stories in *The Big Book of Bible Story Fun* for signs that you could use in your story, and think of any other signs or motions your students might know from worship songs.

• Practice whatever signs or motions you decide on, and make small sketches to use as reminders while telling the story, if needed.

# Shape a Story

Maximize a student's learning and story participation fun through story dough sculpting. Children will understand Bible stories in a fresh way as they keep their hands busy molding play dough during each Bible story. Even during this sitting time, you'll find it easy to keep your students' interest!

## A Step-by-Step Guide to Using Play Dough

To some teachers, using play dough may be a terrific idea; for others, it may be terrifying! But with a little preparation, you'll become an expert in using dough as a Bible story teaching tool! (Note: If dough is not possible in your church, provide chenille wire, yarn or string with which children may form shapes.)

### What do I need?

• Provide hand wipes or a dishpan of soapy water and paper towels for kids to use in cleaning their hands before and after dough use.

• Provide a paper plate or waxed-paper square for each student ("Waxies" are available in bulk at restaurant supply stores). Or simply cover tables with plastic tablecloths that can be folded up and then shaken outdoors. Plastic tablecloths may also be placed on the floor. Students may sit around the edges of the cloths, or cloths may be spread beneath tables where students will work.

• Provide approximately ¼ cup (2 oz.) of play dough for each student (a ball of dough about the size of a child's fist) and a resealable bag or small clean container such as a recycled yogurt container. To prevent sharing of germs, label each container with the student's name. (Optional: The first time you tell a story using dough, provide ingredients, so every student makes his or her own dough, preparing extra for future visitors as well.) Periodically throughout the year, provide a fresh batch of play dough. Refrigerate dough between sessions if needed.

• Occasionally provide flat toothpicks, pencils or craft sticks as tools to vary the ways students model dough during the Bible story. A variety of these tools are suggested when appropriate.

### What's the plan?

• Ask the story-related question in the box at the beginning of the Bible story to spark student interest. As students give their answers, helpers or older students distribute labeled dough containers. (Optional: Students may pick up their own dough as they come to the Bible story location.)

• Seat students so that everyone can see a teacher, helper or older student molding the dough objects. For small groups, push tables into a V shape, so everyone can see the teacher seated at the point of the V. For larger groups, seat helpers around the circle, so a group of students can see the helper's hands clearly. Students will be more likely to follow along with you if they can see the hands of someone who is molding the object.

• Redirect attention to the activity at hand if a student begins using play dough in disruptive ways. **John, have you made a donkey yet? Let me see yours! That's an interesting donkey! Thank you for sharing it.** When students know you are interested in what they are doing, they will be more likely to be making the item for that story section and be ready to show their work.

• Collect play dough at the end of the Bible story. Students place dough in their own containers, and then helpers put the containers away. That way, the teacher is able to continue with the story conclusion and discussion questions without interrupting the flow of the Bible story.

## How do I keep the lesson fresh for all ages?

• Expect that younger students will make fewer objects than older students. Even though younger students may only play with their dough while you tell the Bible story, the activity still helps them keep hands in one place and holds their attention. You may want to allow younger students time to play with their dough before giving instructions to make story objects.

• Encourage older students to make more objects or more complex objects to keep their interest high. Don't worry that older students may grow tired of dough play (we've never heard of it happening yet!). Rather, enlist them as your allies: Before class, give copies of the story to older students. Invite them to be demonstrators of the illustrated dough items.

• When it's time to replace dough, invite students to make and take home special sculptures instead of throwing old dough away.

• For variety, provide two colors of dough for students to use in making objects.

## How can I use play dough with other Bible stories?

• Look in the Bible story for several objects, letters, keywords, facial expressions or actions that can be depicted with play dough. Look through other dough stories in *The Big Book of Bible Story Fun* for ideas.

• Think of a simple way to describe how to form the dough shapes you have chosen. Balls (made by rolling play dough in between palms) can be used for faces or round objects. Ropes (made by rolling play dough against the table or work surface) can be used to form letters or shapes.

• To create add-on scenes, instruct students to divide dough into the needed number of portions at the beginning of the story.

• Bring tools such as plastic forks or knives, straws and toothpicks for students to use in creatively making dough objects.

## What kind of play dough is best?

• A pliable dough that can be easily manipulated by students is best. As often as it's needed (at least every two months), make or purchase a fresh batch of dough. Keep in mind that play dough will eventually dry out, get dirty and even disappear by bits and pieces!

• Purchase commercially made play dough (some come in containers with individual portions) or make one of the recipes on pages 11-12.

• Ask older students or parents of students to make the dough as a service project.

# Dough Recipes

## Salt and Flour Dough

**Ingredients**
2 parts flour
1 part salt
1 tablespoon alum for every 2 cups flour
Food coloring
Water

**Utensils and equipment**
Mixing bowl
Large spoon
Breadboard
Resealable bags or airtight containers

Measure ingredients; mix dry ingredients well. Add coloring to water as desired. Slowly pour colored water into dry ingredients; mix and add water until dough forms a ball around spoon. Knead dough on floured board. If dough is too soft, add more flour. If dough is too stiff, slowly add more water. Divide dough into portions the size of a child's fist; package each portion in a resealable bag or container, labeling each with a student's name and leaving some unlabeled for use by visitors.

## Salt, Flour and Cornstarch Dough

**Ingredients**
1 and 1/2 cups flour
1 cup cornstarch
1 cup salt
Food coloring
1 cup warm water

**Utensils and equipment**
Mixing bowl
Large spoon
Breadboard
Resealable bags or airtight containers

Mix dry ingredients; then add food coloring to warm water. Slowly pour colored water into dry ingredients; mix and add water until dough forms a ball around spoon. Knead dough on floured board. If dough is sticky, dust with flour. If dough is stiff, slowly add water. Divide dough into portions the size of a child's fist; package each portion in a resealable bag or container, labeling each with a student's name and leaving some unlabeled for use by visitors.

## Sand Dough

**Ingredients**
1 cup sand
1⁄2 cup cornstarch
1 teaspoon powdered alum
3⁄4 cup hot water

**Utensils and equipment**
Large pot
Wooden spoon
Heating element
Resealable bags or airtight containers

Mix dry ingredients in pot. Add hot water and stir vigorously. Cook over medium heat until thick, stirring constantly. After dough has cooled, divide dough into portions the size of a child's fist; package each portion in a resealable bag or container, labeling each with a student's name and leaving some unlabeled for use by visitors.

## Sawdust Dough

**Ingredients**
2 parts fine sawdust
(any kind except redwood)
1 part flour
Water

**Utensils and equipment**
Large bowl or bucket
Wooden spoon
Breadboard
Resealable bags or
airtight containers

Mix dry ingredients well. Add water a little at a time, stirring until mixture reaches a stiff but pliable consistency. Add more flour and water if dough is too crumbly. Knead dough until it becomes elastic. Divide dough into portions the size of a child's fist; package each portion in a resealable bag or container, labeling each with a student's name and leaving some unlabeled for use by visitors.

## Dough Options

- Add cake coloring paste instead of food coloring to dough to create more vibrant colors.
- Add unsweetened Kool-Aid to dough to add both color and fruit scent.
- Add drops of essential oils (orange, peppermint, etc.) or small amounts of spice to dough to create interesting scents.

# Leading a Child to Christ

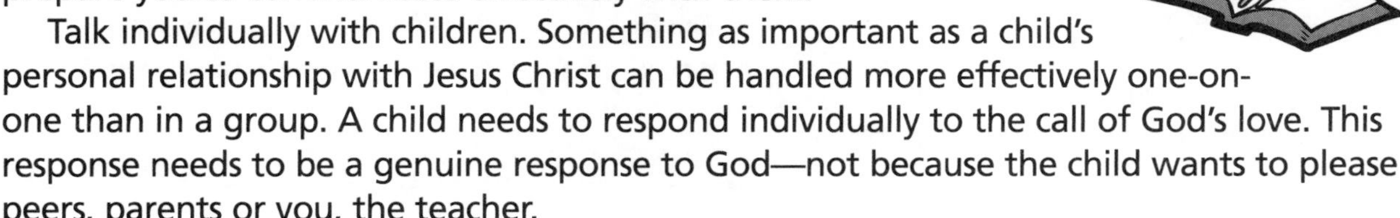

One of the greatest privileges of serving in Sunday School is to help children become members of God's family. Some children, especially those from Christian homes, may be ready to believe in Jesus Christ as their Savior earlier than others. Ask God to prepare the children in your class to receive the good news about Jesus and prepare you to communicate effectively with them.

Talk individually with children. Something as important as a child's personal relationship with Jesus Christ can be handled more effectively one-on-one than in a group. A child needs to respond individually to the call of God's love. This response needs to be a genuine response to God—not because the child wants to please peers, parents or you, the teacher.

Follow these basic steps in talking simply with children about how to become members of God's family. The evangelism booklet *God Loves You!* (available from Gospel Light) is an effective guide to follow. Show the child what God says in His Word. Ask the questions suggested to encourage thinking and comprehension.

**1. God wants you to become His child.** (See John 1:12.) **Do you know why God wants you in His family?** (See 1 John 4:8.)

**2. You and all the people in the world have done wrong things.** (See Romans 3:23.) **The Bible word for doing wrong is "sin." What do you think should happen to us when we sin?** (See Romans 6:23.)

**3. God loves you so much He sent His Son to die on the cross for your sins. Because Jesus never sinned, He is the only One who can take the punishment for your sins.** (See 1 Corinthians 15:3; 1 John 4:14.) **The Bible tells us that God raised Jesus from the dead and that He is alive forever.**

**4. Are you sorry for your sins? Do you believe Jesus died to be your Savior? If you do believe and you are sorry for your sins, God forgives all your sins.** (See 1 John 1:9.)

**When you talk to God, tell Him that you believe He gave His Son, Jesus Christ, to take your punishment. Also tell God you are sorry for your sins. Tell Him that He is a great and wonderful God. It is easy to talk to God. He is ready to listen. What you are going to tell Him is something He has been waiting to hear.**

**5. The Bible says that when you believe in Jesus, God's Son, you receive God's gift of eternal life. This gift makes you a child of God. This means God is with you now and forever.** (See John 3:16.)

Give your pastor the names of those who make decisions to become members of God's family. Encourage the child to tell his or her family about the decision. Children who make decisions need follow-up to help them grow in Christ.

**NOTE:** The Bible uses many terms and images to express the concept of salvation. Children often do not understand or may develop misconceptions about these terms, especially terms that are highly symbolic. (Remember the trouble Nicodemus, a respected teacher, had in trying to understand the meaning of being "born again"?) Many people talk with children about "asking Jesus into your heart." The literal-minded child is likely to develop strange ideas from the imagery of those words. The idea of being a child of God (see John 1:12) is perhaps the simplest portrayal the New Testament provides.

# God's Never-Ending Story

## Materials

Drawing materials/equipment for teacher and each student.

## Tell the Story

As you tell each part of the story, draw each sketch. Students copy your sketches.

***What's your favorite story from the Bible?***

***Today we'll find out how you're part of God's never-ending story!***

1. God's never-ending story began with God creating the world and the first people, Adam and Eve. Even though Adam and Eve sinned, God loved them and promised to send a Savior who would take the punishment for people's sins. God gave a special country to a man named Abraham and called him to be the beginning of His people—the people through whom God would send the Savior.

1. Draw earth. Print "SAVIOR."

2. After God's people lived in Egypt for 400 years, God sent Moses to bring them back to their special land. Because God loved them, He sent judges and kings to lead them. He sent prophets to tell them God's messages—messages telling them to obey God, telling them about the future and telling them that God had promised to send a Savior.

2. Crown from "O" and "V"s, scroll from "S"s. Add "PROMISED" to "SAVIOR."

3. And many years later, what happened? The Savior God had promised came to earth! Jesus was born! When Jesus grew up, He taught people about God. He healed sick people and even brought dead people back to life. But some people hated Jesus. Jesus let them kill Him so that He could take the punishment for all the wrong things people do—their sins. And Jesus came back to life! When He went back to heaven, He sent the Holy Spirit to help all the people who believe in Him.

3. Draw cross around "PROMISED" and "SAVIOR." Add "JESUS."

4. This is the good news, or gospel, that the New Testament tells about. All the stories we read about Jesus' life are part of the New Testament books called the Gospels.

4. Print "GOOD NEWS"; add happy face.

5. The rest of the New Testament books tell about people who listened to this good news and became part of God's family. Many of these books are letters written to the people in the first churches. These letters tell God's family about God's plan and how to live as God wants them to.

5. Envelope and stamp from rectangles; address it "To: God's Family."

6. For instance, one of Paul's letters tells how God's family is like the parts of a person's body—every part is important and all the parts have to work together. "Love each other," Paul wrote. And Paul also wrote that God's plan is so wonderful that no one can imagine what God has prepared for those who love Him!

6. Draw eye, hand, ear. Add heart and face with thought balloon.

7. The last book of the Bible tells about all the things that will happen when Jesus comes back to earth. Everyone will know He is the greatest King!

7. Crown from "O" and "V"s. Add "JESUS."

8. But the story doesn't end there! Because Jesus died to take the punishment for our sins, we can all become part of God's family and live with Him forever. Anyone who asks Jesus to forgive his or her sins will be forgiven. And anyone who asks can become a member of God's family.

That's the best news in the world! If you have asked Jesus to forgive your sins and make you part of God's family, that makes YOU part of God's big picture! The big picture of God's love just keeps getting BIGGER!

8. Frame from rectangle and "3"s. Add happy faces and names of students.

## Conclude the Story

**The whole story of God's big picture is about how much He loves us—and everyone in the world! What are some ways God shows He loves us?** (Gives us friends and family. Forgives our sins. Hears and answers our prayers. Gives us courage to obey Him.) **What are some ways we can help others learn about God's love?** (Pray for them. Tell them about God's love. Tell them what Jesus did to show love.)

Talk with interested students about God's love and salvation (see "Leading a Child to Christ" on p. 13).

**Genesis 1—2:2**

# God Creates the World

## Materials

Drawing materials/equipment for teacher and each student.

***Of all the things in the world, what part would you have liked to have seen God create?***

***Today we're going to talk about how everything came to life!***

## Tell the Story

As you tell each part of the story, draw each sketch. Students copy your sketches. (Optional: Invite students to tell details of this familiar story.)

1. Before God made the world, there was nothing—no houses, no people, no animals, no sun or sky or land. It was just dark and empty. But God was there! And God decided to make something wonderful.

1. Draw dark scribbles.

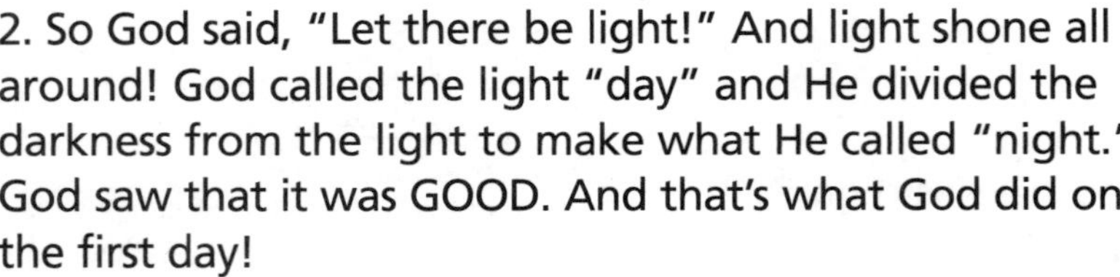

2. So God said, "Let there be light!" And light shone all around! God called the light "day" and He divided the darkness from the light to make what He called "night." God saw that it was GOOD. And that's what God did on the first day!

2. Use "M"s to draw burst of light; add "1."

3. The next day, God said, "Let the sky and the water be made separate from each other." Now there was water below the sky and a sky that arched over the water. And that's what God did on the second day!

3. Sky from curved strokes; clouds from "3"s; "U"s for water. Add "2."

4. On the third day, God spoke and the waters gathered together to make rivers, lakes and oceans. Once the water was moved around, dry land appeared. Now there were mountains and hills, deep canyons and dry deserts. God had shaped a beautiful world. But God was not finished yet! There still was not anything on the earth that was ALIVE.

4. Draw "M"s for mountains. Add "3."

5. So God said, "Let there be all sorts of grasses and plants and trees." Grass sprang up. Flowers bloomed—red, yellow, pink, purple—every color you can think of! Trees of all shapes and sizes grew. Berry bushes and pumpkin vines grew beautiful fruit and bright orange pumpkins. God looked at all the work He had done. And God saw that it was GOOD!

5. Flowers and bushes from "3"s, berries and pumpkins from "O"s.

6. Next, God made a special bright light and put it in the sky to shine during the day. We call that light the sun! And He made the moon and stars to shine at night. God did a lot of things on the fourth day!

6. Sun from circle and "M"s; moon from "C"s, stars from triangles. Add "4."

7. On the fifth day, God filled the water and the sky with living creatures. He put fish and sharks, octopuses and whales into the oceans. Birds flew through the sky. Some birds were tiny; some birds were BIG. And they were every color you can think of!

7. Octopus from upside-down "U" and "S"s. Add "5."

8. On the sixth day, God made land animals. He made little mice and middle-sized anteaters and laughing hyenas—and great big polar bears and water buffalo and even dinosaurs! Now the world was a hopping, buzzing, galloping, wiggling, lively place! This was all very wonderful. But the day was not over yet. The next thing God did was even more amazing.

8. Mouse from triangle, "C," and "S." Add ears, feet and eye.

9. God created a MAN. God called the man Adam. Later, God made a woman called Eve. God made them different from the animals. They could think and make things; they could talk to each other and to God. God loved them. They were His special friends! Adam and Eve lived in a beautiful garden that was full of the wonderful things God had made.

9. Stick figures. Add heart and "6."

10. God looked at the whole world He had created. It was exactly as He wanted it to be! He looked around at everything and said, "This is GOOD!"

10. Draw eyes. Add "G" and "D."

## Conclude the Story

**What did God say about the world He made?** (It was good.) **What made people different from the animals and plants?** (They could love God. They could think and talk.) **How did God feel about Adam and Eve?** (He loved them.)

**When we look at the animals and plants, the moon and the stars, we remember that God is very strong. He can do anything! And what we see around us helps us know He loves us. He wants us to be His special friends, like Adam and Eve were! God made this world to show His love.**

**Genesis 2:4—3**

# God Creates People

## Materials

Drawing materials/equipment for teacher and each student.

## Tell the Story

As you tell each part of the story, draw each sketch. Students copy your sketches.

***What's your favorite animal God made? What was the last thing God made?***

***Today we're going to create some stick people on paper to tell about what happened in the garden of Eden.***

1. Of everything God made, He made people last. The Bible says God took dirt from the ground and formed a body from the dirt. Then, God breathed His breath into the body. And that body became a LIVING PERSON!

1. Draw stick figure. Add face.

2. God named that person Adam. He put Adam in a special garden called the Garden of Eden. And He gave Adam important work to do! Adam took care of the garden and named all the animals. That must have been fun! But God knew it wasn't good for Adam to be alone. So God made another person! When Adam saw her he said, "At last! She is someone like me! I'll call her woman."

2. Draw second stick figure; add small circles for hair.

3. Adam and Eve must have loved living in the garden. They talked with God every evening. And there was lots to eat! In fact, Adam and Eve could eat from any plant or tree in the garden except ONE. God told Adam, "Do not eat from the tree of the knowledge of good and evil. You'll die if you do!" God loved Adam and Eve and wanted them to live and be happy. So He made this one rule for them to obey.

3. Flowers and tree from "3"s.

4. Adam and Eve obeyed this rule UNTIL the day a beautiful snake came along. The snake was really God's enemy, Satan, in disguise. Satan wanted to destroy God's plan and the people God loved so much. The snake slyly asked Eve if God REALLY had said they couldn't eat from that one tree. The snake told Eve that it would be good to try that fruit. He said eating that fruit wouldn't make them die. It would make them like God!

4. Snake from 2 "S"s. Fruit from letter "O."

5. Eve saw the beautiful fruit; it looked DELICIOUS! She reached. She picked the fruit off the tree and took a bite. At that moment, everything changed. A person had disobeyed God's one rule. That's called sin. Eve gave the fruit to Adam and he ate some, too. Now they had BOTH disobeyed!

5. On either side of fruit, draw faces from "C"s and upside down "7"s.

6. When they heard God coming, Adam and Eve HID from God, who loved them and had made them to share His wonderful creation! God called to them. Finally Adam answered and told God that he was afraid. God asked if Adam had broken His one rule. Adam blamed Eve. He said it was Eve's fault. Then Eve blamed the snake.

God was very sad. Adam and Eve were certainly sad. Adam and Eve had to leave the beautiful garden. Now thorns and weeds would grow. There would be pain and death.

6. Draw 2 sad faces.

7. But God still loved Adam and Eve! God made a VERY important promise. He promised to send a special person who would put an end to all the wrong things that Satan had brought into the world. And God's promise came true many, many years later. The person He sent was JESUS!

7. Write "PROMISE." Add "JESUS."

## Conclude the Story

**Who convinced Eve to disobey?** (Satan.) **What happened as a result? What did God promise He would do to stop sin from ruining the world He had made?** (Send Jesus—the only One who could stop Satan.)

**Even though Adam and Eve had disobeyed God, God still loved them. And even when we do wrong, it's good to know that God's love is bigger than ANY sin!**

**Genesis 4:1-16**

# Cain and Abel

## Before the Story

Guide students to briefly practice signs for underlined words.

## Tell the Story

As you tell the story, lead students in responding as shown when you say the underlined words.

***What kind of jobs do you have in your family?***

***Today we're going to hear about two brothers who had very different jobs and very different attitudes!***

1. The very first baby born to the very first people was named Cain. Adam and Eve were thankful to God for their son. Later, they had a second son. They named this baby Abel. As the boys grew up, they learned how to work and help provide their family with food.

1. Baby: Rock crossed arms.

2. As the two brothers grew, they learned how to do different kinds of jobs. Cain, the older brother, became a farmer. He worked with plants and grew food for his family to eat. Abel, the younger brother, grew up to be a shepherd. He took care of the animals that his family used for milk, meat, wool and skins.

2. Grew: Palms face each other; hands flip positions.

3. It came time to give an offering of thanks to the Lord for all the good things He had given Adam and Eve's family. Since the brothers were grown up now, they brought their own offerings to God. Since he was a farmer, Cain brought an offering of some vegetables he had grown.

3. Offering: With palms up, move hands forward.

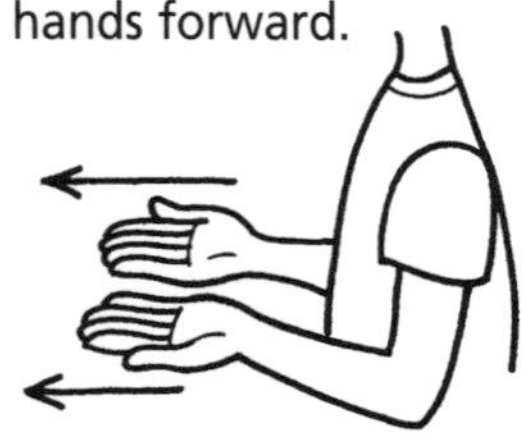

4. Abel also brought an offering to God. Since he was a shepherd, he selected from the first animals that had been born in his flocks. Abel gave his thanks to God by giving Him the best gift he could.

4. Thanks: Place fingertips of both hands against mouth and throw forward and down.

5. God was happy with the offering Abel brought. But God was not pleased with Cain's offering. And here's where the big trouble started. Cain got very angry. God said to Cain, "Why are you angry? If you do what is right, your offering will please Me. But if you do not do what is right, more trouble will come."

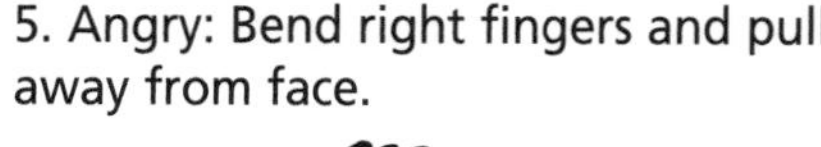

5. Angry: Bend right fingers and pull away from face.

6. And more trouble DID come. Not long after this, Cain and Abel were out in the fields together. And while they were far from home, Cain attacked his brother and killed him. Then God called to Cain, "Where is your brother, Abel?" Cain angrily said to the Lord, "I don't know where he is. Do I have to take care of my brother ALL the time?" Cain didn't want to admit that he had killed Abel.

6. Killed: Point right finger; twist and move under left hand.

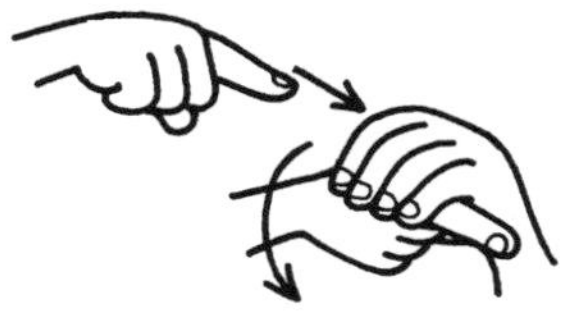

7. The Lord replied, "What have you done? I know you have killed your brother in anger. You are not going to be a farmer any longer. If you work in the soil, it will not grow anything for you ever again. You will have to leave home and travel from place to place." And that's what Cain did. He left home and traveled to another place.

7. Leave, left: Move flat hands up and into fists.

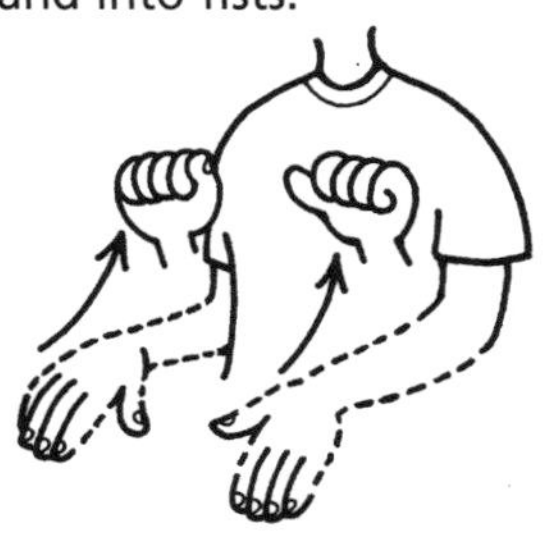

8. Cain was VERY sad. He thought he was being punished too much! But Cain's trouble came because of his own anger and his unwillingness to worship, love and obey God! What a sad end to this family's life together!

8. Sad: Palms in, drop hands down face.

## Conclude the Story

**How were Cain and Abel different? What did they give in their offerings to God?** (Cain gave vegetables. Abel gave from his flock of animals.)

**What are some offerings we can give to God?** (Our obedience by helping others. Our money. Our praise.) **When we want to show God our love and thankfulness, we use the things He has given us—our time, our abilities and our money—in good ways.**

**Genesis 6:9—9:19**

# Noah's Ark

## Materials

Drawing materials/equipment for teacher and each student.

## Tell the Story

As you tell each part of the story, draw each sketch. Students copy your sketches.

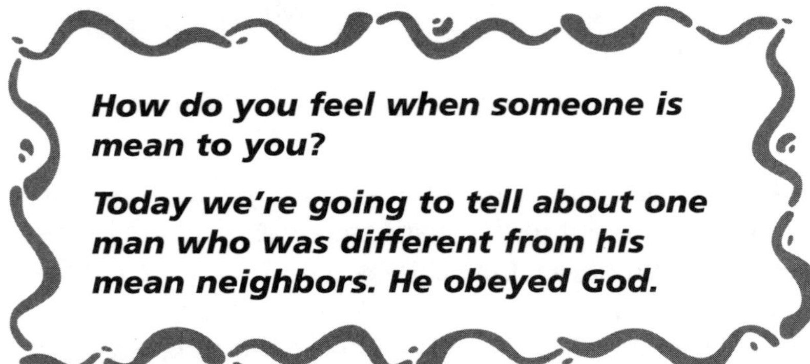

***How do you feel when someone is mean to you?***

***Today we're going to tell about one man who was different from his mean neighbors. He obeyed God.***

1. After God made the world, more and more people were born. Now there were more people than anyone could count! But people had forgotten that God had made them. They had forgotten all about obeying Him. Instead, they were disobeying God—lying, hurting and even killing each other! They didn't care what God wanted. That made God very sad.

1. Use "V"s and "C"s to draw mean faces.

2. But in all that meanness and disobeying, one person DID love and obey God. His name was Noah. When God decided to put a stop to the terrible things going on in the world, He decided to do it with a flood. God told Noah, "I'm going to send a lot of rain. It will rain until the whole earth is covered with water. But I want you to build a big boat, an ark. You, your family and all the creatures I have made will be safe there."

2. Draw as many raindrops as you can.

3. God told Noah EXACTLY how to build the ark, what kind of wood to use and how big to make it. It was going to be BIG—as long as one and a half football fields! Noah obeyed. He chopped down trees; he sawed and nailed. It was a BIG JOB! Noah and his family worked many, many YEARS to build the ark. After it was built, Noah painted it inside and out with tar to keep it from leaking.

3. Ark from sideways "D." Add roof.

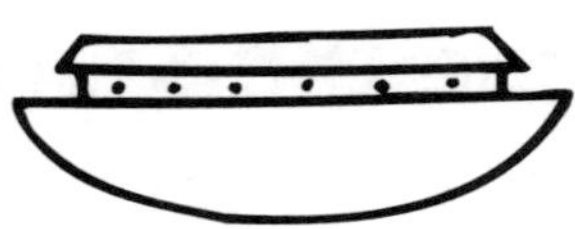

4. One day God said, "Noah, take your family into the ark. And take EVERY kind of animal and bird with you—two of some and seven of others." Again, Noah obeyed! He loaded food for his family and for ALL those animals into the ark. Then God sent animals to Noah. Animals of every kind and size came to the ark! Rabbits and hippos, lions and mice, sparrows and eagles—all these and more found places in the ark. Finally Noah and his family got inside the huge boat, too. As Noah and his family got settled, they began to hear something—plink, plink, plink! Rain was coming down, faster and harder! Then God shut the door of the ark.

4. Draw two rabbits from long and round "O"s.

5. The rain fell harder. Little puddles got larger. Soon, the ground was covered with water! The ark began to FLOAT! For 40 days and 40 nights the rain fell hard and fast. OUTSIDE, the water got DEEPER and DEEPER until even the tallest mountain on earth was COVERED. But inside the ark, Noah and his family and all the animals were snug and dry.

5. "U"s for water. Add rain clouds from "3"s, "Z"s for lightning.

6. One day, it got very quiet. The rain had stopped! But it was a LONG time before the water dried up—almost a YEAR. Then one day God told Noah to bring his family and all those animals and birds out of the ark! What an exciting day THAT must have been! At last, Noah and his family and ALL those creatures could run and stretch their legs and leap in the sunshine!

6. Add sun in front of clouds.

7. The first thing Noah did was thank God for keeping him and his family safe. God was glad that Noah remembered to thank Him. God promised, "I will NEVER again destroy the whole earth with a flood." Then to remind everyone of His promise, God put a beautiful rainbow in the sky. Even today, whenever we see a rainbow, we remember that God promised NEVER again to cover the whole earth with water.

7. Draw "C"s for rainbow (7 "C"s for full rainbow). Add colors.

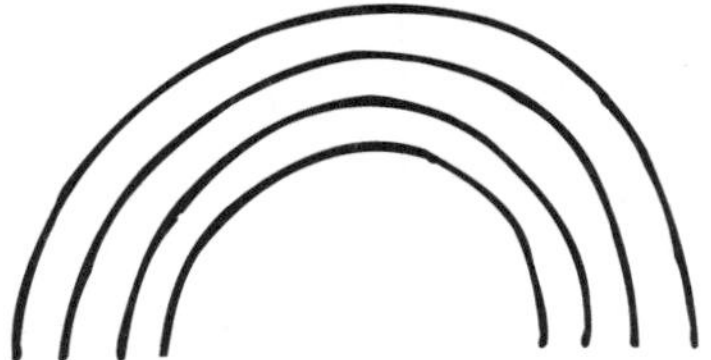

## Conclude the Story

**Who showed love for God by obeying Him?** (Noah.) **What are some ways Noah obeyed God?** (Built ark. Took care of animals. Thanked God.) **What did God do to show His promise?** (Made a rainbow.)

**We may find it hard to obey God. But He will help us obey Him if we ask Him. He loves us and wants us to show we love Him by obeying Him!**

**Genesis 12:1-9**

# Abraham's Journey

## Before the Story

Guide students to briefly practice signs for underlined words.

***When have you gone camping? Who helped you know where to go?***

***Today we're going to hear about some people who took a long camping trip. They had no idea where they were going!***

## Tell the Story

As you tell the story, lead students in responding as shown when you say the underlined words.

1. Abraham and his wife, Sarah, and ALL their family lived in the city of Ur. Ur was a very large city, with harbors for boats that traveled up and down the nearby Euphrates (yoo-FRAY-teez) River. Abraham and Sarah had always lived in Ur, surrounded by their friends and family. They had probably NEVER thought about moving away!

1. Family: With thumbs and index fingers touching, make outward circle until hands touch.

2. While many people in Ur worshiped false gods, Abraham loved and worshiped the one true God. He often talked with God. One day, God told Abraham something VERY surprising.

"Abraham," God said, "I want you to leave your country to go to a new land. I will show you where to go."

2. Abraham: Holding left fist near right shoulder, hit close to elbow with right fist.

3. Even though Abraham didn't have a specific place to go to, he believed God's promise to lead him. He and Sarah began to get ready for this long trip. This journey would be like a long camping trip. They packed food, rugs and blankets, pots and pans. They fastened bundles to their camels and donkeys and filled water bags. Finally they were ready to go.

3. Trip, journey: Two bent fingers of right hand move in wavy forward path.

4. Abraham, Sarah and many of their family began to walk. Traveling through hot sun, cold nights, rain and wind was hard work! There was no air-conditioning, no hotel where they could get a meal or a bath. Each day when they stopped, they had to work to find grass and water for all their animals. They worked to put up their tents, build a fire, cook and eat. Finally, they rolled up in blankets to sleep.

4. Work: Hands in fists, tap left wrist with right.

5. When it was time to move on, they would pack up everything again, put fresh water in the water bags and start walking. Sometimes they must have wondered where they were headed—and if they would ever get to the land God had promised! But Abraham trusted God's promise. He was sure that sooner or later, they were going to reach the new land where God had promised to bring them.

5. Promise: Right index finger on lips; move to open hand on left fist.

6. For days and months, they traveled this way. Sometimes they stayed in one place for a while, but then God would tell them it was time to go. So they would pack up the tents, camels and donkeys. And they'd move on again. They traveled through the desert for a long time. But as they traveled, the land finally began to look very different.

6. Traveled: Two bent fingers of right hand move in wavy forward path.

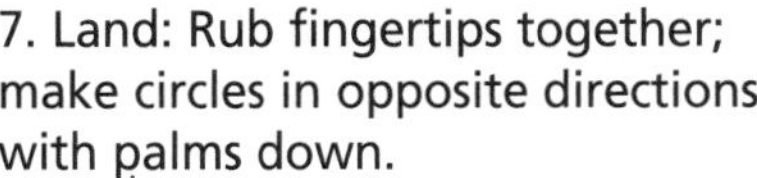

7. Finally, they came to a place of hills and valleys covered with good grass that would feed many sheep, goats and cows.

"This is the land I promised to you," God told Abraham. "Go and walk through it, because it is the land I am giving you." The land was beautiful! It was called Canaan. They traveled on to a place where big, beautiful oak trees grew. They set up their tents and pounded in their stakes. They were STAYING in this land!

7. Land: Rub fingertips together; make circles in opposite directions with palms down.

8. The very first thing Abraham did in this new land was to build a special place: an altar to worship God. He praised God and thanked Him for bringing him ALL that way.

God had led them to the land He had promised to give Abraham. He and his family hadn't gotten lost, even though they had never seen a map and even though there were no signs to point the way! God had kept His promise and brought Abraham and his family to a new land.

8. Altar: Touch thumbs of fists; move apart and then down with palms facing.

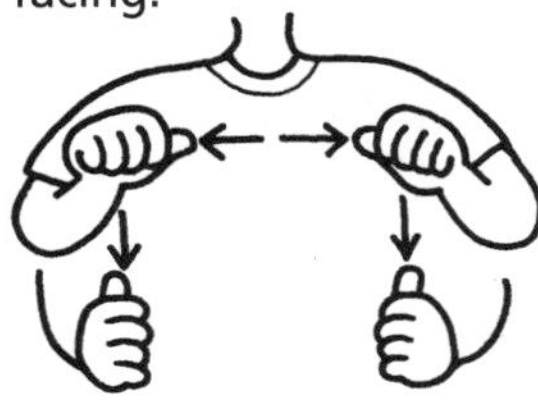

## Conclude the Story

**Why did Abraham leave Ur?** (God told him to. God promised to take him to a new land.) **Was traveling easy or hard? Why?** (Hard. They had to carry everything they needed.) **How do you think Abraham felt when he came to the land God had promised him? What did he do?** (Happy. Thanked and worshiped God.)

**Just like God guided Abraham, God is leading and guiding each of us in our lives. We can trust God to lead us and guide us because He loves us and He always keeps His promises.**

## Genesis 12:1-4; 13

# Abraham Gives Lot First Choice

### Materials

Play dough (¼ cup, or 2 oz.) and pencil for each student.

### Tell the Story

**Follow along with me as we use our dough to tell today's story.**

***Have you ever had to sit around a crowded table? How do people act when they are crowded?***

***Today we'll hear what happened when some people got crowded!***

1. **Use your dough to make a house with a flat roof.** Abraham was a man who lived in the city of Ur. Ur was a big city, full of fountains and trees and houses made of brick and plaster. Abraham and his wife, Sarah, had lived in Ur all their lives. They had a home and many servants. Abraham loved God. He often talked with God. And one day, God told Abraham something VERY SURPRISING. He told Abraham, "I want you to go to a new land. I will show you where to go."

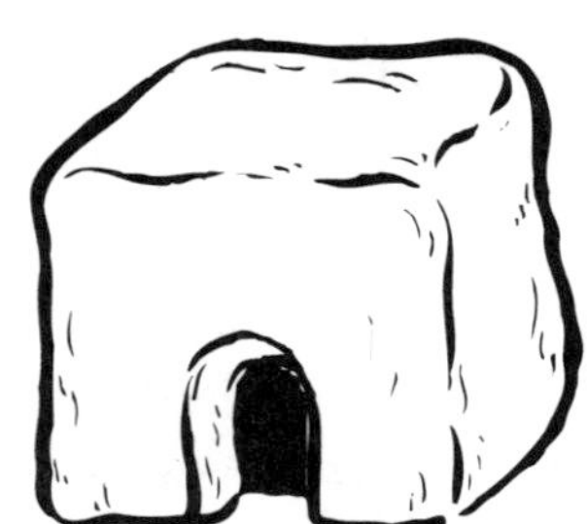

Abraham believed God and began to get ready to move. Since this move would be like a long camping trip, the people in Abraham's household packed up everything they would need for traveling—pots and pans, clothes and tents, rugs and blankets, water and food. They tied the bundles onto camels and donkeys and herded the sheep and goats. Abraham's father and his nephew Lot also went with them on this journey. Soon the whole family was off—walking to a place they knew nothing about!

2. **Roll a long rope and then flatten it to make a long path.** Abraham's family walked for weeks and months and then years! Sometimes Abraham's family must have wondered if they would ever get to the land God had promised! But Abraham trusted God. He was sure God would take care of him. He knew that, sooner or later, they were going to reach the new land where God had promised to bring them.

After many years of traveling and many adventures, they came to a place of hills and valleys covered with good grass that would feed many sheep and goats and cows. "This is the land I promised to you," God told Abraham. It was beautiful! The land was called Canaan.

3. **Make tiny dough balls to be herds of animals.** During all this time Abraham and his family had traveled, their flocks of sheep and herds of goats had grown and grown. There were so MANY animals, there wasn't enough water or grass for all of them. Both Abraham and his nephew Lot had HUGE flocks of animals. And in the crowded valley, the servants who took care of these animals began to fight over whose flocks should get the water and the grass.

When Abraham heard about the fighting, he said to Lot, "Let's not have any quarreling between you and me, or between your herdsmen and mine. Look around! The whole land is here for us. You may choose where you would like to go. Take your herds in that direction and I'll go the other way. Then there will be plenty for all of us."

4. **Make some flat land and some hilly land.** Lot looked and saw that the whole plain, or flat area, that went down to the sea was beautiful. He could see bright streams of flowing water and fields of green grass. So Lot chose this plain for himself and his family. He said good-bye to Abraham's family and moved down to the plain.

5. **Write "peace" or the letter P on flat dough with pencil.** Because Abraham gave Lot first choice, the fighting stopped! There was peace.

After Lot had moved away, God said to Abraham, "Look around. All the land that you can see I will give to you and your family forever. Your family will grow and I will give you many grandchildren! Go, walk all through the land. I am giving it to you."

So Abraham moved his tents, his family and his herds of animals to live in the hills. Now Abraham and Lot and their servants would never have to quarrel again. God had given Abraham all the land he could see! And best of all, from Abraham's descendants would come the Savior God had promised to send.

## Conclude the Story

**Why did Abraham and his family leave Ur?** (God commanded him to leave.) **Why did the herdsmen fight?** (There was not enough food and water for all the animals.) **How did Abraham solve the quarrel?** (He let Lot choose where he wanted to live.)

**It can be hard or even scary to try to make peace and stop a quarrel. But God will help us know what to do. One way to be a peacemaker is to give other people first choice. When we put others first, we treat them in ways we would like to be treated. It's a great way to show God's peace to others!**

Genesis 12:1-5; 15:1-7; 18:1-19; 21:1-7

# God Keeps His Promises to Abraham

***Where has someone promised to take you?***

***Today we're going to use shapes and letters to draw about people who trusted God's promises.***

## Materials

Drawing materials/equipment for teacher and each student.

## Tell the Story

As you tell each part of the story, draw each sketch. Students copy your sketches.

1. In the city of Ur lived a man named Abraham. Ur was a big city, with trees and fountains and buildings. Abraham and his wife, Sarah, had always lived there. But one day, God told Abraham, "I want you to leave Ur. I will show you a new land."

1. Draw fountain from 3 half circles. Add water.

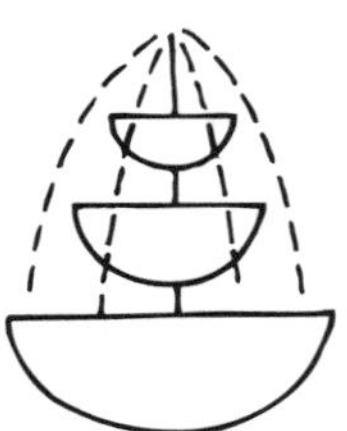

2. Abraham and Sarah and all their helpers packed pots and pans, clothes and tents, food and water, and put their bundles on camels and donkeys. Abraham, Sarah and some of their family began to walk. Traveling was hot, hard work! There were no cars or air conditioning. When they stopped, they put up tents, built a fire, cooked dinner and slept rolled up in blankets. When it was time to move on, they packed up everything, got fresh water and walked some more.

2. Tents from upside-down "V"s and trapezoids.

3. They must have often wondered where they were going—and if they would ever get to the land God had promised! But Abraham believed God. And one day, they came to a place of hills and valleys covered with good grass. It was beautiful! "This is the land I promised to you," God told Abraham. The land was called Canaan. God had kept His promise!

3. Small lines for grass.

4. Now God had also promised that Abraham would have many grandchildren and great-grandchildren. But Abraham and Sarah didn't have ANY children yet! And they were old! But God told Abraham again, "You will have a son. And from him there will come more grandchildren than you can imagine! Look at the stars. Can you count them? You'll have more grandchildren than there are stars in the sky!" And Abraham believed God.

4. Stars from triangles. Make as many as you can.

5. More years went by. Abraham and Sarah grew even older. But God told Abraham His promise again. And again, Abraham believed God, even though it made him laugh! Abraham wondered, *How can we have a son? I am 100 years old and Sarah is 90!*

5. Faces from "100" and "90," adding noses and mouths from "C"s.

6. Even more time went by and still no baby. But one day, three VERY important visitors came to Abraham's tent. In fact, ONE of the visitors was really God, although He looked like a man! As Abraham and the visitors talked, Sarah listened at the tent door. She heard God say that she would soon have a son! Sarah laughed! She thought, *I'm so OLD! Will I really have a child?* But God said, "NOTHING is too hard for the Lord! Sarah really will have a son!"

6. Laughing face.

7. At the EXACT time God had promised, Abraham and Sarah DID have a baby boy! They named him Isaac, which means "laughter!" Sarah and Abraham remembered God's promise every time they called Isaac's name!

7. Baby from oval and circle. Add "C"s for face.

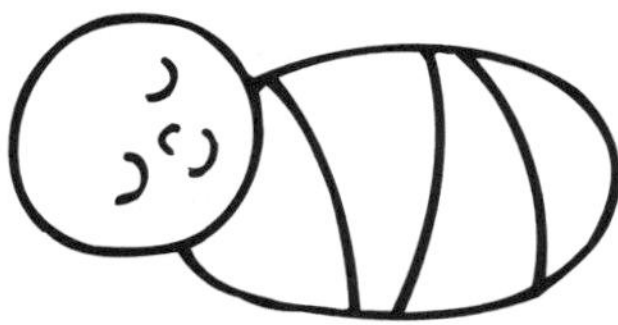

## Conclude the Story

**How did Abraham and Sarah show their trust in God?** (Moved to a new land. Believed God would give them a child.) **What did Abraham and Sarah learn about God?** (He keeps promises. He is faithful.)

**Sometimes it is hard to believe God's promises. But God shows us that even if we have to wait, He never forgets us. And He never, EVER forgets to keep His promises! That's why the Bible says God is faithful. He always keeps His promises. The Bible is filled with wonderful promises God makes to us.**

## Genesis 26:1-6,12-33

# Isaac Builds Many Wells

## Materials

Play dough (¼ cup, or 2 oz.) for each student.

## Tell the Story

**Follow along with me as we use our dough to tell today's story.**

***When has someone taken something that was yours? How did you feel?***

***Today we'll find out how one man acted when some people took things from him.***

1. **Make as many sheep as you can.** One hot and dusty day in Old Testament times, Isaac, Rebekah, their family and herdsmen trudged along beside their sheep and cattle. There was a famine where they had been living. A famine is a time when there isn't enough rain for crops to grow and drinking water becomes scarce. Isaac and his family were going to the city of Gerar (JIHR-ahr). Isaac's father, Abraham, had lived there long before. They hoped that there was still water in the wells Abraham had dug years before.

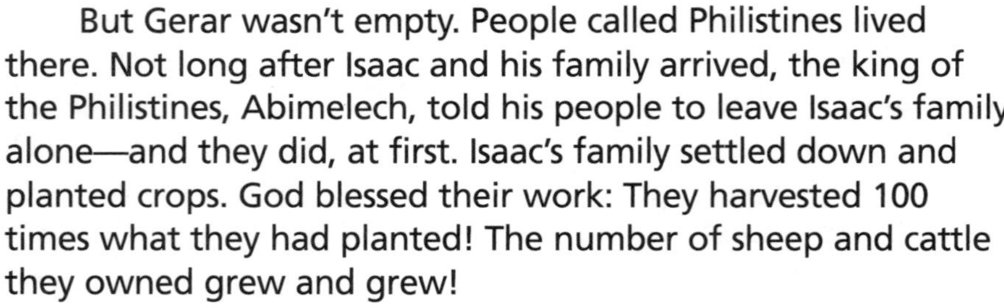

But Gerar wasn't empty. People called Philistines lived there. Not long after Isaac and his family arrived, the king of the Philistines, Abimelech, told his people to leave Isaac's family alone—and they did, at first. Isaac's family settled down and planted crops. God blessed their work: They harvested 100 times what they had planted! The number of sheep and cattle they owned grew and grew!

When the Philistines saw Isaac's BIG harvest and BIG flocks, they got jealous! So they filled with dirt all the wells Isaac's father had dug! And King Abimelech told Isaac to move AWAY.

2. **Make a well from small balls.** Even though Isaac, his family and all his servants had settled in and made themselves at home, Isaac did what the king asked. He didn't argue; he didn't try to change Abimelech's mind. He simply moved away from Gerar and settled in a valley away from the town.

After they looked for a place to set up camp in the valley, they searched for the most important thing—WATER! Isaac's men found more old wells that Isaac's father, Abraham, had dug. After long days of cleaning out the wells, they had water to drink! They also dug a new well that gave cool, fresh water. BUT it wasn't long until they had unhappy visitors.

"Didn't we tell you to LEAVE?" the herdsmen from Gerar asked Isaac's men. "THIS is OUR well because this is OUR land," they growled.

The Bible says that Isaac and his people moved on and dug another well in a new place. GUESS who came to take THIS well away? That's right, the herdsmen of Gerar came after them AGAIN and told them to leave!

No doubt some of Isaac's herdsmen grumbled as they packed up to move AGAIN. It wasn't FAIR! They hadn't hurt anybody. But Isaac was determined to keep the peace.

Once again, Isaac and his family, his herdsmen and their families settled at a new place Isaac found. And they began to do the FIRST thing they had to do—dig another WELL. They must have been pretty good at it by now!

But this time, they had moved far enough away. No one came to fight with them over the water! And although Isaac was glad to have some peace, he moved on after a while to a place called Beersheba. There God talked to Isaac and reminded him of His promises to Isaac's father, Abraham. Isaac settled in at Beersheba and guess what they did next? That's right! They dug a WELL!

3. **Make a crown.** Meanwhile, King Abimelech and one of his advisors came to Beersheba. Isaac met them and said, "Why have you come here? You sent me away from your land!"

King Abimelech answered, "We saw clearly that God has helped you. We decided that we should make an agreement with you. Promise us that you will do us no harm because we have never harmed you but only sent you away in peace."

WELL! That wasn't exactly how Isaac remembered it! But he was glad that the king wanted peace. So he made the agreement and made a feast for the visitors. That day, Isaac's servants found water in the newest well they were digging. Now they had water AND peace!

## Conclude the Story

**Why did Isaac's family move?** (Famine. No rain. Needed water.) **How did Isaac react when the herdsmen took his wells?** (Didn't fight back. Moved away.) **Why didn't Isaac fight the herdsmen for the wells?** (Wanted to keep peace.) **How did King Abimelech finally treat Isaac?** (With respect. Wanted to make peace.)

**Keeping peace with others isn't always easy, but looking for ways to keep peace often helps us make friends with others. God promises to help us make peace if we ask Him.**

Genesis 25:19-34; 27—33

# Jacob and Esau

## Materials

Drawing materials/equipment for teacher and each student.

## Tell the Story

As you tell each part of the story, draw each sketch. Students copy your sketches.

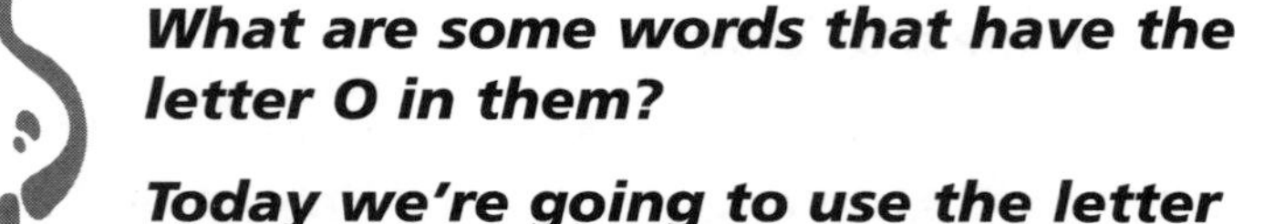

***What are some words that have the letter O in them?***

***Today we're going to use the letter O to tell about twins who were oh, so much trouble!***

1. Abraham was a new grandfather! His son Isaac had married a woman named Rebekah. And she gave birth to TWINS! The oldest one was named Esau. The younger twin was named Jacob. But OH, were these twins different! Esau was hairy and strong. He loved to be outdoors and grew to be a hunter. Jacob was smooth-skinned and liked to work around the family tent.

1. Draw two babies from long and small "O"s. Add hair to one.

2. One day after the boys were grown, Esau came in from a long day of hunting. He hadn't caught any food and he was VERY hungry. He could smell stew cooking. When he saw Jacob by the pot, he said, "Give me some stew!" Jacob slyly answered, "Sure! If you promise to give me your birthright."

Esau's birthright meant he would inherit twice as much as Jacob because Esau was born first. But he didn't care about that birthright at all! He just wanted FOOD. (That word has two Os!) So Jacob gave him food and got Esau's birthright. OH-OH!

2. Bowl of stew from long "O" and "U"; add "S"s for steam.

3. Later, Jacob tricked his father, Isaac, so he could get the special blessing that Isaac would normally have given to Esau. While Esau was gone, Jacob dressed up like Esau and made his father's favorite food. Because Isaac was now blind, Jacob was able to make him think he was Esau. Once Isaac's words of blessing were said, they couldn't be taken back! Esau was OH, SO ANGRY that he wanted to KILL Jacob! So Jacob ran away, afraid of what his brother might do to him.

3. Esau's angry face with 2 "V"s. Jacob's scared face from "O"s.

4. Jacob traveled and traveled. In one place, he lay his head on a rock and slept. And OH, what an amazing dream he dreamed! He saw a beautiful stairway that went up into heaven, with angels going up and down. And he heard God tell him, "I will bless you and help you. You will have many, many children and will inherit the land where you are. Your children will bless all the earth." Jacob woke up and called the place Bethel, or "house of God." He promised to honor God because of the promises God had made to him.

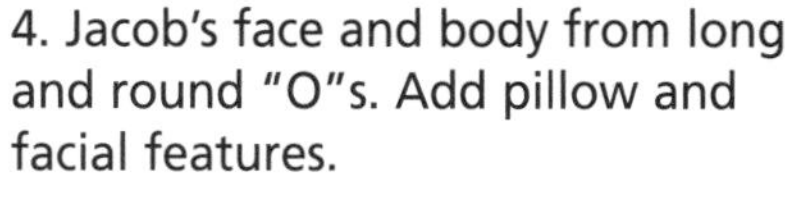
4. Jacob's face and body from long and round "O"s. Add pillow and facial features.

5. Jacob went to live with his uncle, far away. He became very wealthy! He got married and had children—oh, did he have a lot of children! He had 12 sons and only one daughter. He lived far from home for many years. But finally, God told Jacob it was time to go back. Jacob was still very afraid of Esau because Jacob remembered that Esau had wanted to kill him! But God promised to be with him. So Jacob and his family packed up and set out.

5. Draw 13 "0"s for children; add faces.

6. As Jacob and his family traveled, Jacob sent many presents on ahead of him for Esau—cattle and sheep and camels and goats. He kept his family far behind all of these gifts, in case Esau was still angry. At long last, he could see dust rising. Esau was coming—with 400 men! OH-OH! But God had told Jacob that He would be with him. So Jacob went on ahead. He bowed low to his brother. And Esau didn't KILL him—he KISSED him! The two brothers cried and Esau forgave Jacob for the mean tricks he had played.

6. Cow face from "U","O"s and "C"s.

Write "KILL"; change "L"s to read "KISS."

## Conclude the Story

**Who was a cheater?** (Jacob.) **Who didn't care about his birthright?** (Esau.) **How did Jacob's and Esau's feelings change during this story?**

**When we do wrong, we sometimes think that God doesn't love us. We might think that God will give up on us. But God loves us even when we do wrong. He is always waiting for us to come to Him and ask His forgiveness. He never gives up on us!**

**Genesis 37; 39—45**

# Joseph and His Brothers

## Materials

Drawing materials/equipment for teacher and each student.

***How would you feel if a brother, sister or friend got a better gift than you?***

***Today we're going to use faces to tell our story about a boy who had a lot of trouble because his brothers were jealous.***

## Tell the Story

As you tell each part of the story, draw each sketch. Students copy your sketches.

1. Jacob had 12 sons and one daughter. Joseph was his eleventh son. And he was Jacob's FAVORITE son. This made his brothers jealous! Joseph also had dreams that he told to his family—dreams about his family bowing down to him. This made his brothers MORE jealous! And if that weren't enough, Jacob made a special coat for Joseph. That coat showed everyone that Jacob had chosen Joseph to be in charge of his brothers. WOW, were his brothers ever jealous!

1. Draw Joseph's face from "U"s. Add "Z"s for hair and "L"s for coat.

2. Joseph's brothers had gone off to find new pastures for their animals. One day, Jacob sent Joseph to check on them. When they saw Joseph coming (it was easy to spot his coat!), they decided to take his coat from him and throw him into a nearby pit.

2. Draw mean faces.

3. A traders' caravan was coming. So the brothers sold Joseph to the traders. His brothers told their father, Jacob, that Joseph was dead. But really, Joseph was now a slave in Egypt.

3. Draw a sad face.

4. But Joseph trusted God and did his best and became his Egyptian owner's most trusted servant. But the man's wife lied about Joseph. Joseph was put into JAIL! Once again, Joseph trusted God. He did his best and helped other prisoners. He even told two other prisoners what their dreams meant.

4. Write "Jail." Add face to "a," bars from other letters.

5. Some time later, Pharaoh, the ruler of all Egypt, had a dream. No one could tell him what it meant! But one of the men Joseph had helped in jail told Pharaoh about Joseph. Soon Joseph was in front of Pharaoh! He told Pharaoh that his dream meant there was going to be a famine. There wouldn't be any rain or much food.

So Pharaoh made Joseph second ruler in Egypt! Joseph had granaries built to store food to eat during the famine. He was in charge of everybody except Pharaoh!

5. Pharaoh from 2 "F"s, "V"s, and sideways "D"s.

6. But there was also a famine back where Jacob and all of Joseph's brothers lived. Soon the brothers came to Egypt and bowed low before Joseph. They begged him to sell them food. Joseph didn't tell them who he was just yet. But he gave them lots of grain and sent them home. He also kept one brother with him, just to be sure they would come back!

6. Bowing man: sideways "L" and 3 "C"s; "7" for nose.

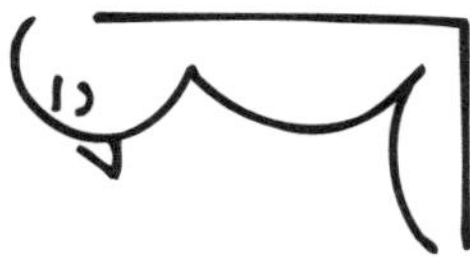

7. Joseph's brothers did come back. And finally, he told them who he was! His brothers were afraid he would punish them all, but Joseph told them that even though they had meant to hurt him, God had used it for good! Now Joseph forgave his brothers and invited them all to come and live in Egypt.

7. Draw happy face.

## Conclude the Story

**Who had the most trouble in this story?** (Joseph.) **Why were his brothers mean to him?** (They were jealous.) **How did God turn the brothers' mean actions into something good?** (Joseph was in Egypt, so they could get food and move there.)

**When things are hard for us, it's easy to forget that God is with us. But He never forgets where we are or what we need. Even in the worst times, He loves us and will help us!**

**Exodus 1—20**

# Moses Obeys God

## Materials

Drawing materials/equipment for teacher and each student.

## Tell the Story

As you tell each part of the story, draw each sketch. Students copy your sketches.

***What is something hard you are learning to do?***

***Today we're going to use letters and numbers to tell about someone who learned to do right even when it was hard.***

1. Joseph's brothers had gone to live in Egypt. Their families had children. Those children had MORE children. The family grew to be thousands of people! Many years later, something awful happened to this family called the Israelites.

The king of the Egyptians was called Pharaoh. Egyptian pharaohs (or kings) had been kind to the Israelites because of the way Joseph had helped Egypt. But now there was a new pharaoh. He didn't care about what Joseph had done. What he DID care about was that there were so many of those Israelites! He was worried that the Israelites might take over his country.

1. Draw Pharaoh from 2 "F"s, "V"s, sideways "D"s.

2. So Pharaoh made the Israelites slaves. They were forced to build cities. They had to make bricks out of mud and straw. It was hard, hot work. The Israelites were sad and angry at the way they were being treated. Then life got even worse. Pharaoh made a law that all Israelite baby boys were to be killed. But one baby boy was saved—Moses. His mother floated him on the river in a basket. The daughter of Pharaoh found him and raised him.

2. Baby in basket: long "O," "C" for bottom. Face: "M"s and "C"s.

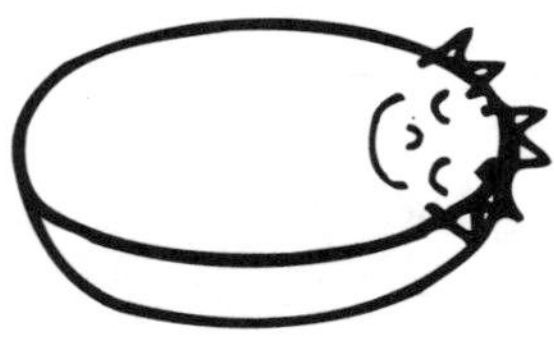

3. When Moses grew up, he had to leave Egypt. For many years he lived in the desert tending sheep. One day he saw a bush that was on fire, but it didn't burn up. Moses came closer; then he heard a voice. It was GOD! God told Moses that He had heard the Israelites's cries for help. And Moses was going to be the one to lead the people out of Egypt, so they wouldn't be slaves anymore. Moses wasn't sure he could do this job! But God told Moses He would be with

3. Bush: "3"s, "M"s. Add "I"s for trunk.

Moses and that his brother, Aaron, would go with him to help him.

Moses and Aaron obeyed God and went to talk to Pharaoh. They told him God wanted the Israelites to leave Egypt. But Pharaoh kept saying no. So God sent the Egyptians 10 troubles—called plagues—to make Pharaoh obey God!

4. One trouble God sent was frogs! Frogs were everywhere! They were in beds and cooking pots and jumping out of trees onto people's heads. There were nine other awful things God sent, too. After all 10 plagues were sent, Pharaoh finally said the Israelites could leave. In fact, now he WANTED them out of his sight!

4. Frog: "P"s and "C"s for body. Add "I"s, "V"s and "W"s for legs and feet.

5. So Moses led the people away from Egypt, following God's instructions exactly. By the time the Israelites reached the Red Sea, however, Pharaoh had changed his mind. He sent an army to capture them!

God told Moses to hold up his walking stick. Moses obeyed and God sent a wind. The wind was so strong that it blew a path through the sea. Moses led the people to safety on the other side of the sea. When the Egyptian army tried to follow, the sea went back to its place! But the Israelites were safe!

5. Draw many "C"s. Tall "C"s for water. Add Moses' stick.

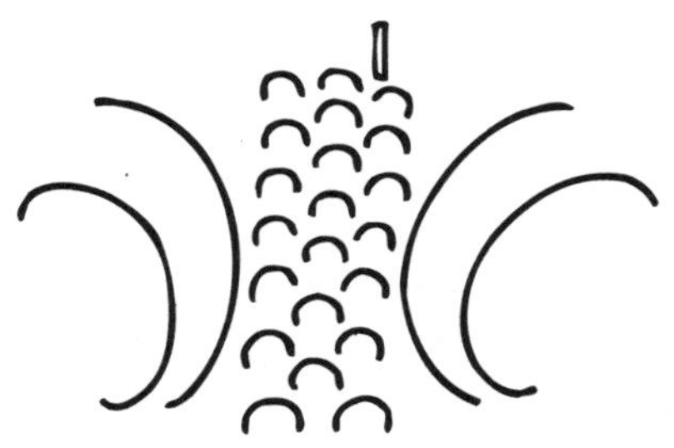

6. Moses led the people into the desert to a mountain called Mount Sinai. God gave Moses 10 special commands to teach all the people to follow. They are called the Ten Commandments. God gave many other instructions that Moses wrote down. Now Moses and all the Israelites knew God's instructions for them.

6. Draw sideways "B." Add details and "10."

## Conclude the Story

**Who obeyed God and did what was right?** (Moses. Aaron.) **How?** (Talked to Pharaoh. the people.) **When do you think it might have been hard for Moses to do what was right?**

**Sometimes you might think that it's just too hard for a kid to do what God wants or that God only cares about the lives of grown-ups like parents, teachers or coaches. But God wants everyone to do what's right. Ask God to show you what's right. And ask Him to help you do it. He will help you do it. He'll even give you family and friends who will make it easier—just like He did for Moses.**

**Exodus 2:1-10**

# Baby Moses

## Materials

Play dough (¼ cup, or 2 oz.) for each student.

*Have you ever helped care for a baby? What are some of the things you did for the baby?*

*Today we'll hear about the unusual way one baby was cared for.*

## Tell the Story

**Follow along with me as we use our dough to tell today's story.**

1. **Make at least six bricks from your dough.** For 400 years, the Israelites (also called the Hebrews) lived in Egypt. During those years, the number of Israelites grew and grew and GREW! Pharaoh, the ruler of Egypt, was worried that the Israelites might become more powerful than the Egyptians!

"Those Hebrews will become my slaves," the Pharaoh decided. "They will work in the hot sun from morning to night making bricks."

The taskmasters used whips to make the Hebrews work very hard. The Hebrew slaves built two large cities. But the harder the Israelites worked, the more of them there seemed to be. Pharaoh was hoping to DECREASE the number of Hebrews, but instead their numbers INCREASED.

2. **Make a baby from one brick.** Soon Pharaoh thought of another plan. He sent for the Hebrew midwives, women who helped the Hebrew mothers when they were having babies. Pharaoh told the midwives to KILL any baby boys that were born. These women knew God would not want them to obey Pharaoh's order, so they protected the baby boys instead. Then Pharaoh gave a terrible order. "Drown all the Hebrew baby boys," he said. "Throw them into the Nile River!"

3. **Make a basket from two bricks. Put the baby in the basket.** One Hebrew family was determined they would NOT let Pharaoh kill their baby boy. For three months the family kept their baby a secret. Soon the baby's mother, Jochebed (JAHK-eh-behd), had a new idea about how to keep the baby safe. She smeared some gooey, sticky tar all over the outside of a basket and lined the inside of the basket with soft blankets. Then Jochebed gently laid her baby inside the basket.

4. **Make lid from a brick to cover basket.** Jochebed put a lid on the basket, picked it up and carried it all the way to the Nile River. Miriam, the baby's big sister, followed. She watched as Jochebed carefully set the basket in the water. The basket floated right on top of the river. The baby was safe and dry.

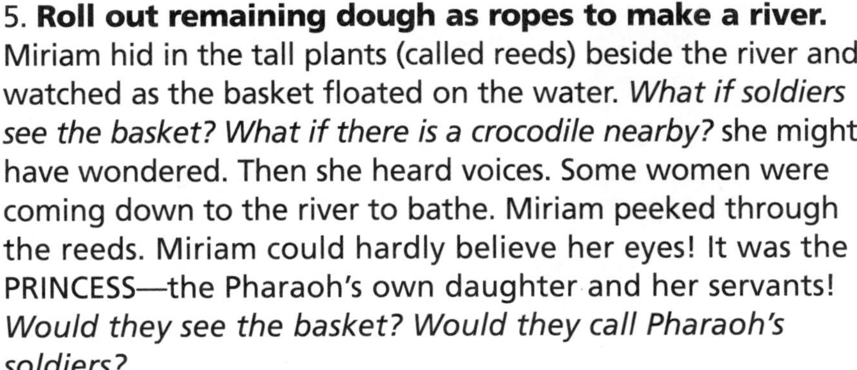

5. **Roll out remaining dough as ropes to make a river.** Miriam hid in the tall plants (called reeds) beside the river and watched as the basket floated on the water. *What if soldiers see the basket? What if there is a crocodile nearby?* she might have wondered. Then she heard voices. Some women were coming down to the river to bathe. Miriam peeked through the reeds. Miriam could hardly believe her eyes! It was the PRINCESS—the Pharaoh's own daughter and her servants! *Would they see the basket? Would they call Pharaoh's soldiers?*

"That looks like a basket over there," the princess said. "Go and get it," the princess told her maid. When the basket was opened, the baby was crying. The princess felt sorry for him. "This is one of the Hebrew babies," the princess said.

Miriam left her hiding place and ran over to the princess. "Would you like me to get one of the Hebrew women to help you take care of this baby?" Miriam asked politely.

"Yes," answered the princess, "go and do that." So Miriam ran all the way home to get her mother.

When Miriam introduced Jochebed to the princess, the princess said, "I'll pay you to take care of this baby for me." Now the baby was safe! No one would try to hurt a baby that belonged to the princess—and the baby still got to live with his own family while he was little!

6. **Make a K for the word "kindness."** The baby grew to be a little boy. Finally the time came when he was old enough to live in the palace with the princess. The princess named the baby Moses and treated him as kindly as if he were her very own son.

## Conclude the Story

**How did the Hebrew midwives show kindness? How did Jochebed show kindness? Miriam? The princess?** (The midwives protected the baby boys. Jochebed made a warm, dry basket for Moses and put it where someone would find it. Miriam watched over Moses when he was in the basket. The princess treated Moses like her own son.)

**Each of the people who helped Moses used the abilities God had given them to show kindness. In the same way, we can use whatever abilities we have to show kindness to others.**

**Exodus 14—15**

# Red Sea Crossing

## Materials

Play dough (¼ cup, or 2 oz.) and plastic knife for each student.

## Tell the Story

**Follow along with me as we use our dough to tell today's story.**

***What are some reasons people sing songs?***

***Today we're going to hear about some people who sang a song to praise God.***

1. **From most of your dough make a large sea with waves. Save a small part of your dough.** Hundreds and thousands of Israelite people followed Moses away from Egypt. During the day, God sent a big cloud to move across the sky in front of them. At night, God sent a pillar of fire to guide them. The Israelites walked day after day through the desert until they finally set up camp by the edge of a big body of water called the Red Sea.

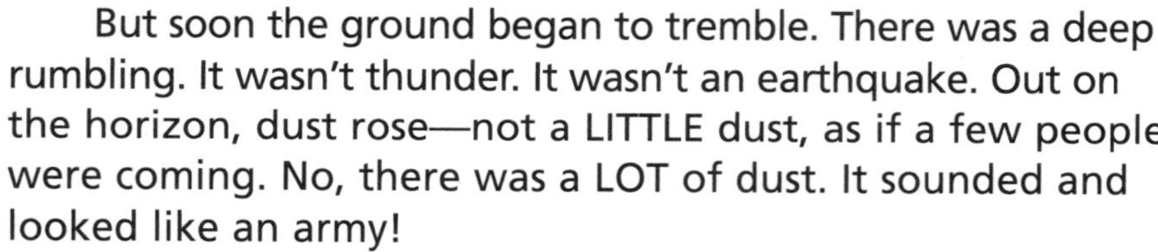

But soon the ground began to tremble. There was a deep rumbling. It wasn't thunder. It wasn't an earthquake. Out on the horizon, dust rose—not a LITTLE dust, as if a few people were coming. No, there was a LOT of dust. It sounded and looked like an army!

Remember Pharaoh, the king of Egypt? After the Israelites had left, Pharaoh decided he had made a huge mistake in letting the Israelite slaves get away! Hundreds and hundreds of angry Egyptian soldiers were pursuing the Israelites, determined to bring them back to slavery!

"Oh no, Pharaoh has changed his mind!" someone shouted.

The Israelites felt like running, but the sea was in front of them. The whole Egyptian army with its chariots and swift horses was coming! (Chariots are two-wheeled carts pulled by horses.)

The people were angry and afraid. "Why did you bring us here to die?" they shouted at Moses. "We can't go forward because of the sea and we can't go back toward the soldiers!"

"Don't be afraid," Moses said. "You will see how God will bring you out of trouble. He will fight for you!"

And Moses was right! Before Pharaoh and his soldiers could get close to the Israelites, God moved the huge cloud to stand between the Egyptians and the Israelites! The sky over the Egyptians became so dark that the army had to stop. But for the people of Israel, it was still light!

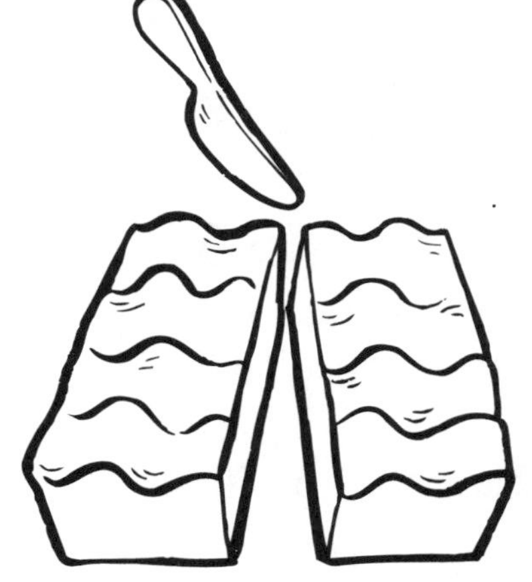

2. **Cut the water in two, making a path down the middle of the water.** God told Moses to hold his staff high in the air over the sea. All night long God sent a strong wind. It blew so hard that it blew a path through the waters of the sea. By morning, the water was stacked up in a wall of water on the right and a wall of water on the left. There was a wide, dry path right through the sea!

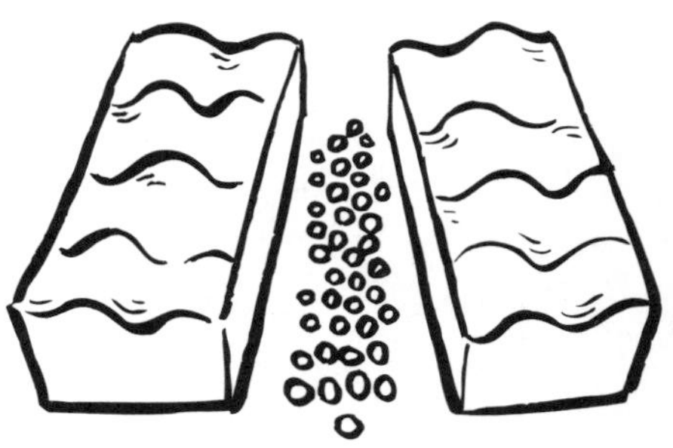

3. **From the small part of your dough, make small balls for Moses and the people. Move them from one side of the water to the other.** The people followed Moses over that dry path. Every single person and animal made it safely across. No one even got their feet wet!

Well, Pharaoh's army wasn't about to let the Israelites get away so easily! The chariots and soldiers rushed down that path to catch the Israelites. But God showed His power and protection once again. God told Moses to stretch out his hand over the sea. When Moses did, those walls of water came CRASHING down! The soldiers and the chariots were all GONE.

4. **Make a musical note.** God's people were so happy they just had to sing and praise God! Moses made up a song, right there on the far shore of the Red Sea! Moses' sister Miriam got the women together to play tambourines and sing.

"Sing to the Lord,
  for He is highly exalted.
The horse and its rider
  He has hurled into the sea."

Everyone sang and danced and played instruments to thank God for His amazing power and help. It was the biggest, noisiest, happiest party ever held in that quiet desert!

## Conclude the Story

**What are some ways God took care of the Israelites?** (He rescued them from slavery in Egypt. He made a dry path through the water. He protected them.) **What did the Israelites do when they saw God take care of them?** (They sang songs of praise and thanksgiving to God.) **How would you describe God's actions?**

**God's power is just the same today as it was in Old Testament times, and He is always glad to help us. God shows His love and care in many ways. We can joyfully celebrate God's help and protection!**

**Exodus 16—17:7**

# God Provides Food for the Israelites

## Before the Story

Guide students to briefly practice signs for underlined words.

***When you really need something, who do you ask to help you?***

***Today we're going to find out about some people who thought they would die if they didn't get what they needed!***

## Tell the Story

As you tell the story, lead students in responding as shown when you say the underlined words.

1. God's people, the Israelites, had been slaves in a country called Egypt. They had prayed to God for help, and He had sent a man named Moses to lead them away from Egypt. God had even parted the waters of the Red Sea, so His people could escape from the Egyptian army. After all the ways God had helped them, you would think the Israelites would have been happy. But they were UNHAPPY.

2. One day, the Israelites gathered around Moses. They grumbled, "When we left Egypt, you said we would go to a new home where we could be happy. Well, Moses, we're NOT happy. We don't have houses to live in! We're stuck out here in the desert, and our food is all GONE. We're HUNGRY. We're going to starve to death and it's ALL YOUR FAULT!"

3. Moses turned and walked away from the people. He was TIRED of all this complaining! He sat down on a rock and sighed. But he knew what to do. He talked to God about this grumbling. God told Moses, "I have heard the people. I will send you all the food you need. There will be so much that you will think the sky has opened up and rained food!"

4. Just as God had promised, the food came! Later that day, thousands and thousands of small birds called quail came flying over the camp. The quail flew so low that the people could just reach out and grab as many as they wanted! There were quail EVERYWHERE! Soon everyone was eating roasted quail. They ate and ate until they were FULL.

1. Moses: Extend thumb and index finger of both hands at temples; close fingers as you move hands to sides.

2. Grumbled: With right hand curved, strike chest with fingertips a few times.

3. God: Point right index finger; lower and open hand at chest.

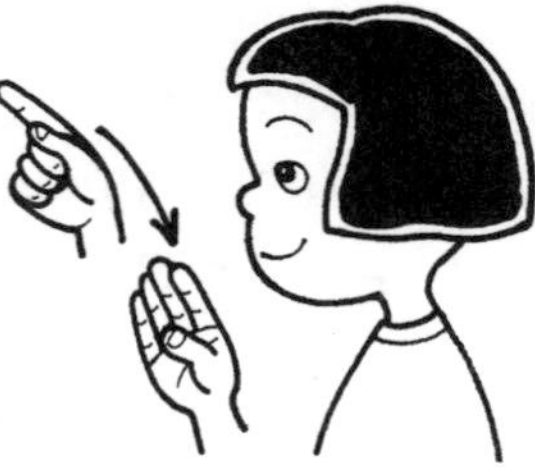

4. Birds, quail: Right thumb and index finger at mouth; open and close fingers a few times.

5. But that wasn't ALL God did! The next morning the people woke to find something on the ground they had never seen before. It looked like little seeds. Moses told the people, "This is bread God has given you to eat." It was delicious! It tasted like little cakes made with honey. The Israelites called it manna.

5. Bread: Move edge of right hand down back of left a few times.

6. God told the people to gather only as much manna as they needed for each day. Before the Sabbath, they were to gather enough for two days. That way, they could rest on the Sabbath. When people gathered too much manna or kept it too long, it smelled awful and got worms in it!

6. Sabbath: Fists with thumbs facing out; move in opposite-direction circles.

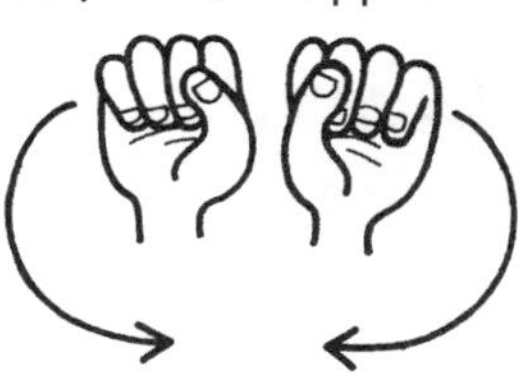

7. Every single day, God sent food to feed all those people. But now the Israelites were THIRSTY. NOW all they wanted was cool, clear water. So what did they do? They grumbled to Moses AGAIN. Moses couldn't wait to get away from them and pray to God. After all, God had taken care of them so well up to now! Moses knew that God would take care of them here. Moses asked God what to do. And sure enough, God had a plan! He had a way to give them water, right there in that dry desert!

7. Take care of: Cross hands, right over left, each with two fingers extended; move in outward circle.

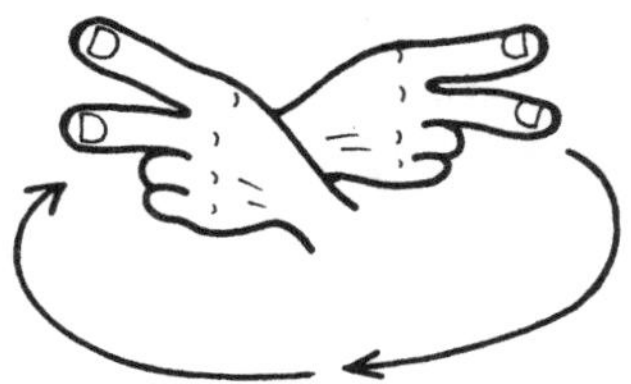

8. As soon as he got back to camp, Moses called the leaders of each family. Moses and the leaders walked and walked until they came to a big rock. Before anyone else could open his mouth to complain, Moses did what God had told him. Moses lifted his walking stick high over his head and swung it toward the rock. CRACK!!! Something AMAZING happened! Water came out of the rock! And guess what? Those Israelites quit complaining! God gave them water right out of a rock in the middle of a desert! Once again, God gave them EVERYTHING they needed!

8. Water: Extend three fingers of right hand; touch mouth a few times.

## Conclude the Story

**Why were the Israelites unhappy?** (They were hungry. They were out of food.) **What did God do to give them food?** (Sent quail. Sent manna.) **What else made the people complain?** (They had no water. They were thirsty.) **How did God give them water?** (Moses hit a rock in the desert.)

**What kinds of things do kids your age need?** (Food. Water. Loving family.) **What does God promise to do?** (Give us the things we need.) **Because God loves us, He gives us everything we need.**

**Exodus 19—20:21**

# The Ten Commandments

## Before the Story

Guide students to briefly practice signs for underlined words.

## Tell the Story

As you tell the story, lead students in responding as shown when you say the underlined words.

***What kinds of rules do you have to follow at school or when playing a game?***

***Today we'll hear about a time when God gave His people some rules to follow.***

1. For three months after the Israelites escaped from Egypt, they walked through the desert. They were on their way to the land God had promised to give them. God guided them with a <u>cloud</u> during the day and a fire by night. One day, the <u>cloud</u> that guided them stopped at the base of steep, rocky Mount Sinai. As the Israelites set up their tents and put their sheep out to graze, they had no idea what an important event was about to take place!

2. Moses <u>climbed</u> the mountain to talk to God. Somewhere, WAY UP among the rocks and boulders, the Lord told Moses how He wanted the Israelites to be His special people, a nation that belonged to Him. Moses listened carefully and then <u>climbed</u> back down the mountain to the Israelite camp. He told all the leaders what God had said. The people all responded, "We will do everything the Lord has said!"

3. For the second time, Moses climbed up Mount Sinai and told the Lord that the people wanted to obey. God answered, "I am going to visit the people. When I speak with you, everyone will <u>hear</u> the sound of My voice. Then they will always believe you. Have the people get ready," the Lord continued. And once again Moses <u>listened</u> carefully to God's instructions and then hurried down the mountain to call the people together.

4. "The day after tomorrow the Lord is going to visit us in a special way," Moses said. "Get <u>ready</u> for His visit!" So the people did the things God had told them to do to get <u>ready</u> for His visit—including washing all their clothes. Moses also told the people to set up a boundary around the mountain. NO ONE was to go up on the mountain—or even touch it!

1. Cloud: Curve raised hands; make circular movements to side.

2. Climb: Curve index and middle fingers; alternately move up in small arcs.

3. Hear, listen: Cup right ear; turn head to left.

4. Ready: Facing hands bounce left to right.

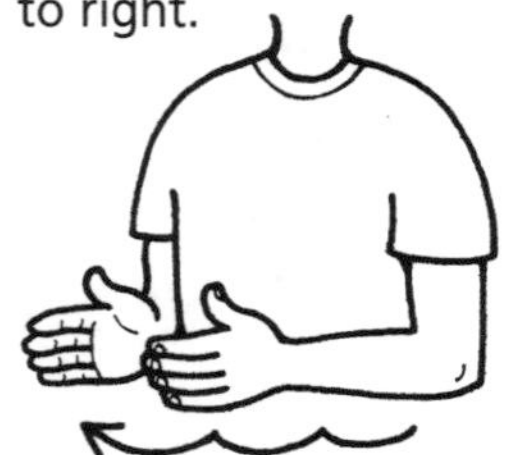

5. Everyone got busy and prepared for the visit. Finally, the day of the Lord's visit arrived. Thunder and lightning came over the mountain and a LOUD trumpet blast rang out. The people trembled as it thundered and billows of smoke rose from the mountain. The Lord CERTAINLY had their attention now! And that was just what He wanted, for God had some VERY important things for Moses to tell them!

5. Thunder: Point to ear; move fists alternately back and forth.

6. God called Moses up to the top of the mountain and began to speak. He gave Moses 10 commandments written on two stone tablets. The first four commandments that God gave were about how to worship and respect Him. He said the people were not to make or worship any idols (false gods) as the people around them did. They were not to misuse God's name in any way. And they were to keep the Sabbath (the seventh day of the week) holy and special by resting on that day and not doing any work.

6. Worship: Left hand over right fist; move hands to body and bow head.

7. Then God gave six commandments about how people should treat each other. God said children should treat parents with respect. God told Moses that the people should never murder, take each other's wives or husbands or steal anything from each other. God also commanded not to give false testimony against a neighbor, which means we should not lie about others. Finally, God warned against wanting what others have.

7. Command: From lips, move index finger out and down with emphasis.

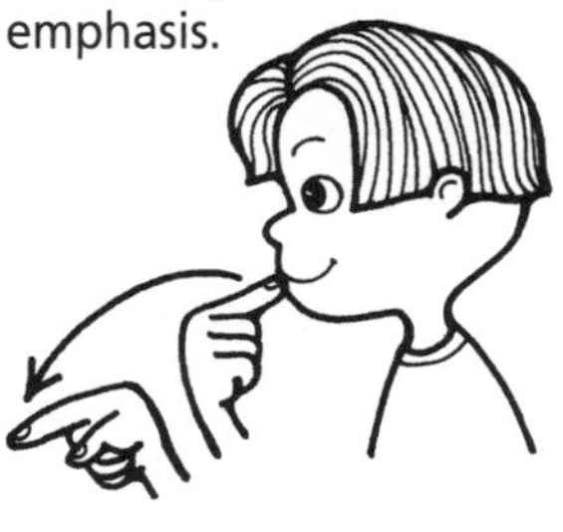

8. Then God was quiet. But the smoke rose and the thunder and trumpeting continued. The people stayed far away. They were all terrified! They said to Moses, "YOU listen to God and then tell us God's message! Don't let God speak to us or we will die!"

"Don't be afraid," Moses told them. "God has shown you His mighty power so that you will have respect for Him and won't sin against Him." But the people stayed at a distance while Moses returned to the mountain to talk with God. Moses listened carefully as God gave him more instructions for the Israelites.

8. Terrified, afraid: Fingertips touching, open hands and cover chest.

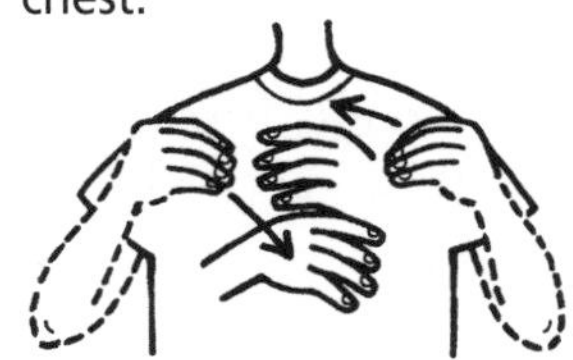

## Conclude the Story

**How did the Israelites know God had come to the mountain to talk with Moses?** (They saw and heard smoke, thunder, lightning and trumpet sounds.) **What are some of the things God commanded the people? Why did God show the people His power?** (So that they would not sin against Him.)

**We don't have to figure out the very best way to live all by ourselves. God's commands teach us the best way to live. That's a GOOD reason to celebrate!**

**Joshua 1; 3; 6**

# Joshua Leads the Israelites

## Materials

Drawing materials/equipment for teacher and each student.

***What are some street signs you see on your way to school or church?***

***Today we'll draw some signs to tell our story!***

## Tell the Story

As you tell each part of the story, draw each sketch. Students copy your sketches.

1. The Israelites were camped by the Jordan River. Moses, their leader, had died. Now Joshua was their leader. Leading God's people was a big job. Joshua must have felt afraid! But God told him over and over, "Be strong and courageous. Don't be afraid. I am giving you this land." God told Joshua to get all the people ready to cross the Jordan River.

1. Draw sign: "FEAR" with "no" slash.

2. God's people were excited! After many years, they were going to enter the Promised Land. But the river was so high and moving so fast, it looked dangerous.

2. Sign: 2 "V"s, "DANGER." Add water behind sign.

3. Now God had told Joshua exactly what to do. Joshua told the people, "Follow the Ark of the Lord!" (The Ark of the Lord was a big, beautiful box covered with gold. It was set on poles and had God's laws inside it.) The priests carried the Ark to the edge of the rushing river. God had that wild river under control, for as the priests' feet touched the water, it stopped upstream! All the people walked across the riverbed without getting their feet wet!

3. Sign: "RR" crossing; add "IVE." Footprint: "J," backward question mark, "O"s. Students add more footprints.

4. The leader of each family picked up a big, smooth stone from the riverbed. When everyone except the priests were safely across, God told Joshua, "Tell the priests to come up out of the Jordan." As the priests stepped out—CRASH!—the water roared back in place! God's people stacked up the stones from the riverbed as a sign to remind them how God helped them cross that scary river!

4. Draw 12 stones from "O"s. Students add details.

5. God's people were finally in the Promised Land. But other people lived in that land already. These people had known that God's people were coming for a long time. And their strong armies wanted to keep God's people out!

5. Sign: "STOP."

6. Jericho was the first big city. A huge stone wall was around it. When the city gates closed, no one could get in or out. That wall looked like it would NEVER come down!

But God told Joshua that He would help His people take over the city of Jericho. God told Joshua, "March around Jericho with your army once a day for six days while the priests blow trumpets made from sheep horns.

"On the seventh day, march around the city SEVEN times. That day, have the priests blow one long, loud blast on the horns. When everyone hears it, tell them to SHOUT! The walls of the city will fall down. They can walk right in!"

6. Sign: "DO NOT ENTER."

7. Joshua told the people all about God's plan. That big wall looked strong, but God had said it would fall! So the Israelites did EXACTLY what God had told them to do. For six days, the army, the priests and all the Israelites marched around Jericho. There was no sound but the horns and the STOMP, STOMP, STOMP of marching feet. The people marched like a big parade for six days.

7. Horn: "6," "C"s.

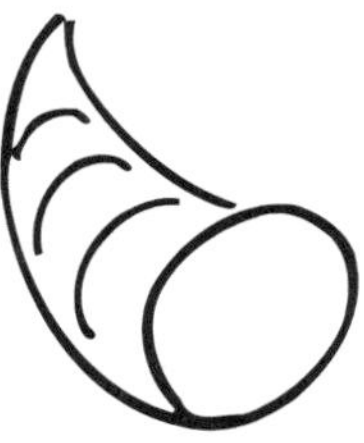

8. On the seventh day, everyone came together to march around that huge high wall. The first six times around there was no sound but the priests' horns and the marching feet. Nothing happened—yet!

But the SEVENTH time around, the priests blew their horns long and loud together. Joshua called, "SHOUT! The Lord has given you the city!"

The Israelites SHOUTED! The high, strong wall rumbled. It CRACKED! And then—CRASH!—the wall came down. And the Israelites marched right in, just as God had promised!

8. Sign: "PROBLEM" with a "no" slash.

## Conclude the Story

**Who was the new leader?** (Joshua.) **What river did the Israelites cross?** (Jordan.) **What did God tell the people?** (Don't be afraid. I will make the wall of Jericho fall.) **What do you think the people learned about God?**

**When we are afraid, God encourages us and promises to be with us. He will help us by giving us courage and by giving us good ideas of what to do.**

### Judges 4:1-16; 5:1-23

# Deborah the Judge

## Materials

Drawing materials/equipment for teacher and each student.

## Tell the Story

As you tell each part of the story, draw each sketch. Students copy your sketches.

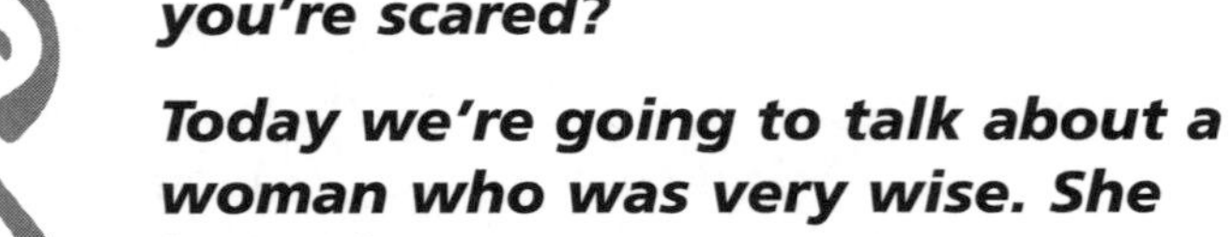

***What makes you feel better when you're scared?***

***Today we're going to talk about a woman who was very wise. She knew how to encourage someone who was afraid.***

1. The Israelites were disobeying God by worshiping idols (gods who weren't real). And so the Israelites had trouble! The trouble was that for 20 YEARS a man named Sisera had been attacking Israel. Sisera's army had 900 iron chariots! Things looked bad. But in the middle of all this trouble, the Israelites finally remembered that God had helped them before. They began to pray to Him to help them again.

1. Draw chariot from triangle, circle and straight line. Add stick-figure driver.

2. A woman named Deborah was a judge for the Israelites. She helped people settle their arguments. People came from all over to a palm tree near her home to get her help. Deborah sat under the palm tree while she helped people. She loved God and listened to Him. She was also a prophetess. That means God gave her messages to tell the Israelites.

2. Palm tree from "W"s and "C"s. Deborah from upside-down "U" and "B." Add face.

3. One day Deborah sent for a man named Barak (BEAR-uk). When Barak came, she said, "The Lord has a job for you. God says, 'Get 10 thousand men and go to Mount Tabor.' God will bring Sisera, his chariots and his army to the river there. God will help you defeat Sisera."

3. Draw Barak.

4. Barak was afraid! *Was this really God's plan?* he wondered. Barak said, "Deborah, if you go with me, I will go. But if you don't go, I'm not going either." Deborah was not afraid. And she wanted Barak to trust God, too. So she said, "Very well. I will go with you."

4. Draw scared faces and "3"s for hair.

5. Barak and Deborah went together to Mount Tabor. Barak sent messengers to the Israelites to ask them to join his army. Soon 10 thousand men were hiking up that mountain. But they weren't the ONLY ones getting ready for a battle!

5. Draw large "M" for mountain.

6. Sisera had heard about all the people coming to Mount Tabor. He prepared for battle, too. And he was sure he'd win. After all, he had the chariots! But Sisera didn't know that the Israelites had GOD'S help!

One morning, Deborah and Barak looked out across the wide, flat valley below. First, they saw a little cloud of dust. It became a BIG cloud of dust! It was the chariots of Sisera and his men! They came closer and CLOSER, until Sisera's army filled the valley below Mount Tabor.

6. Below mountain add wide "U" for valley; add sideways "C"s for people.

7. Deborah turned to Barak and smiled! "Go!" she said. "God will help you defeat Sisera's army!" Deborah encouraged Barak just when he needed it! So Barak and his men came down the mountain. And what do you think happened? God sent a THUNDERSTORM! Lightning flashed. Rain poured down.

7. "Z"s for lightning; add raindrops and "3"s for clouds.

8. Sisera and his chariots were in the wide, flat valley where they could go very fast—over dry ground. But they hadn't counted on RAIN! Soon, water was everywhere! The ground was thick mud! And those horses and chariots were stuck. Sisera and his men left their chariots in the mud and ran! All Barak's army had to do was to chase the enemy until there was no one left to chase! God had won the battle, just as Deborah had told Barak.

8. Draw running stick figures.

9. Deborah and Barak made up a song about how God won the battle! This song is written in Judges chapter 5. Deborah showed how encouraging someone can help that person trust God.

9. Draw musical notes.

## Conclude the Story

**What was Deborah like?** (Prophetess. Wise. Believed God.) **Why do you think Barak needed her help?** (He was afraid.) **When God sent a storm, what happened?** (The chariots were stuck in mud. The soldiers ran.)

**Sometimes we might be afraid to obey God, like Barak was. One way God helps us is by giving us people to encourage us like Deborah encouraged Barak to trust God. We can be encouragers, too—by our kind words and the things we say!**

**Judges 6—7**

# Gideon the Prophet

## Materials

Drawing materials/equipment for teacher and each student.

## Tell the Story

As you tell each part of the story, draw each sketch. Students copy your sketches.

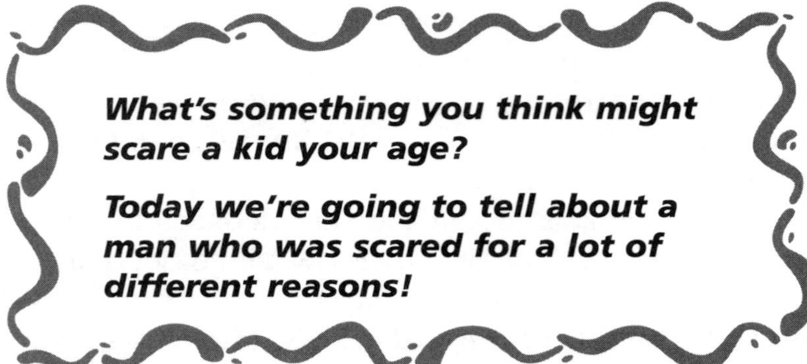


1. Gideon was threshing grain—tossing it into the air to separate the hulls from the grain. Usually people do this in the open air, so the breeze carries off the hulls. But Gideon was doing it while he HID! He was down in a large pit under an oak tree! You see, the Midianites were everywhere. And they were taking everything! Gideon was scared and was hiding and hoping the Midianites wouldn't find him and take his grain! But someone DID find him.

1. Draw 2 "I"s and add "3"s for oak tree. Add figure in "U" for pit.

2. Gideon looked up. A stranger looked down at him and said, "The Lord is with you, mighty warrior!" How do you think Gideon felt, hearing that? The stranger said that Gideon was going to defeat the Midianites! Gideon didn't see how THAT could happen! He wasn't brave or strong—he was scared! But the stranger said, "I will be with you." The stranger was God. GOD would help Gideon!

2. Draw scared face.

3. So Gideon blew a ram's horn and sent messengers to call warriors from all over the country of Israel. Thousands of Israelites came to help defeat the Midianites!

3. Horn from "6" and "C"s.

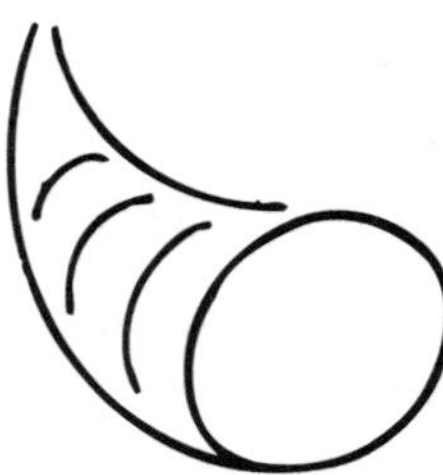

4. But Gideon was still afraid. He asked God to do something to prove he would really defeat the Midianites. Gideon laid a sheepskin out at night and asked God to make the ground around it dry but the sheepskin wet. Well, God did just that! And God did it again in a different way, just so Gideon would know God was helping him.

4. Draw sheepskin from "C"s, "L"s and "3"s.

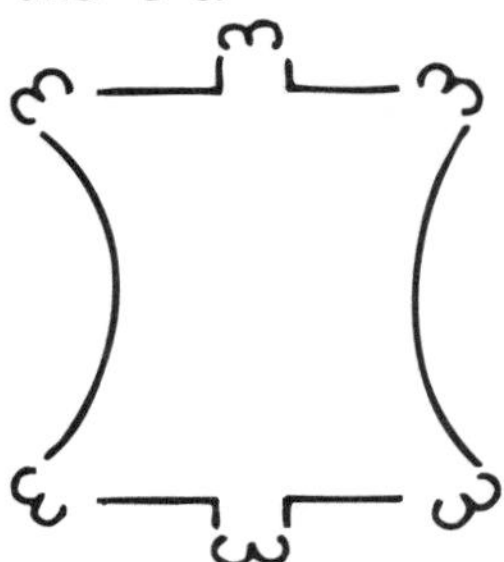

5. Next, God told Gideon, "There are too many soldiers. With so many, Israel might think they beat the Midianites by their own strength. Send anyone home who is afraid!" Gideon obeyed, and all but 10,000 men went home. And Gideon obeyed again when God told him to send even MORE people home! Now there were only 300 soldiers. There were THOUSANDS of Midianites! But God had told Gideon that He would defeat the enemy.

5. Draw scared face. Add "Z"s for legs and "I"s for arms.

6. Gideon and his men got ready. Instead of weapons, they carried horns and torches inside clay jars. Gideon told them, "God has said we will defeat the Midianites. Now watch me and do what I do!" In the middle of the night, they made a big circle around the valley where the Midianites were sleeping. They blew their horns, broke their jars, lifted their torches and shouted!

6. Make "V"s for torches.

7. The shouting and bright lights woke the Midianites. Scared and confused, they began to fight EACH OTHER! They began to RUN! All Gideon and his men had to do was CHASE them! Gideon had trusted God and obeyed, even when he was afraid. And God HAD defeated the Midianites!

7. Write "FEAR." Add circle and "no" slash.

## Conclude the Story

**What did God tell Gideon to do?** (Defeat the Midianites.) **When Gideon was afraid, what did he do? What did God do?** (Asked God to prove He would help; God proved to Gideon He would help him.)

**Even when we are afraid, we can still obey. God's love and power are bigger than all our fears. We can tell Him when we are afraid, like Gideon did. He knows we need His help. And He hears us when we pray to Him!**

**Judges 13—16**

# Samson's Strength

## Materials

Drawing materials/equipment for teacher and each student.

***What might happen if a person didn't follow instructions while baking a cake?***

***Today we're going to tell about a person who ignored some of God's instructions.***

## Tell the Story

As you tell each part of the story, draw each sketch. Students copy your sketches.

1. Once again God's people forgot to obey God's instructions. And once again, God had a plan to get them out of all the trouble they had caused by doing evil instead of doing good. One day God sent an angel to a woman. He told her that she would have a son who would obey God in some special ways. The angel told her some special rules for her son to obey: not to eat any grapes or drink any wine, not to touch anything dead and never EVER to cut his hair.

1. Draw circles for grapes. Head from a wiggly upside-down "U" and knife from 2 "D"s. Add "no" slash over grapes and knife.

2. So Samson was born. He grew up to be VERY strong. His hair was very long and braided into seven braids. But although he was strong, he was not always wise.

2. Face from "7" and "C"s. Add 7 rows of "X"s for hair.

3. You see, the Philistines lived nearby. They had made trouble for the Israelites for years. And God had told the Israelites never to marry Philistines because the Philistines worshiped false gods. But Samson wanted to get married—to a Philistine girl!

3. Draw "P"s for Philistines. Add faces and details for man and girl.

4. This led to lots MORE trouble with the Philistines. When the Philistines fought with Samson, he destroyed their fields. When their army came to kill him, he killed them all. He pulled down the gates of a town! No one could stop him! This really scared the Philistines. They began thinking they had better not attack Israel while Samson was around!

4. Gates from upside-down "U"s and lines.

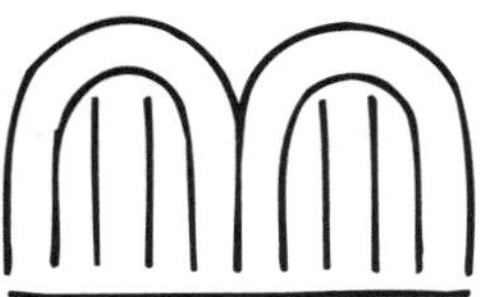

5. Well, all this trouble didn't keep Samson from liking those Philistine ladies! He fell in love with another lady named Delilah. The Philistines paid her to find out how to make Samson as weak as other men. Delilah asked and asked, and Samson told her one story after another. But she nagged him until he told her that if she cut his hair, he'd be like other men. Guess what she did?

5. Knife from 2 "D"s.

6. Sure enough, with no hair Samson had broken the promise he had made to God and God's power left him. He became as weak as other men. The Philistines tied him up and made him a slave. They even blinded him and forced him to grind grain every day in prison. But slowly, Samson's hair began to grow back.

6. Draw face with sad eyes made from "C"s Add growing hair.

7. One day, many Philistines had a big party at their temple to honor their idol! They brought Samson into the temple and put him between the two main pillars that held up the roof. The Philistines wanted to make fun of their once-great enemy. But Samson wanted to stop the Philistines one more time. So he prayed.

7. Draw ovals and lines to make temple pillars, leaving space between the pillars.

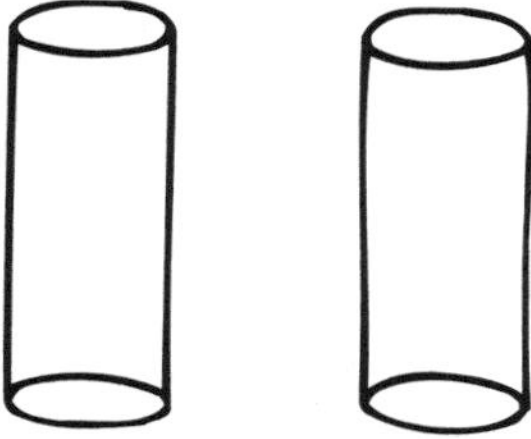

8. He prayed, "God, let me be strong once more, so I can knock down this temple full of Philistines." He began to push on the pillars! Soon, WHAM! the whole BUILDING fell down! Samson died, too. But the Philistines left Israel alone for a long time.

8. Add stick-figure Samson between pillars.

## Conclude the Story

**What was Samson like?** (Strong. Chosen by God for a special job.) **What kind of choices did he make?** (Disobeyed God.) **What were the results of Samson's disobedience?** (Lots of trouble.)

**Sometimes we think we can get away with doing wrong, like Samson did. But disobeying God always causes problems. God loves us and knows what is best for us. That's why we obey Him!**

Ruth

# Ruth's Faithfulness

## Before the Story

Guide students to briefly practice signs for underlined words.

***When was a time you really needed someone's help? What happened?***

***Today we'll find out what happened when someone needed help just to have food to eat!***

## Tell the Story

As you tell the story, lead students in responding as shown when you say the underlined words.

1. For years in Israel, there had been famine—no rain and no food. Many Israelites had moved from Israel to nearby Moab in search of food. Ruth was a young woman who grew up in Moab. She met and married one of these Israelite men. Ruth and her husband lived with her husband's family. After a time, her husband's father died and then her husband and his brother died. Now Ruth, her husband's mother, Naomi, and Ruth's sister-in-law were widows! They had no husbands.

1. Husband: Close fingers of right hand while moving out from forehead; clasp hands.

2. In those days, a woman who had no husband usually had no way to make a living. All three women must have wondered, *Who will help us now that our husbands are gone?*

Naomi told her daughters-in-law, "Go back to your own families. Perhaps you will marry again. I will leave for Israel." Ruth and her sister-in-law did not want to leave Naomi. But finally, Ruth's sister-in-law left for home.

2. Leave: Flat hands move up and into fists.

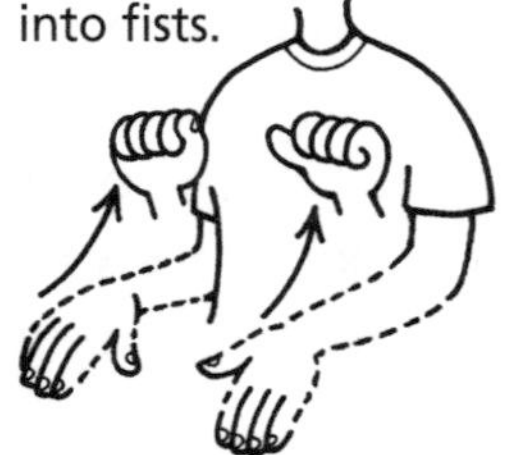

3. Ruth, however, said, "I'm going with you! I will be like your daughter. Your people will be my people, and your God will be my God. I have promised God that I will not leave you!" Naomi could see that Ruth WASN'T going to change her mind! So Ruth set off with Naomi for Bethlehem, Naomi's hometown. During this hard time in her life, Ruth must have been glad that God had provided her with a caring mother-in-law like Naomi.

3. With: Touch fists together.

4. When they got to Bethlehem, the farmers were just beginning to harvest, or cut down, the ripe barley plants. Barley is a grain, like wheat. In Bible times, people harvested the barley and tied the plants into bundles.

4. Plant: Open right hand as it comes up through left.

5. Ruth must have been VERY glad there was a harvest going on! God had made laws about harvesting food. God said that grain that fell to the ground and grain that grew in the corners of the fields were to be left for poor people to gather (called gleaning). Well, Ruth and Naomi were poor people now, so Ruth could glean enough barley so that she and Naomi could eat for a while.

5. Poor: Right hand cups left elbow; move hand down and close fingers.

6. Ruth went to a barley field where she saw people harvesting grain. She followed the harvesters, picking barley off the ground and cutting barley stalks in the corners of the field. Ruth didn't mind the hard work. Naomi had been kind to her and helped her. Ruth wanted to make sure that she was kind, too, and that she had enough food for Naomi.

6. Kind: Left hand at chest level; right hand circles left.

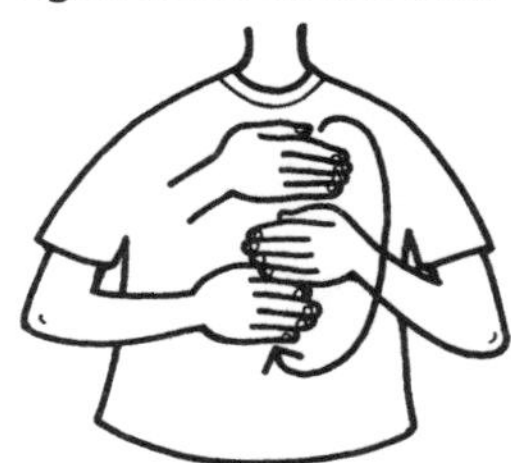

7. The field where Ruth gleaned belonged to a relative of Naomi. His name was Boaz. When Boaz saw Ruth working in his field, he asked his helper about her. "She's the woman from Moab who came with Naomi," the helper said. "She asked if she could glean in our field, and she's worked very hard since she got here!" Boaz had already heard about Ruth and how she had taken care of Naomi. Boaz went to Ruth and invited her to stay and glean in his fields.

7. Work: Hands in fists, tap left wrist with right.

8. So Ruth gleaned in Boaz's fields all during the harvest. And once Naomi heard that it was her relative Boaz who owned the field where Ruth was gleaning, she made a wise plan. Her plan would mean that she and Ruth would be able to get back some of her family's land. Naomi guided Ruth in following Naomi's plan exactly. And as a result of Naomi's guidance, Boaz bought back the land Naomi's family had owned. Now Naomi and Ruth had a home! And Boaz also MARRIED Ruth! When Ruth and Boaz had a baby, Naomi's friends came to celebrate with her. Because of her wise plan, Naomi and Ruth had a home and family again!

8. Wise: Bend right index finger; move up and down on forehead.

## Conclude the Story

**Why did the Israelites go to Moab?** (There was no food in Israel.) **When Naomi decided to go back to Israel, what did Ruth decide?** (To go with Naomi and care for her.) **When Naomi found out that Boaz was her relative, what did she do?** (Made a plan to get Boaz to help her.) **How did Naomi help and guide Ruth?** (She brought her back to Bethlehem. She told her what to do to get some land and a home.)

**Even in hard times, God gives us people to love and care for us. It's one way God guides us.**

**1 Samuel 1—2:11,18-21,26; 3:1-19**

# Samuel Listens to God

## Materials

Drawing materials/equipment for teacher and each student.

## Tell the Story

As you tell each part of the story, draw each sketch. Students copy your sketches.

***Who is someone you know very well?***

***Today we'll use the letter U to tell about a boy who grew to know God better and better.***

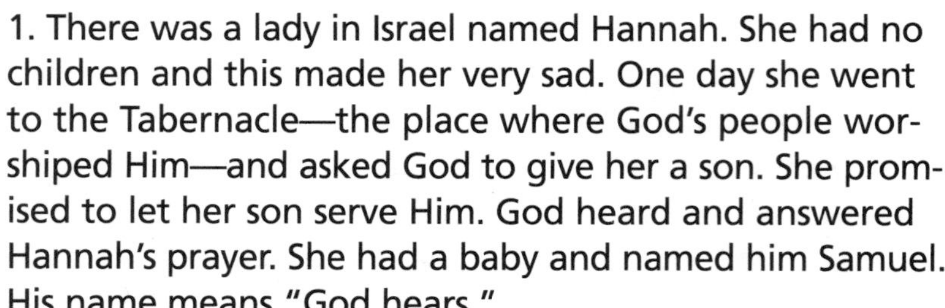
1. There was a lady in Israel named Hannah. She had no children and this made her very sad. One day she went to the Tabernacle—the place where God's people worshiped Him—and asked God to give her a son. She promised to let her son serve Him. God heard and answered Hannah's prayer. She had a baby and named him Samuel. His name means "God hears."

1. Draw upside down "U"s and add lines for praying hands.

2. Baby Samuel grew and grew! When he was old enough, Hannah took him to the Tabernacle where she had prayed. Samuel stayed there with Eli, the priest. Hannah loved and missed Samuel. Every year, she visited Samuel and brought him a special coat she had made him, just to remind him of her love.

2. Draw "U"s and add faces for Hannah and Samuel.

3. As Samuel grew, he helped Eli take care of the Tabernacle. By now Eli was old and he couldn't see well, so he must have been very glad to have Samuel's help! Samuel made sure there was oil for the lamps and wood for the fire. He opened the Tabernacle doors in the morning, closed them at night and probably helped Eli do many other things, too!

3. Draw lamp and wide "U"s for oil. Add wick.

4. One night, Samuel finished all his chores as usual. He got into bed, lay down and closed his eyes as usual. Suddenly, he heard a voice. Someone was calling his name. "Samuel! Samuel!" *Who was it?* Samuel thought. *Was it Eli?*

4. Draw face of sleeping Samuel.

5. Samuel sat up. Maybe Eli needed him. He ran to where Eli lay asleep. He shook Eli. "Here I am!" he said.

5. Add open eyes and mouth to Samuel.

6. Eli woke up and looked at Samuel. He said, "I didn't call you, Samuel. Go back to bed." Now Samuel KNEW there was NO ONE else in the Tabernacle. He had checked when he shut the doors! But after Samuel went back to bed, he heard the same voice calling his name. Samuel got up again and went back to Eli. "Here I am!" he said. And again, Eli said, "I didn't call. Go back to bed."

6. Draw second sleeping face. Add details for Eli's face.

7. When Samuel heard the voice call his name a THIRD time, he went to Eli and said, "Here I am! I KNOW you called me!" *Was Eli playing tricks on him?* Samuel wondered.

Suddenly, Eli realized what was going on: GOD was calling Samuel! Eli said, "Samuel, go back to bed. When you hear the voice again say, 'Speak, Lord. Your servant is listening.'"

7. Turn closed eyes to surprised face.

8. So Samuel went back to bed. But he probably wasn't sleepy! Amazed and excited, he waited quietly, straining to hear. Then, he heard it—the voice calling his name! Samuel said, "Speak, Lord! Your servant is LISTENING."

8. Add head and large ears to Samuel.

9. The Bible says that God talked with Samuel. He told Samuel important things that were going to happen. After that night, God often talked with Samuel. And Samuel always listened and obeyed. As Samuel grew up, God helped him to become a person everyone in Israel respected. All the people of Israel knew that Samuel was a person who listened to God! He became the priest and was the leader of God's people for many years.

9. Write "SAMUEL." Add "LISTENS" and "OBEYS."

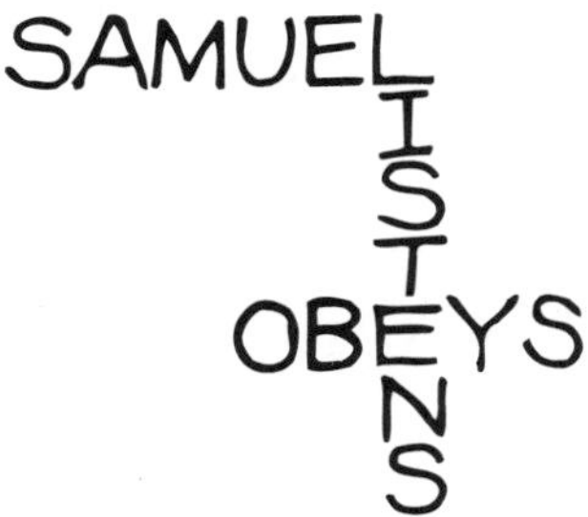


## Conclude the Story

**What does Samuel's name mean?** (God hears.) **How would you describe Samuel? Why do you think Samuel chose to listen to God?**

**Because Samuel listened to God, he knew how to obey God. We can listen and obey, too—from the time we're young until we're old!**

**1 Samuel 8—10; 13:1-14; 15**

# Samuel Anoints Saul

## Materials

Drawing materials/equipment for teacher and each student.

## Tell the Story

As you tell each part of the story, draw each sketch. Students copy your sketches.

***What is something you've made an excuse for not doing?***

***Today we're going to hear about Israel's first king who made some excuses for not obeying God.***

1. Samuel had been God's leader, or judge, for a long time and now he was old. Although his sons were helping him judge, they weren't honest. So the people told Samuel, "You are old. Your sons are NOT good judges. Find a king for us instead!"

1. Write "old." Add face.

2. Samuel was upset because he knew that God was really their king! But God told Samuel, "Warn them. Tell them a king will take their children, their food, their land and their animals. They will be like slaves!" Samuel told the people God's warning. But the people wanted a king ANYWAY, so God told Samuel He would give them a king.

2. Draw "O" and "V"s for crown.

3. Now about this time, a young man named Saul was looking for his father's lost donkeys. He and his helper came to ask Samuel if he knew where the donkeys were. When Saul came toward Samuel, God said, "Here's the man who will be king." Samuel invited Saul and his helper to a special dinner. Later Samuel poured olive oil on Saul's head and said, "God has chosen you to be the leader of His people."

3. Donkeys from "U"s, "V"s and lines.

4. Not long after that, Samuel called all of Israel together and brought Saul to the front. Samuel said, "Here is the king God has chosen." God let the people have what they wanted, but God's warning about the trouble from a king came true.

4. Add "Saul" to crown.

5. King Saul seemed to want to do everything his own way instead of God's way. God was patient with him. But one day, God gave Samuel a message for King Saul. Samuel told Saul, "God will help you win your battle against the enemy. But God says that after the battle, you must get rid of EVERYTHING that belongs to the enemy." God had good reasons for His rule. And God expected Saul to obey!

5. Write "ENEMY." Add "no" slash.

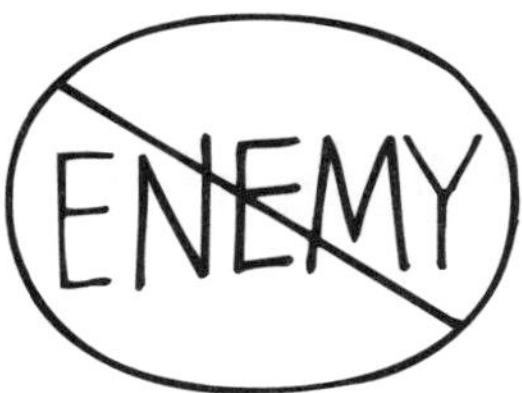


6. Soon, Saul and the Israelite army charged into battle. They won, just as God had said they would. But Saul decided to bring home some of the best cattle and sheep. Saul disobeyed God's command! God told Samuel what had happened. The next morning, Samuel went to meet Saul who was returning from the battle. Sure enough, cows and sheep were coming along behind—cows and sheep that proved Saul had disobeyed!

6. Draw cow and sheep from "U"s and "O"s.

7. Saul made excuses. He said that disobeying was the soldiers' idea. Then he said the soldiers wanted to offer the animals to God! Then he said he was so afraid of the soldiers that he disobeyed! Samuel told Saul that NOTHING is more important than obeying God—not even gifts! He said, "Because you no longer obey God, you will not be king."

7. Conversation balloon for excuses. Add "no" slash.

8. As Samuel walked away, Saul grabbed Samuel's robe, trying to stop him. A piece of the robe tore off. Samuel said, "Just like you tore a piece off my robe, God has torn the kingdom from you. God doesn't lie or change His mind. When He tells you something, He means it!" Saul was sorry for what he had done, but he couldn't undo it! God still loved Saul, but he was not going to be king for much longer.

8. Add "no" slash over Saul's crown.

## Conclude the Story

**Why did God make Saul king?** (The people wanted their own way.) **Why do you think Saul disobeyed God? How do you think Saul felt when he heard he would no longer be king?**

**Sometimes we make excuses for not obeying God. Our excuses may even seem pretty good! But deep down we know we are not obeying. God wants us to obey Him, not make excuses—not even good excuses! Nothing is more important than obeying Him.**

**1 Samuel 16—18:16; 2 Samuel 5:1-10; 6:1-19**

# David Loves God

## Materials

Drawing materials/equipment for teacher and each student.

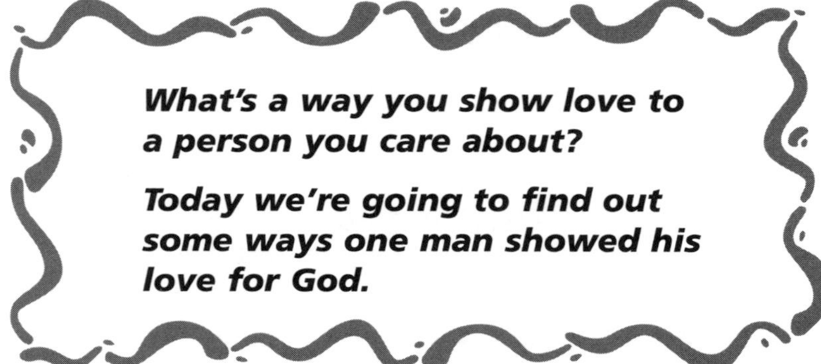


## Tell the Story

As you tell each part of the story, draw each sketch. Students copy your sketches.

1. King Saul had not obeyed God. He had done things his own way. Although Saul was still the king, God had chosen a new king. God sent Samuel to Jesse's house in Bethlehem, so He could show Samuel the next king. Samuel met seven fine-looking sons of Jesse, but God said NONE of them was the one He had chosen. Jesse had one more son—his youngest son David, who was out watching the sheep. When Samuel met him, God told Samuel, "HE is the one!" Samuel poured olive oil on David's head to show that God had chosen David as king.

1. Draw seven circles; add faces.

Write "8." Add details for David.

2. Some time later, King Saul needed a person to play soothing music for him. Someone told the king about this young man named David, so David was brought to the palace to play his harp for Saul. David was soon living in the palace some of the time.

2. Harp from "D."

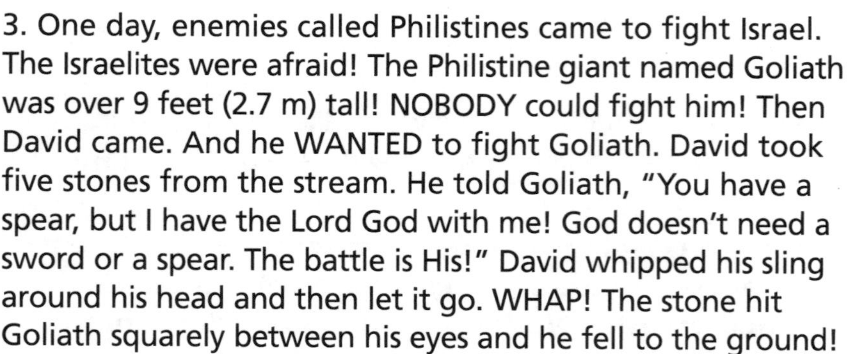

3. One day, enemies called Philistines came to fight Israel. The Israelites were afraid! The Philistine giant named Goliath was over 9 feet (2.7 m) tall! NOBODY could fight him! Then David came. And he WANTED to fight Goliath. David took five stones from the stream. He told Goliath, "You have a spear, but I have the Lord God with me! God doesn't need a sword or a spear. The battle is His!" David whipped his sling around his head and then let it go. WHAP! The stone hit Goliath squarely between his eyes and he fell to the ground!

3. Goliath from "9."

The Philistines ran! The Israelites chased them away. David became a hero!

Write 2 "5"s; add details for David's head.

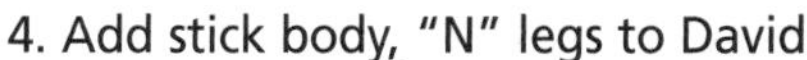

4. David married King Saul's daughter and lived in the palace. But Saul was jealous that everyone in Israel loved David. Saul even tried to KILL David. David ran from Saul, but he never tried to hurt Saul. David showed by his attitude and his actions that he trusted God to make him king at just the right time. After Saul died, the people came to David and made him their king.

4. Add stick body, "N" legs to David.

5. Now that David was king, he didn't want to be like Saul, doing things his own way. Instead, David wanted to honor God and help the Israelites remember that God was their real King! One way David helped his people was by helping them worship God. David loved to worship God. He had made up songs for God when he was a shepherd boy. Now he wrote many songs, called psalms, to help the people worship God. He also chose people to sing and play instruments, so everyone could praise God together!

5. Draw new David; add crown. Add musical notes; harp from "D."

6. David did many other things, too. He fought many battles so that there would be peace in his country. He helped people who had problems. Sometimes, David did wrong things. But David always talked to God. He asked God for help with his hard choices and asked for God's forgiveness when he had done wrong. David showed his love for God by praying whether he was glad or sad. And because David showed his love for God in the things he did and said, the people of Israel learned to honor and obey God.

6. Draw new crowned David with eyes closed. Add praying hands from "U" and "W."

## Conclude the Story

**How did David show that he loved God and wanted to please God?** (Trusted God when he fought Goliath. Obeyed God when he was king. Wrote songs to worship God. Prayed.)

**It's easy to say we love God. But God wants us to show our love for Him by our attitudes and actions, too.**

**1 Samuel 18:1-9; 19–20**

# David and Jonathan Are Friends

## Before the Story

Guide students to briefly practice signs for underlined words.

## Tell the Story

As you tell the story, lead students in responding as shown when you say the underlined words.

***Why might someone be jealous of another person?***

***Today we'll hear about all the trouble one man caused because of his jealousy!***

1. David was an ordinary boy who lived in Bible times—at least his family and neighbors considered him ordinary. But everything changed when Samuel the prophet came to David's home in Bethlehem. Samuel told David and his family that God had chosen David, that ordinary boy, to be KING. Not long after that, David depended on God for courage to fight the giant Goliath—and won! Suddenly, that ordinary boy was a <u>hero</u>. Everyone in Israel loved David. People made up songs about what a great <u>hero</u> he was.

1. Hero: Right fingertips close as hand moves out from forehead; touch chest with fingertips and then move forward to fists.

2. King Saul decided that since David had won such a great victory for Israel's army, David should live in the palace. As David grew, King Saul made him an army officer. Every time Saul sent David to do something, David did it well! As Saul saw how everyone loved David, Saul began to grow <u>jealous</u>. People liked David better than Saul, the KING! Saul grew more and MORE <u>jealous</u>. He even hoped that David would be killed in battle!

2. Jealous: With little finger at mouth, twist right hand forward.

3. Although King Saul was jealous and hateful, his son Jonathan wasn't like that at all. Jonathan became David's best <u>friend</u>! He and David were like brothers and they promised to be true <u>friends</u> always. After David and Jonathan made this promise, Jonathan gave David his prince's robe and belt and sword to tell David, "You're my best <u>friend</u>."

3. Friend: Interlock index fingers; repeat in reverse.

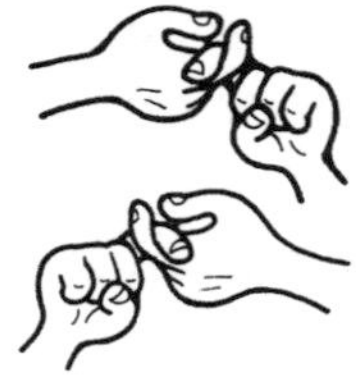

4. Jonathan did more than give David gifts. He helped save David's life! You see, King Saul's jealousy got worse and WORSE. One day, Saul threw a SPEAR at David! Jonathan knew he needed to help his friend <u>hide</u>. If David didn't <u>hide</u> well, he might be found by King Saul and KILLED!

4. Hide: Touch lips with right fist; move right fist under cupped left hand.

5. In fact, whenever King Saul was angry, David had to run away or hide. Jonathan was courageous and <u>helped</u> David each time. Jonathan watched King Saul and talked to him to find out how Saul was feeling. Then Jonathan would find a way to tell David if it was safe to come back to the palace or safer to stay away.

5. Help: Raise right fist with left palm.

6. Finally, things got so dangerous that Jonathan told David to hide in the bushes near a field where Jonathan usually went to practice shooting arrows.

Jonathan told David, "If it's <u>safe</u> for you to come back, I'll tell the boy who chases my arrows, 'Bring the arrows back.' But if it is NOT <u>safe</u>, I'll say, 'Look. The arrows are beyond you!' Then you'll know it is God's time for you to stay hidden from my father."

6. Safe: Crossed fists facing chest, pull apart and face out.

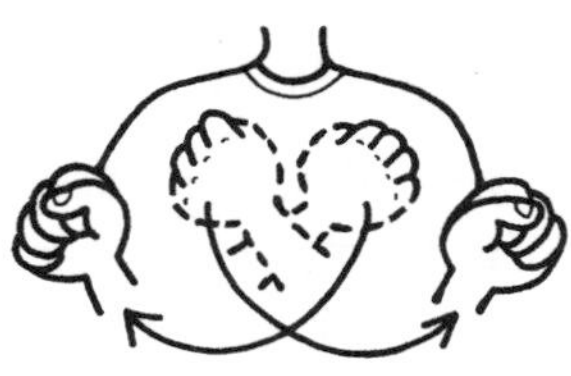

7. So David hid. He <u>watched</u> and listened to find out his friend's message. Jonathan shot three arrows and then said to the boy who chased the arrows, "The arrows are beyond you. Hurry. Go quickly! Don't stop!" David must have been VERY sad as he <u>watched</u>. He now knew it was not safe to come back to the palace as long as Saul was alive. Now David had to depend on God once again to give him courage.

7. Watch: Move right two fingers away from eyes.

8. After Jonathan sent the boy away, David stepped out of his hiding place. He and Jonathan talked and hugged and cried together. They reminded each other about another <u>promise</u> they had made to each other: they would always take care of each other's families, no matter what happened. Even though David and Jonathan never saw each other again, David had an opportunity to keep that <u>promise</u> later, when he became king.

Jonathan knew that God had chosen David to be king. He knew that helping David meant he himself would NEVER be king. But Jonathan always chose to be David's friend, and God gave them both courage, reminding them that He was with them and helping them do right.

8. Promise: Right index finger on lips; move to open hand on left fist.

## Conclude the Story

**Why did Saul grow jealous of David?** (People loved David. ) **How did Jonathan show his friendship to David?** (Gave him gifts. Made promises.) **How did Jonathan tell David it was not safe to come back?** (He spoke orders to a boy in a certain way.)

**God gave David and Jonathan courage to do what was right. When we ask God, He can give us courage in any situation, too!**

1 Samuel 24

# David Spares Saul's Life

## Before the Story

Guide students to briefly practice signs for underlined words.

***How do you think most enemies treat each other?***

***Today we'll find out how one man in Bible times treated an enemy who wanted to kill him!***

## Tell the Story

As you tell the story, lead students in responding as shown when you say the underlined words.

1. Many years had passed since David was a young boy in Israel. He had been chosen to be king and had killed the giant Goliath. He had come to work for King Saul and married King Saul's daughter. After all this time, David was not yet the king. Saul was STILL the king of Israel. And Saul HATED David. He wanted to kill David. But David did NOT want to kill Saul. God had said David would be king someday. And David knew that GOD would decide when Saul should stop being king.

2. King Saul was so jealous of David and so angry at him, he took 3,000 men with him to the desert to chase and capture David! One time when Saul was chasing David, David and his men hid way back in a deep, dark cave. Then guess who walked right into the front of the cave? SAUL!

3. Saul was all alone, away from his soldiers. One of David's men whispered, "Look! It's Saul! God has given you this chance to capture Saul, or even kill him!" As quiet as a shadow, David slipped to the front of the cave. He silently took his knife from his belt, but he didn't hurt Saul. He sliced a piece from Saul's clothes. David's men wanted to attack Saul, but David would not hurt him.

4. When Saul left the cave, he heard someone call, "My lord, the king!" It was DAVID! Saul whirled around. David lifted the piece of Saul's clothes high and said, "Why do you listen to people who tell you I am going to hurt you? Look! I cut this from your clothes! My men wanted me to kill you, but I said, 'I can't hurt Saul. He is God's chosen king.'"

1. King: Right thumb between index and middle fingers; move from shoulder to waist.

2. Chase: With left in front of right, move fists outward; wiggle right fist as it moves.

3. Quiet, silent: Index finger at lips; move hands outward, palms down.

4. Clothing: Flat hands down over chest several times.

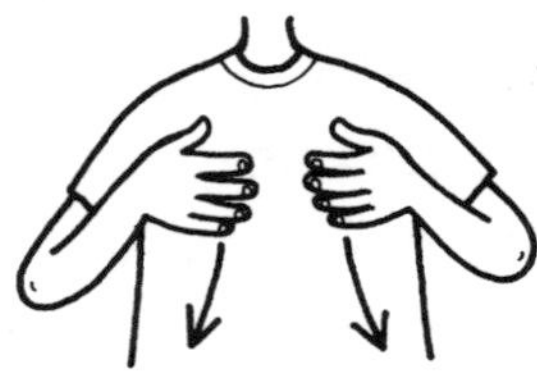

5. David continued, "King Saul, I will not hurt you, no matter what you do to me."

Saul felt SO ashamed! He said, "David, you have treated me kindly, but I have treated you badly. May God reward you for being kind to me today." Then Saul left safely. David made sure of that.

5. Kind: Left hand at chest level; right hand circles left.

6. Even though King Saul was glad David had not killed him, it wasn't long before Saul was chasing David AGAIN! Saul took his 3,000 soldiers and went looking for David. They camped for the night near a hill. Saul lay down to sleep, right in the center of his soldiers. God put Saul and all his men into a deep sleep. Meanwhile, David and one of his men quietly made their way into Saul's camp.

6. Sleep: Draw hand down to chin, closing fingertips.

7. David tiptoed past the sleeping men guarding Saul to where a spear and a water jug lay near Saul's head. David stood over the sleeping king who wanted so badly to kill him. He could have taken Saul's spear and killed Saul, right there and then! But David would not do it. Instead, David picked up the jug and spear and climbed up the nearby hill.

David shouted out, "Who's guarding the king of Israel? Where are the water jug and the spear that were beside his head?"

7. Guard: Move fists outward together.

8. Saul sat up. He saw David, holding up Saul's spear and water jug. David called, "Why are you chasing me? God put you into my hands again, but I would not hurt you." Saul promised not to try to hurt David again. But it didn't take long for Saul to forget his promise. In fact, Saul kept trying to kill David until the day Saul died! All those years, even though Saul was cruel to David, God gave David the courage to show love to Saul. David knew God would make him the king one day. And until then, he could love even his enemy Saul!

8. Love: Cross fists over heart.

## Conclude the Story

**Why was Saul trying to kill David?** (He was jealous and afraid.) **Why didn't David kill Saul?** (Saul was God's chosen king.) **How did David need God's gift of courage?** (Needed courage to show love to Saul, instead of anger.)

**It's never easy to love those who are unkind or to do kind things for people who are mean to us. But God says His love and forgiveness are for everyone. God promises to give us the courage to do what's right and good. He will help us.**

## 1 Samuel 25

# Abigail Is Kind to David

## Materials

Play dough (1/4 cup, or 2 oz.) and a plastic spoon for each student.

***When have you argued with a friend instead of being kind? What happened?***

***Today we'll hear about some people who argued and some who treated each other kindly.***

## Tell the Story

**Follow along with me as we use our dough to tell today's story.**

1. **Divide your dough in half. From one half make some hills. Use a plastic spoon to shape hills.** Before David became the king of Israel, he and his men spent a lot of time living out in the hills. For one thing, they were trying to stay away from King Saul. King Saul wanted to KILL David because he knew David would one day become the king. But because David did not want to hurt Saul AND because he wanted to stay safe, he and his men stayed far from the palace and camped out in places where there were very few people.

2. **From the other half of your dough, roll tiny balls to make a flock of sheep.** But out in the hills there were robbers who would raid the flocks belonging to others. So while David and his men were living out in the hills, they often protected flocks of sheep and the shepherds who took care of the sheep. One year, David and his men protected the sheep and shepherds of a man whose name was Nabal.

Later that year, David and his men were still living out in the hills. And they were very HUNGRY! They needed food and water. So David sent some of his men to the place where Nabal was shearing his sheep. They greeted Nabal and politely reminded Nabal that while his shepherds and sheep were out in the hills, David and his men had protected them.

David's men then asked if Nabal might please give them whatever food and drink he could spare. Now MOST people would have gladly given David and his men whatever they asked for, because David was a hero in that country!

But no matter what ANYONE else might have done, NABAL wasn't about to share anything! The Bible says he was mean and selfish in the way he treated people. The name "Nabal" meant "fool," and this was one time he lived up to his name!

"Who IS this David?" Nabal asked, as if he had never HEARD of David! He went on to insult David. Then Nabal finished up by saying he saw no reason to share his food and water with some stranger! Nabal probably thought he had really shown David who was boss!

3. **Make a sword.** David's men returned and told him everything Nabal had done and said. David then instructed his men to put on their swords. They were going to have to TAKE food and water from this selfish, foolish man who would not share.

But in the meantime, one of Nabal's workers ran home and told Nabal's wife, Abigail, what had happened!

"See what you can do," the worker told Abigail. "I think we're going to have trouble with David, because our master is such a wicked man. No one can talk to him!"

4. **Make a donkey. Add bundles to its back.** Abigail was a wise woman and immediately made plans to stop the quarrel her husband had started with David. Abigail quickly had her servants pack many pounds of bread, figs, raisins, grain and good things to drink on donkeys. She told her servants to go on ahead of her.

Soon Abigail, herself, came riding up to David's camp. She greeted David humbly and said, "Sir, let me take the blame for Nabal's meanness. Ignore him—he is a fool, just as his name says. Please accept these gifts I bring and forgive Nabal's actions."

David was impressed with this wise and kind woman. He thanked God that she had come and stopped the trouble between him and Nabal. David told Abigail to go in peace; he would not hurt Nabal. Soon after this, however, Nabal died. When David heard that Nabal died, he remembered Abigail. He remembered her generosity and kindness. David sent his servants to ask Abigail to become his wife! And kind and generous Abigail married David, who later became king of Israel!

## Conclude the Story

**What made Nabal a foolish man?** (He didn't listen to others. He was mean and would not share.) **Why did David ask him for help?** (David and his men had been kind and had protected Nabal's sheep.) **How did Abigail show she was kind and wise?** (Brought food to David and his men. Apologized for her husband's actions.) **Abigail's kindness made a big difference by helping to keep peace between David and Nabal.**

**Being generous and kind can make a difference in our lives, too. Kindness in our lives pleases God and helps us make and keep good friends!**

## 2 Samuel 6; 1 Chronicles 15—16

# David Brings Home the Ark

## Before the Story

Guide students to briefly practice signs for underlined words.

***What's something you like to do when your family is together?***

***Our Bible story today is about something God's people did together. Listen to find out what happened.***

## Tell the Story

As you tell the story, lead students in responding as shown when you say the underlined words.

1. A long time ago in Old Testament times, God had told His people to make a special box called the Ark of the Covenant. The Ark was beautifully carved from wood and covered with gold. It showed the people that God was always with them. One important rule God had told His people was that only priests were to carry the Ark, and they were to use poles to make sure they didn't touch the Ark itself. A person who broke the rules would die. By obeying these rules, the Israelites showed their respect for God.

2. The Ark was not where it belonged, however. Years before, the Ark was captured by enemies in a battle. Then for more years, the Ark was kept in a house a few miles from the city of Jerusalem. Now that David was king, he wanted to bring the Ark to Jerusalem. So David and some of his men put the Ark on a brand-new wagon that was pulled by powerful oxen. But they DIDN'T carry the Ark on poles as God had told them.

3. Everything seemed to be going well. Then suddenly, the oxen stumbled! A man named Uzzah (UHZ-uh) reached out and touched the Ark to keep it from falling. Instantly, Uzzah fell to the ground—dead! The happy day had become very sad. Even though Uzzah was trying to do something good, he had disobeyed.

4. After this, David left the Ark at the home of a man named Obed-Edom. While the Ark was at his house, God caused good things to happen to everyone at Obed-Edom's house. When the Israelites saw that God was blessing Obed-Edom, they wanted to keep the Ark in Jerusalem so that God would bless them, too!

1. Rule: Right crossed fingers move down left palm.

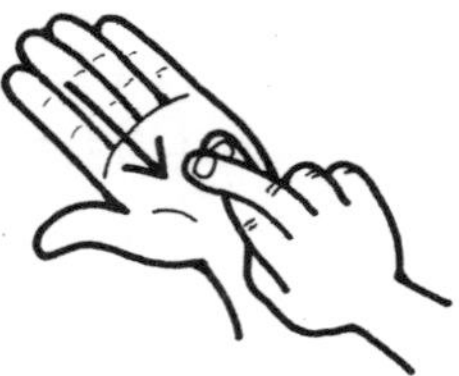

2. Jerusalem: With little finger outline a J; touch fingertips of flat hands and repeat, moving hands to the side.

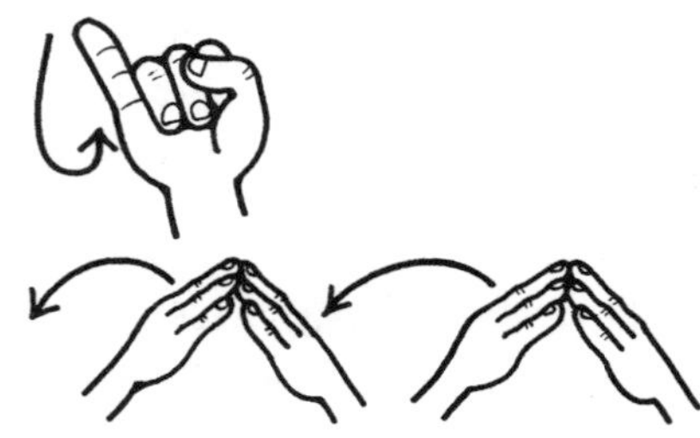

3. Disobey: Touch fists to forehead; twist fists forward and out.

4. Bless: Fists at mouth; open hands and move forward and down.

5. So again, David took his men and went to bring the Ark to Jerusalem. David said to his men, "The last time we tried to bring the Ark to Jerusalem, we failed because we didn't talk to God first and obey His rules. This time, we're going to obey God's rules EXACTLY." The priests were the only ones to carry the Ark, and they carried the Ark on poles—just as God had told them!

5. Obey: Hold fists near forehead; bring down and palms up.

6. King David led the big crowd of people. David sang and danced to show his joy that God was really with His people! All along the way, people stood by the road, singing and shouting and playing music to show their love for God. They joyfully played cymbals, harps and trumpets. They wanted God to know how happy they were to have the Ark in Jerusalem.

6. Sing, music: Move right hand back and forth in front of left palm.

7. But David's wife, Michal, didn't join in the celebration of praise to God. She was upset by David's actions. She didn't think it was proper for a king to sing and dance in the streets. Later that day when she complained, David answered, "Michal, I was singing, dancing and celebrating to show love to God. God is pleased with me and that is what matters."

7. Celebration: Right index finger and thumb touching, make small circles.

8. When the Ark was safely placed in the special tent made for it, David gave gifts to God and prayed. David finished the wonderful day of music, celebration and worship by giving gifts of delicious breads and fruits to EVERY person who had come to the great celebration.

That night as the stars began to come out, everyone returned to their homes and remembered their joyful day of celebrating and worshiping God. The people were glad to show their love for their great God!

8. Give: Hands down and fingertips touching, flip hands forward and open, palms up.

## Conclude the Story

**What had God said about carrying the Ark?** (The Ark was to be carried on poles. No one was supposed to touch the Ark.) **How did David and God's people celebrate the Ark's return to Jerusalem?** (Sang and played music. Gave gifts to God and prayed.)

**We don't need the Ark to remind us that God is always with us. We can remember the ways God has helped us in the past and we can talk about the ways He's helping us now! Any day, any time and whenever members of God's family get together, we can celebrate and praise God!**

2 Samuel 4:4; 9

# David Cares for Mephibosheth

## Materials

Play dough (1/4 cup, or 2 oz.) for each student.

## Tell the Story

**Follow along with me as we use our dough to tell today's story.**

***When have you made a promise to a friend?***

***Today we'll hear about someone who was glad to keep a promise he had made to his best friend!***

1. **Roll two ropes from your dough.** A long time ago, in the palace at Jerusalem, there lived a little boy named Mephibosheth (Muh-FIHB-oh-shehth). He was the grandson of King Saul and the son of David's best friend, Jonathan. But in one terrible day, Mephibosheth's father, Jonathan, and his grandfather Saul were killed in a battle. Mephibosheth's nurse (the woman who took care of him) heard the sad news.

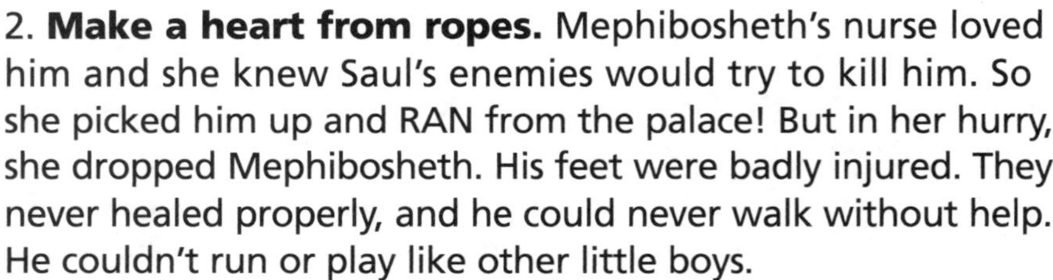

2. **Make a heart from ropes.** Mephibosheth's nurse loved him and she knew Saul's enemies would try to kill him. So she picked him up and RAN from the palace! But in her hurry, she dropped Mephibosheth. His feet were badly injured. They never healed properly, and he could never walk without help. He couldn't run or play like other little boys.

3. **Remove half of heart and add a dot to make a question mark.** Years later, David was crowned king. He was sad that his best friend, Jonathan, had died. David remembered how he and Jonathan had promised to always take care of each other's families. So now David asked his servants, "Is there anyone from Jonathan's family to whom I can show kindness for Jonathan's sake?"

One servant was a man named Ziba (ZEE-buh). He had been Saul's family servant. He told King David, "There is still a son of Jonathan's. He is crippled in both feet and lives quite a distance from here."

4. **Make a letter *M*.** David was delighted to hear about Jonathan's son named Mephibosheth! He sent servants to the house where Mephibosheth lived. They knocked on the door and told Mephibosheth that King David wanted him to come to Jerusalem!

5. **Make a Bible-times crutch shaped like a *T*.** Now because Mephibosheth was crippled, he might not have been treated too kindly before this. He surely must have wondered if King David was bringing him to Jerusalem to lock him in prison or even KILL him! When he arrived at the palace, he probably shook with fear.

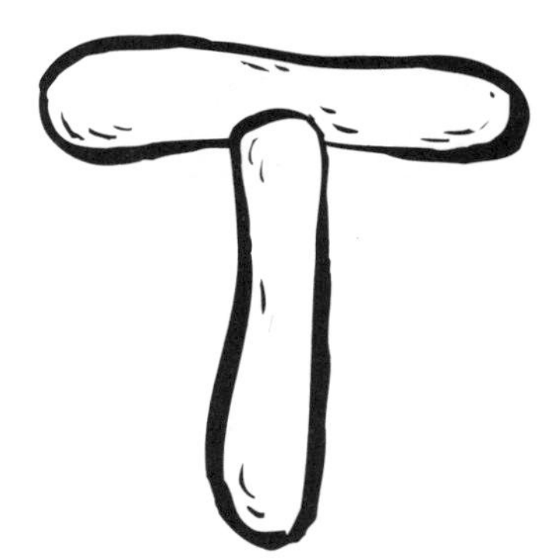

"Mephibosheth!" King David called out excitedly.

"I am your servant," said Mephibosheth, too afraid to look up.

David could see that Mephibosheth was frightened. He said, "Don't be afraid. I will be kind to you for Jonathan's sake. I will give you all the land that belonged to your grandfather Saul. And I want you to stay here in the palace and eat at the royal table every day!"

6. **Make a bowl.** WELL! Mephibosheth must have been VERY surprised—and relieved, too! He probably could hardly believe what he had heard! The KING had invited him to eat with him every day! Mephibosheth bowed down and said, "Why would you notice me and treat me so well? I am not important at all!"

7. **Make a heart.** "Your father Jonathan was my best friend. I promised to care for you years ago!" King David explained.

King David had spoken. Now Ziba and all the people who had been the servants of King Saul became Mephibosheth's servants. They farmed his land for him and took care of his animals. He now had a great deal of land, many servants and, best of all, he was treated as part of David's family! King David was as kind to Mephibosheth as if he were his own son. Mephibosheth lived in Jerusalem and ate at King David's table every day. King David showed him great kindness because of the loving promises he had made to Jonathan.

## Conclude the Story

**How did Mephibosheth become crippled?** (He was dropped when his nurse ran away with him.) **Why did King David want to help Mephibosheth?** (Because David had promised to care for members of Jonathan's family.) **How did King David help Mephibosheth?** (Gave him back his family's land. Gave him servants. Treated him as a son.)

**Sometimes it isn't easy to be kind without expecting anything back. But that is what King David did. And God can help us grow kindness in our lives, too!**

**1 Kings 2:1-12; 3:1-15; 4:29-34; 10:1-13; 11:1-13**

# Solomon's Wisdom

## Materials

Play dough (¼ cup, or 2 oz.) for each student.

***Who is a famous person you would like to have visit you?***

***Today we're going to hear about a man who had many famous visitors. Let's find out why they came to see him.***

## Tell the Story

**Follow along with me as we use our dough to tell today's story.**

1. **With your dough, make an *S* for Solomon.** Solomon was still a young man when his father, King David, made him the new king of Israel. Shortly before King David died, he gave Solomon some advice. "Be strong and always obey God," David told his son. "Follow God's laws and commands, and you will prosper in everything you do and everywhere you go."

2. **Make a crown.** Solomon had older brothers who might have been expected to take David's place as king. After all, they had much more experience and knowledge than a young man of 20! But unlike his brothers, Solomon loved and trusted God and followed God's ways. So Solomon was chosen by God to be the next king of Israel.

After David died and Solomon was proclaimed king, he went to a city called Gibeon to worship God.

While Solomon was at Gibeon, God appeared to him in a dream. "Solomon," God said, "ask Me for anything and I will give it to you."

3. **Make a *W* for wisdom.** Solomon could have asked for great wealth so that he could live in luxury. Or he could have asked for great power to keep himself safe from his enemies. He could have asked to be very popular or to have a long life. But instead Solomon asked for wisdom. "I am so young to be king," Solomon said, "I need Your wisdom in order to know right from wrong so that I can lead Your people well."

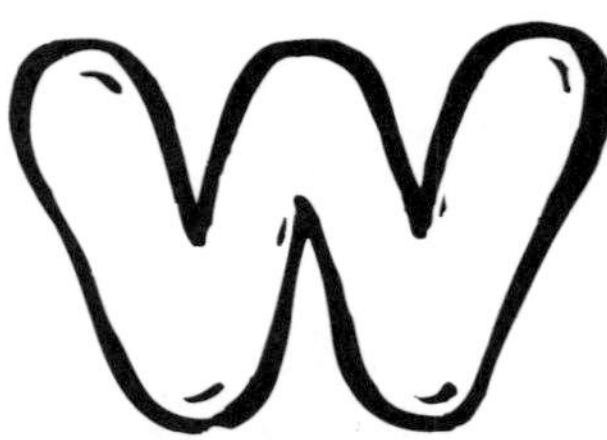

God was very pleased with Solomon's request. He gave Solomon the wisdom he wanted. In fact, God told Solomon that he would be the wisest man ever! In addition, God gave Solomon what he didn't ask for: riches and honor so that there wouldn't be another king like him anywhere on Earth! God made one more, very special promise. "As long as you obey my commands as David your father did, I will give you a long life as well!"

4. **Make a book like a Bible.** Solomon studied plants, animals, birds, reptiles and fish. The Bible tells us that Solomon also wrote 1,005 songs and 3,000 proverbs! Most of the book of Proverbs in the Bible was written by Solomon. Proverbs are wise sayings that help people know the right way to live. Because God had given him such great wisdom, Solomon had a lot to say about living life wisely!

For many years, Solomon ruled God's people wisely. The news of his wisdom traveled around the world. Leaders from all over the world traveled to see King Solomon and ask for his advice.

5. **Make a question mark.** One of Solomon's most famous visitors was the queen of Sheba. The Bible tells us that when she heard about Solomon, she couldn't believe such a great king existed! So she came to Jerusalem to talk with Solomon. She asked him very hard questions to see if he really was the wisest man on Earth. When Solomon was able to answer all of her questions, she realized what a great king he was. She saw the food, the clothes and everything else Solomon had.

"I did not believe what I'd heard about you until I could see for myself, but in wisdom and wealth you are even richer than I'd heard! Praise the Lord God, for He has shown His great love for Israel by making you a great king!" she said.

As long as Solomon followed God's laws and instructions, he was a wise, wealthy and powerful king. But later in his life, Solomon stopped listening to God and started listening to his wives instead. Solomon had wives who worshiped false gods. Instead of doing what was right, Solomon built temples for those false gods. And then he made an even BIGGER mistake and worshiped those false gods! Since Solomon did not obey God, he didn't get to live a long life like his father, David.

## Conclude the Story

**What did Solomon ask God for? Why did he want that?** (Wisdom. In order to do a good job leading God's people.) **What did God give Solomon?** (Wisdom, wealth and honor. God promised Solomon a long life if Solomon would obey His commands.) **Why did Solomon end up not living a long life?** (Solomon disobeyed God.)

**Every day we can make choices that show self-control. We show self-control when we do what is right and obey God. God's Word, including the books written by Solomon, show us how to have self-control and live wisely.**

# Solomon Solves a Problem

## Before the Story

Guide students to briefly practice signs for underlined words.

***Who is a person you know who is very wise? What wise actions or words does that person do or say?***

***Today we're going to meet the wisest man who ever lived. And we'll find out how he became so wise!***

## Tell the Story

As you tell the story, lead students in responding as shown when you say the underlined words.

1. David, the king of Israel, had lived to be a very old man. Before he died, he chose his son Solomon to be the next king. Solomon loved God and he wanted to obey Him. And God loved Solomon! One way Solomon showed his love for God was by worshiping Him. After one special time of worshiping God, Solomon was sleeping. God talked with him in a dream.

2. God said to Solomon, "Ask Me for whatever you want Me to give you." For ANYTHING? That meant Solomon could ask for all the money in the world or to be the most powerful king ever! But what do you think Solomon asked for?

Solomon said to God, "You have been very kind to my father and to me. You have made me the king. But I'm so young! I don't know how to do this job. Please give me wisdom, so I'll know what is right and wrong. I don't know how to be king of all these people without Your help!"

3. God was glad to hear what Solomon had asked. God said, "I will give you wisdom. You will be the wisest person that ever lived. And since you have asked for wisdom instead of money or power, I will also give you riches and honor. If you obey Me, I'll give you a long life, too."

4. Solomon woke from his dream. He must have been excited! God was going to make him wise! But how would he know if he was really wise or not? Solomon's chance to find out came along soon.

1. Worship: Left hand over right fist; move hands to body and bow head.

2. Wisdom: Bend right index finger; move up and down on forehead.

3. Give: Hands down and fingertips touching, flip hands forward and open, palms up.

4. Dream: Right index finger at forehead; move up and out, repeatedly bending finger.

5. One day, two women came to Solomon in his throne room. The women were having a TERRIBLE fight. They wanted King Solomon to decide what should be done.

The first woman said, "Your majesty, this woman and I live together in the same house. We both had brand-new baby boys. This other woman's baby died. And while I was asleep, she took my little son and put him in her bed. Then she laid her dead baby beside me. When I woke up, I thought my baby was dead! But in the morning light, I could see it wasn't my baby at all."

5. Baby: Rock crossed arms.

6. The other woman broke in. "No! This baby is mine! Your baby is dead!" Solomon didn't argue with either woman. He said to his servant, "Bring me a sword." The two women didn't know why Solomon wanted a sword, but Solomon had a plan in mind in order to find out the real mother.

When the servant brought back a sword, Solomon said to the servant, "Cut this baby in half. Give half a baby to each mother!"

6. Sword: Slide right index and middle fingers off left index finger; pantomime drawing out sword and thrusting forward.

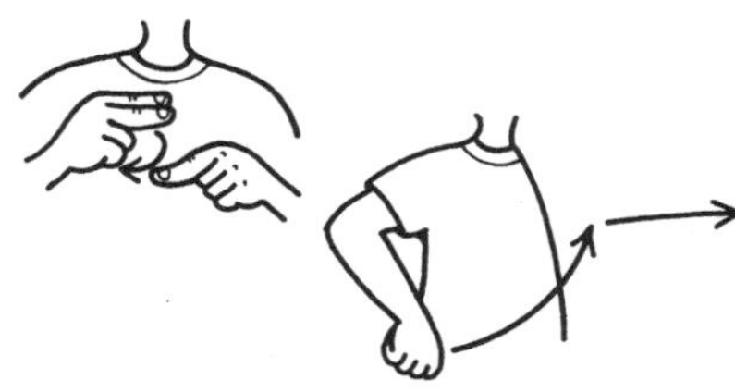

7. The woman who was NOT really the baby's mother said, "Fine. If I can't have him, YOU can't have him either. Cut him in two!" But the woman who was REALLY the baby's mother said, "Oh, no, Your Majesty! Give the baby to the other woman! Don't hurt him!"

Then Solomon said, "I have made my decision. Give the baby to the woman who said, 'Don't hurt him!' She is his real mother. She would rather let someone else have him than let him be hurt."

7. Don't hurt: Uncross crossed hands; jab index fingers toward each other.

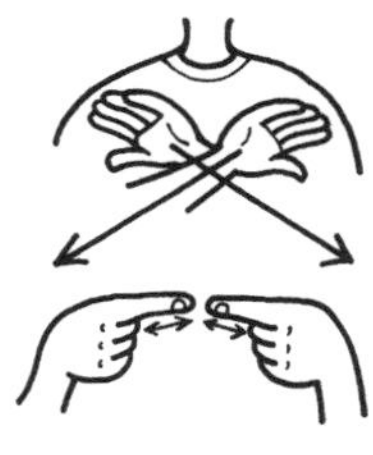

8. Everyone in the throne room looked at Solomon. Solomon had been very WISE! He figured out who the real mother was! Soon the story of Solomon's wise decision was heard all over Israel. Then the people knew that he was going to be a wise king! God had done what He promised. He had given Solomon GREAT wisdom!

8. Wise, wisdom: Bend right index finger; move up and down on forehead.

## Conclude the Story

**How did Solomon show he loved God?** (He worshiped God.) **What gift did Solomon ask God to give him?** (Wisdom.) **When a person is wise, he or she is able to make choices that show love for God and others. How was Solomon able to show God had given him wisdom?** (Solved a quarrel between two women. Found who the baby's real mother was.)

**What are some times a kid your age needs God's wisdom? God's gift of wisdom is a gift we can ask for, too. God's wisdom shows us the best way to live. All we have to do is ask Him.**

**1 Kings 3; 4:29-34; 5—9:9**

# Solomon Builds the Temple

## Materials

Drawing materials/equipment for teacher and each student.

***When is a time you and a friend both wanted the same thing?***

***Today we're going to hear about a king who asked God to help him solve a problem between two women who wanted the same thing.***

## Tell the Story

As you tell each part of the story, draw each sketch. Students copy your sketches.

1. King David lived to be a very old man. Before he died, he chose his son Solomon to be the next king. Solomon loved God and wanted to obey Him. And God loved Solomon! One night, while Solomon slept, God talked with him in a dream. He told Solomon to ask for whatever he wanted God to give him! He could ask for money or power or for God to get rid of all his enemies! But Solomon told God that to be a good king he needed wisdom to know right from wrong. God was glad to answer that prayer! Besides wisdom, God gave Solomon riches and respect, too.

1. Draw "C"s to make sleeping Solomon.

2. Solomon soon had a chance to see if he REALLY had wisdom. Two women who were having a terrible fight came to see Solomon. They lived in the same house and both had new babies. One woman's baby died. While the other woman slept, she traded babies. When the other woman woke, she thought her baby had died! But in the morning light, she could see it wasn't her baby at all.The first woman argued that the other woman was lying!

2. Woman's face from "2." Add 2 "U"s for scarf.

3. Solomon didn't argue with either woman. Instead, he had his servant bring a sword. Loudly, Solomon told the servant to cut the baby in half! Of course, the baby's REAL mother said, "Oh, no! Give the baby to the other woman! Don't hurt him!" Then Solomon knew that this woman was the baby's real mother and gave the baby to her. Everyone in Israel soon heard how Solomon had been very WISE!

3. Write a large "1/2." Add sword.

4. Solomon loved God very much. He was grateful for all the gifts God had given him. God had made him very rich. So Solomon wanted to give a gift to God. He decided to use his riches to build a beautiful Temple to show his love for God. The Israelites could come to the Temple to worship God.

4. Draw a gift box.

5. Solomon had the strongest wood brought in. He hired many workers and famous artists. The workers made the Temple of white stone that sparkled in the sunlight. The floors were covered with gold. It took seven years to build the Temple—not because it was so big, but because it was so beautiful!

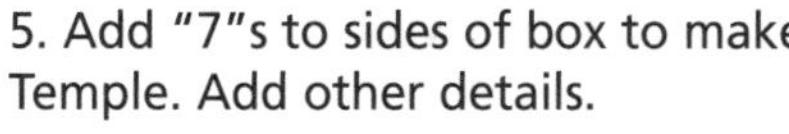

5. Add "7"s to sides of box to make Temple. Add other details.

6. When the Temple was finally finished, Solomon led a joyful parade to bring the Ark of the Covenant to its permanent home in the Temple. (The Ark was a special wooden chest that reminded people that God was with them.) A huge crowd of people joined in the parade. Everyone wanted to see the beautiful new Temple.

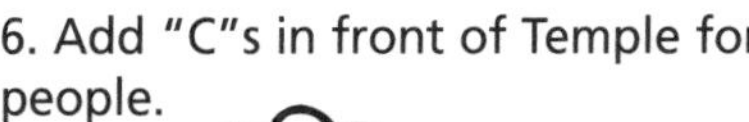

6. Add "C"s in front of Temple for people.

7. After the Ark was placed in the Temple, an amazing thing happened. The whole Temple filled with a bright cloud. Solomon knew the cloud was God's way of saying that He was there and that He was very, very pleased with this Temple. Solomon stood in front of the Temple and thanked God for keeping His promises to Israel. He also asked God to take care of all the people forever. God listened to Solomon's prayer. The people were so happy! They all stayed at the Temple and celebrated for 14 days! Because of his wisdom and his love for God, Solomon helped the people worship Him.

7. Add "3"s above Temple for cloud.

## Conclude the Story

**How did Solomon show his wisdom?** (Solved argument over baby. Built Temple.) **How did he get this wisdom?** (Asked God.)

**As long as Solomon paid attention to God's wisdom, God helped Solomon know what was best to do. God helped him do many wonderful things. When we don't know what is best to do, God promises to give us wisdom, too. We only need to ask!**

1 Kings 17—19

# God Cares for Elijah

## Materials

Drawing materials/equipment for teacher and each student.

## Tell the Story

As you tell each part of the story, draw each sketch. Students copy your sketches.

***What did you want to eat the last time you were really hungry?***

***Today we're going to find out how God fed a hungry man in amazing ways!***

1. After King Solomon died, his son became king and caused big, big problems! Soon, there was so much fighting that Israel split into two kingdoms: Israel in the north and Judah in the south. Both kingdoms had many rulers through the years, but they usually weren't wise like Solomon or loving toward God like David. God often sent prophets to these rulers with warnings for them.

1. Draw zigzag lines; add names.

2. When King Ahab ruled Israel, he worshiped false gods like Baal instead of the true God. So God gave His prophet Elijah an important message for King Ahab. Elijah declared that there would be no rain for the next few years. Without rain, no food would grow. Everyone in Israel was going to be hungry!

2. Draw raindrop and hamburger. Add "no" slash to each.

3. God promised He would take care of Elijah, so God sent Elijah to live by a little stream of water. And God sent birds called ravens to bring food to Elijah every morning and evening. Elijah drank water from the stream and ate what the ravens brought him. But finally, the stream dried up.

3. "U"s for water. Sideways "3"s for birds. Add "no" slash to water.

4. God told Elijah to go to a faraway town. Elijah met a widow at the town gate. He asked her for water—and for bread, too. But she said she had only flour and oil to make one last loaf of bread for herself and her son. Elijah told her God had promised there would be enough flour and oil for all of them. So she fed Elijah first. Then she looked in her flour jar to make more bread. She saw more flour! And there was more oil in the oil jar!

4. "U" and "O" for flour jar. Teardrop shape and "O" for oil jar. Add oil and flour spilling out.

5. After that, there was always enough flour and oil to make more bread. The flour and oil NEVER ran out! The Lord had taken care of Elijah again! And He helped this family who had nothing. Later, when the widow's son got sick and died, God brought him back to life!

5. Draw "D"s for loaves of bread.

6. Now it had been three YEARS without rain. God sent Elijah to see King Ahab again. Elijah told King Ahab to call the prophets of Baal and all the people together for a contest at Mount Carmel. When the crowd was there, Elijah told the false prophets, "Call on your god, Baal. If he is really a god, he can send fire down to burn up your offering. I will call on the Lord. If He is really God, He will send fire down to burn up my offering. We will see who is the true God!" Everyone agreed.

6. Draw "O"s for stone altar; add lines for wood.

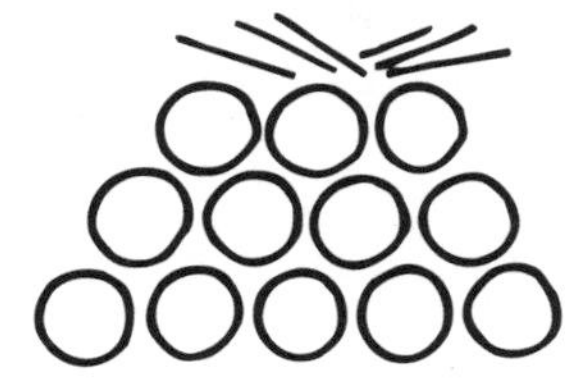

7. The test began. The priests and prophets of Baal prayed and cried and even cut themselves all day long, trying to get Baal to send fire down. But nothing happened! When evening came, Elijah had people pour water three times over the offering he had prepared! He wanted everyone to know that he hadn't hidden any fire or tried any tricks. Elijah prayed, "Lord, answer me so that everyone will know that You, O Lord, are God."

7. Add water drops and wavy lines.

8. God's fire fell! It didn't just burn up the offering; it burned up the stones, the dirt and even the WATER! When the people saw this miracle, they said, "The Lord is God!" That day, the people got rid of the false prophets. The rain came again and food began to grow. But the queen was very angry at Elijah and wanted to kill him. So Elijah ran away. God fed him again and told him what to do next. Even as Elijah hid in a cave, God talked with him and showed him that He would care for him.

8. Draw blackened "O."

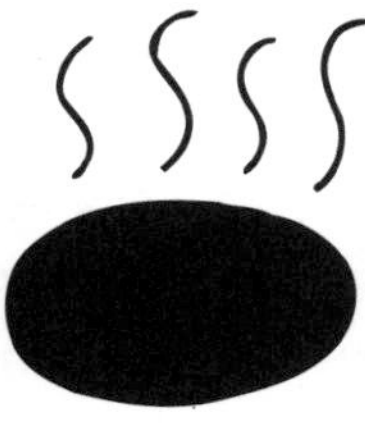

## Conclude the Story

**How did God care for Elijah?** (Fed him. Sent fire.)

**God cared for Elijah in amazing ways. God is big enough to care for us in any situation! He'll give us what we need.**

## 1 Kings 19:19-21; 2 Kings 5; 6:8-23

# Elisha Shows God's Love

### Materials

Drawing materials/equipment for teacher and each student.

***When have you seen or swum in a river?***

***Today we're going to meet a man who told a sick man to wash in a river he didn't want to get into!***

### Tell the Story

As you tell each part of the story, draw each sketch. Students copy your sketches.

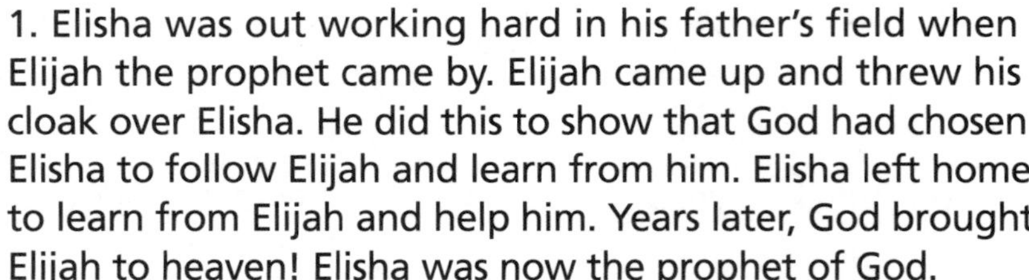

1. Elisha was out working hard in his father's field when Elijah the prophet came by. Elijah came up and threw his cloak over Elisha. He did this to show that God had chosen Elisha to follow Elijah and learn from him. Elisha left home to learn from Elijah and help him. Years later, God brought Elijah to heaven! Elisha was now the prophet of God.

1. Draw "M" and lines for cloak.

2. God gave Elisha power to do amazing things, even to help people who didn't believe in or care about God. One man who didn't care about God was the commander of the Aramean army (Israel's enemy). This man, Naaman, got a terrible skin disease called leprosy. He tried everything he could think of to get rid of his disease. But nothing worked!

2. Hand and arm from "U"s. Add spots to arm.

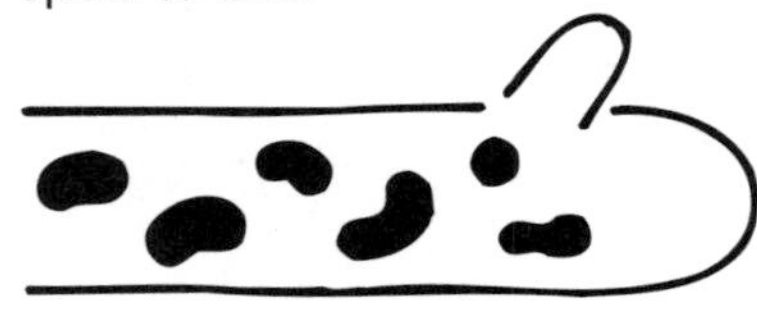

3. Living in Naaman's house, however, was a girl who had been taken from Israel as a slave. Even though Naaman was really an enemy of her people, the slave girl helped him. She told Naaman's wife that God's prophet in Israel could help her husband! So Naaman traveled to Israel to see Elisha. Elisha sent a messenger to tell Naaman to go to the Jordan River and wash himself seven times. Then he would be well. Naaman didn't like this advice at first, but finally he did what Elisha said. And God made Naaman completely well!

3. Water from wide "U"s. Add stick figure and "7."

4. Another time, the Arameans were at war with Israel. And God kept telling Elisha all of the Arameans' battle plans! Finally, one officer told the king that Elisha the prophet was the one who was finding out all the king's plans. So the king sent soldiers to CAPTURE Elisha.

4. Sideways "C"s and lines for helmets of soldiers.

5. When Elisha's servant got up early the next morning, there were Aramean soldiers all around the city! Elisha's servant was AFRAID! But Elisha knew God had armies of His own all around them! Elisha asked God to show his servant that the hills all around them were full of soldiers and horses and chariots of fire! God was ready to protect them!

5. Amazed face from "O"s.

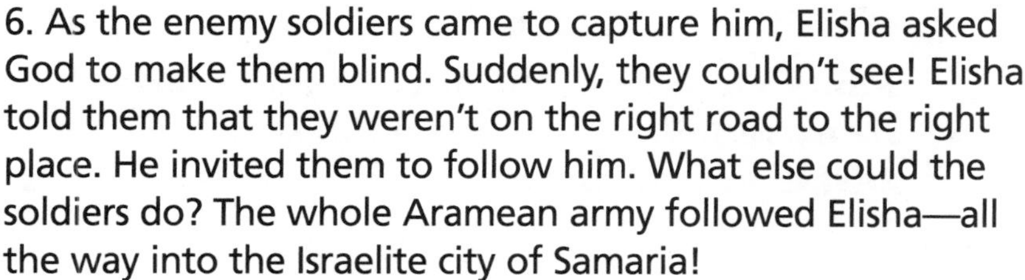

6. As the enemy soldiers came to capture him, Elisha asked God to make them blind. Suddenly, they couldn't see! Elisha told them that they weren't on the right road to the right place. He invited them to follow him. What else could the soldiers do? The whole Aramean army followed Elisha—all the way into the Israelite city of Samaria!

6. Draw closed eyes on soldiers drawn in #4.

7. Once the soldiers were inside the gates of the city, the Lord took away their blindness. NOW the Arameans could see they were in TROUBLE—surrounded by Israelites! The king of Israel thought this was the perfect time to get rid of these enemies. He wanted to kill the Aramean soldiers! But Elisha told the king God's plan: to feed the soldiers and send them home.

7. Draw gates behind soldiers. Make eyes wide. Add "O" mouths.

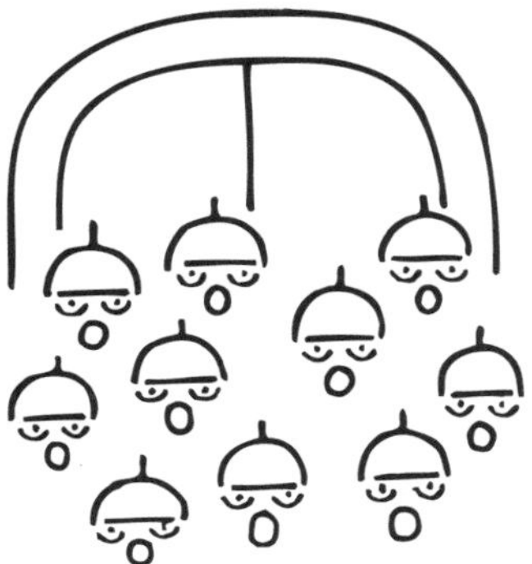

8. So the people of Samaria prepared a big feast for the soldiers. When the soldiers were full, they were allowed to go home. And for a very long time, the Arameans didn't bother the Israelites at all! Elisha had helped show God's love and care for people who didn't care about Him.

8. Add crowd around soldiers.

## Conclude the Story

**How did Elijah show Elisha that God had chosen him to be his helper?** (Threw his cloak over Elisha.) **What did Elisha do to help Naaman?** (Told him to wash seven times in the Jordan.) **What did Elisha do for the Aramean army?** (Fed them. Sent them home.)

**Elisha showed God's love to many people. Some of these people didn't care about God, but God cared about them because God loves all people. When we are kind to others, even those who don't know or care about God, we help them learn about God's love, too.**

**2 Kings 4:8-37**

# Elisha's New Room

## Materials

Play dough (1/4 cup, or 2 oz.) and a plastic spoon for each student.

## Tell the Story

**Follow along with me as we use our dough to tell today's story.**

***When has someone done something kind to surprise you?***

***Today we'll find out how some people surprised Elisha. And we'll hear how Elisha surprised them!***

1. **Make a house with a flat roof.** Elisha was a prophet of God. He traveled from city to city in the country of Israel to teach people about God and give them God's messages. Elisha often passed through a town called Shunem (SHOO-nehm). Whenever he did, a woman who lived there invited Elisha and his servant, Gehazi (gih-HAY-zi), to eat dinner with her and her husband.

One day the woman said to her husband, "Elisha is a man of God. Let's build a room on the roof for him. Then he can stay here whenever he comes."

2. **Make a bed, a table, a chair and a Bible-times lamp. Use a plastic spoon to shape objects.** The flat roof was a perfect place to build a guest room for Elisha! His friends put a bed, a table, a chair and a lamp in the room, so Elisha would be comfortable. When Elisha came to town, they led him to the roof and showed him the room they had prepared for him. Elisha and Gehazi must have been amazed at such kindness! The room was a wonderful surprise!

As Elisha rested in the room, he asked his servant, "Gehazi, tell our friend that we're thankful for this wonderful room. Ask her what we can do for her."

When Gehazi asked her, the woman replied, "Thank you for asking. But I don't need anything."

Elisha still wanted to show kindness to her somehow. He asked Gehazi if he had any ideas of ways to do this.

Gehazi said, "She doesn't have a child. Maybe she would like to have a son to love and care for."

Elisha thought that was a great idea. And God must have, too! Elisha told the woman that within a year, she and her husband would have a baby boy. When the baby was born as Elisha had promised, the family was very happy!

3. **Make a little boy, his mom and his dad.** But there was more to this story of kindness! The baby grew into a boy. One day when he was out in the fields with his father, he cried out in pain. "Father!" he said. "My head! My head!" Although a servant quickly carried him to the house, where his mother held him on her lap and rocked him, he soon died.

The boy's mother carried his body to Elisha's room and laid it on the bed. She called for a servant and a donkey and hurried to Elisha's house in the other city as fast as the donkey could go!

Gehazi came out to meet her and asked her if everyone in her house was well. The woman didn't tell him what was wrong. Instead, she hurried into Elisha's house and grabbed his feet. She was VERY upset! She said to Elisha, "You asked God to give me a child," she cried. "Now he is DEAD!"

Elisha gave Gehazi his walking stick and told Gehazi to run back and lay it on the boy. But even after Gehazi left, the woman kept hold of Elisha's feet and said she wouldn't leave without him! So Elisha hurried with her back to her house.

As they traveled, Gehazi came running back to meet them. "I did as you said," he reported, "but he is still dead!"

Elisha hurried to the room where the boy's body lay. He knew only God could make the boy live again. First, Elisha PRAYED! He laid his own body over the boy's until the boy's body grew warm. He did this again, no doubt praying as he lay there! Then the boy SNEEZED seven sneezes! He was ALIVE! The boy's mother came running upstairs. Elisha handed him to his mother. The boy's parents were SO happy!

The couple had shown kindness to Elisha. God had shown kindness to them in return. They must have been glad they had a friend like Elisha, who didn't just talk about God's kindness. He SHOWED it by caring for them and helping them.

## Conclude the Story

**How did the woman and her husband show kindness to Elisha?** (Fed him. Built him a room.) **How did Elisha show them kindness?** (Elisha promised them that God would send them a son. Prayed for God to use His power to bring the son back to life.)

**In today's story, people showed kindness in some unusual ways. But there are many ordinary ways we can show kindness to each other. Each day we can look for ways to be kind to and care for the needs of others.**

**Isaiah 6:1-8; 9:1-7**

# Isaiah Tells God's Messages

## Materials

Drawing materials/equipment for teacher and each student.

## Tell the Story

As you tell each part of the story, draw each sketch. Students copy your sketches.

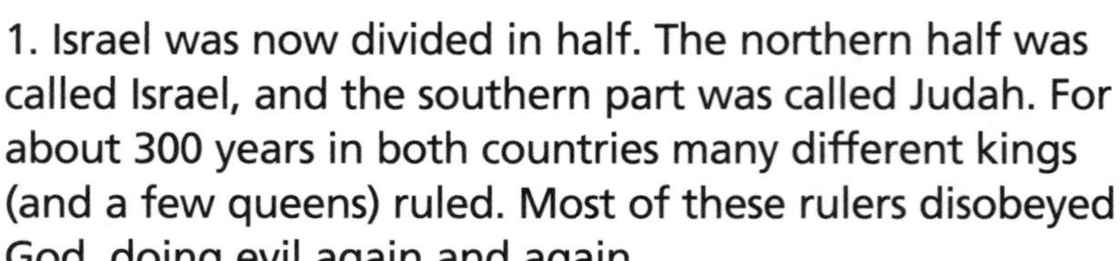

***What's the last thing you remember a grown-up telling you to do?***

***Today we'll write some words that begin with W and we'll hear about a time God gave a man a special job to do.***

1\. Israel was now divided in half. The northern half was called Israel, and the southern part was called Judah. For about 300 years in both countries many different kings (and a few queens) ruled. Most of these rulers disobeyed God, doing evil again and again.

1\. Draw a stop sign. Add "Wicked."

2\. But God never gave up on His people! God wanted His people to stop cheating each other, stop hurting each other and stop worshiping idols, gods who weren't real. God sent many prophets to give His messages and warnings to the people of Israel and Judah, as well as to the other countries around them. Elijah and Elisha were prophets who told God's messages. Another prophet, named Isaiah, lived in Judah, about 100 years after Elisha.

2\. "Warning" on a yield sign.

3\. God chose Isaiah to be a prophet in a special way. Isaiah had a vision—like a dream. Isaiah could see that he was in heaven! WOW! Isaiah saw God on a throne, sitting very high up with fiery angels on either side of Him. These angels called out, "Holy! Holy! Holy! is the Lord Almighty. The whole earth is full of His glory!"

3\. "Wow!" in a thought balloon.

4. When these angels spoke with their powerful voices, everything shook. Smoke filled the throne room! Isaiah thought he was going to die because he had seen God. Isaiah knew he had disobeyed God and was not good enough to be in God's presence. One of the fiery angels brought a glowing coal and touched Isaiah's lips. The angel explained that now Isaiah would be clean and ready for the job God had for him. Whew! Isaiah thought.

4. "Whew!" on a piece of coal.

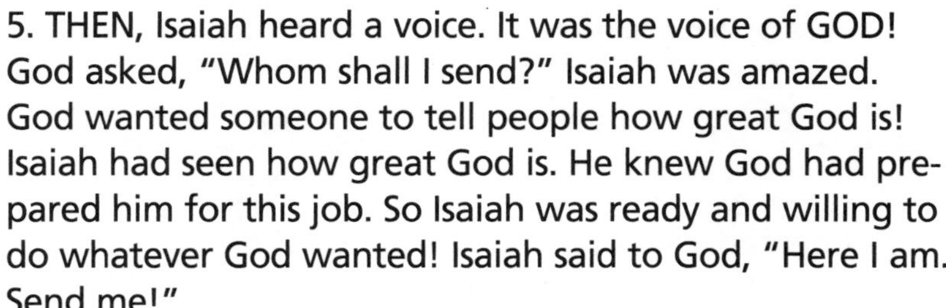

5. THEN, Isaiah heard a voice. It was the voice of GOD! God asked, "Whom shall I send?" Isaiah was amazed. God wanted someone to tell people how great God is! Isaiah had seen how great God is. He knew God had prepared him for this job. So Isaiah was ready and willing to do whatever God wanted! Isaiah said to God, "Here I am. Send me!"

5. "Who" inside a question mark.

6. And God DID. He gave Isaiah many, many messages to tell to kings, to ordinary people and even to people in other countries! Some of these amazing messages were about things that would happen in the future. Many of Isaiah's messages told about Jesus hundreds of years before Jesus was born! One message was that Jesus was going to be the great King! Isaiah also told that Jesus would die to defeat sin. He told many things about how Jesus would take the punishment for our sins.

6. Draw a crown and a cross. Write "Won!"

7. Isaiah told about many other events that were going to happen. Many of them have already happened, like the things Isaiah told about Jesus' birth and death. Some of the things God told Isaiah to write and tell haven't happened yet. But because Isaiah was ready to follow God's commands, God gave him an amazing and very important job.

7. Draw arrows for past and future. Add "Write!"

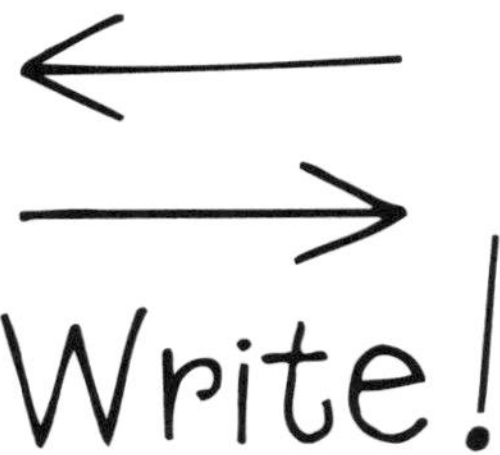


## Conclude the Story

**Whose voice did Isaiah hear? What was Isaiah's job going to be? Why do you think Isaiah wanted to tell God's message?** (He knew how great God is. He wanted to obey God.)

**Knowing how great God is makes us want to trust Him and obey His commands—right away!**

**2 Chronicles 20:1-30**

# Jehoshaphat Praises God

## Before the Story

Guide students to briefly practice signs for underlined words.

***What's something you're glad you know how to do?***

***Today we'll find out what some people did with their abilities!***

## Tell the Story

As you tell the story, lead students in responding as shown when you say the underlined words.

1. Many years before Jesus was born, a king named Jehoshaphat (jih-HAHSH-uh-fat) was the king of Judah. (That's what is now the southern part of Israel.) King Jehoshaphat loved and trusted God. One day some men came to him with very frightening news: "A HUGE group of three armies is on its way to fight you!" King Jehoshaphat was worried about this frightening news. But before he did anything, he decided to pray to God.

1. Frightened: Fingertips touching, open hands and cover chest.

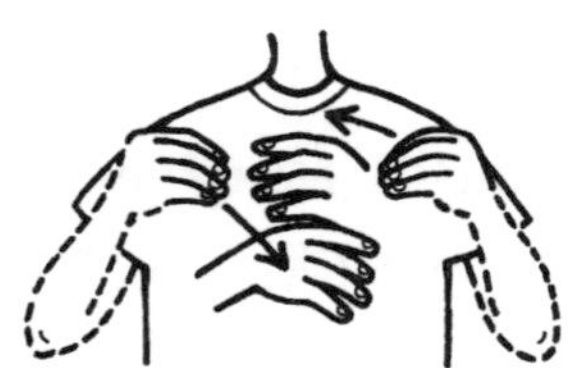

2. King Jehoshaphat sent messages to the people in EVERY town of his kingdom. He told them about the terrible trouble. He told them to come together to fast and pray to God for help. The king wanted his people to stop eating as a way to show great concern and as a way to remember to pray. When all the people were gathered at the Temple, the king stood up in front of everyone and prayed.

2. Pray: Touch palms in front; move hands to body and bow head.

3. The king prayed, "O Lord, You are the God who rules over every kingdom. We know that if any trouble comes to us, we can cry out to You to save us. Now there are three armies who want to take away the land that You gave us, O God. We aren't strong enough to fight against them. We don't know WHAT to do. So we are looking to You, Lord, to see how You will save us!"

3. Save: Open crossed arms.

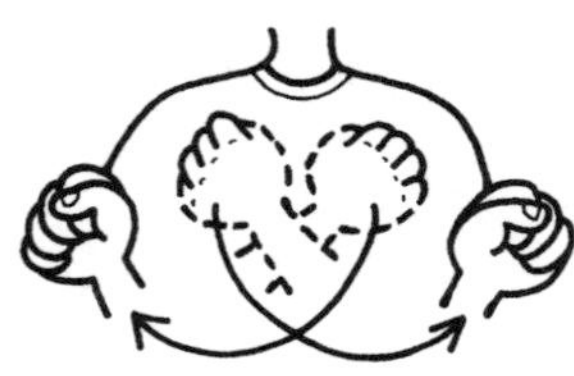

4. EVERYONE—even the littlest children—prayed with the king. They asked God for help. Then God told one of their leaders, a priest, what to do next.

The priest said, "This is what God says: 'Don't be afraid of this huge army. This battle is MINE, not yours.'" GOD promised to help them. He would fight FOR them!

4. Help: Raise right fist with left palm.

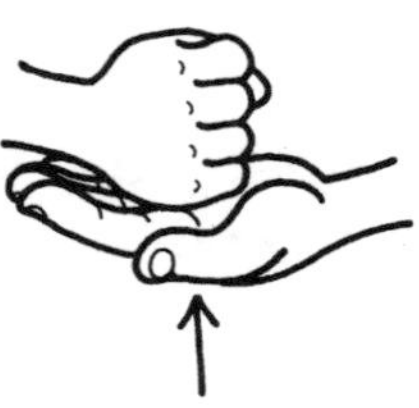

5. The priest told the people God wanted them to march to a mountain ridge and take their battle positions. They weren't supposed to fight, but God's people were to stand on the mountain ridge. They were not to run away; God wanted them to believe that He was with them and watch and see how God would fight their enemies for them.

5. Mountain: Strike right fist on left; move flat hands in wavy motion.

6. Jehoshaphat's army gathered. To show that they believed God's promise to fight the battle for them, they chose singers to lead the army instead of soldiers! The singers didn't carry swords—they carried cymbals and harps and other instruments!

"Give thanks to the Lord," they sang out, "for His love endures forever."

Instead of the bravest soldiers going first, the singers marched on ahead, praising God for what He was going to do.

6. Singer: Move right hand back and forth in front of left palm; move open hands down sides.

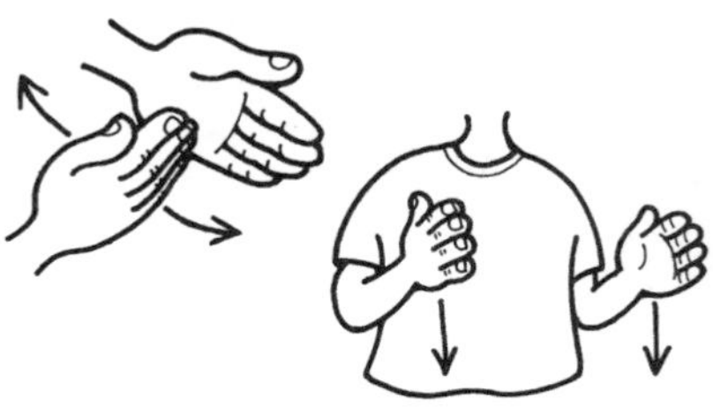

7. While God's people were singing praises to Him and marching to the mountain ridge, something AMAZING happened. God caused those three enemy armies to begin fighting each other! By the time Jehoshaphat's army reached the mountain ridge and looked down on the valley, there was NO ONE left to fight! Jehoshaphat's army went into the valley and picked up all the leftover valuables. After three days, the army gathered right there in the valley and praised God! They called the place the "Valley of Praise."

7. Valley: Flat hands moving down from shoulders come together in center.

8. Then the king led the army and everyone else back to the Temple. They sang songs of praise to God, playing harps and lutes (lutes are Bible-times guitars) and trumpets, too. It must have sounded WONDERFUL!

Everyone around heard how God had fought the battle for His people. After this battle, the armies around them were afraid to attack the Israelites! There was peace for a long time because God's people had trusted God—and praised Him!

8. Praise: Clap hands a few times.

## Conclude the Story

**Why was King Jehoshaphat afraid?** (Three armies were coming to fight.) **What did the people do when they heard the news?** (Fasted. Prayed.) **What happened in the battle?** (The singers marched in front of the soldiers and sang praises to God. There was no battle for God's people to fight.)

**We can use our abilities to praise God like those singers did. God wants us to praise Him for His power and the amazing ways He cares for us.**

**2 Kings 20:12-19; 2 Chronicles 29—31:1; 32:1-6,20-33**

# King Hezekiah Obeys God

## Materials

Drawing materials/equipment for teacher and each student.

## Tell the Story

As you tell each part of the story, draw each sketch. Students copy your sketches.

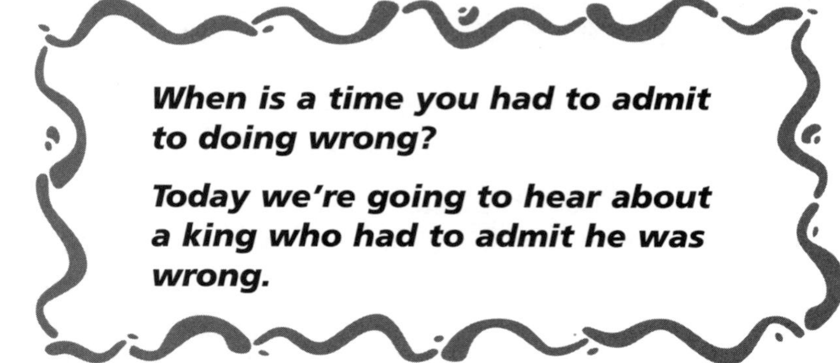


1. Hezekiah was one of the kings of Judah. His father, Ahaz, had been a very evil king; he disobeyed God all of his life and worshiped the false gods and idols of the countries around him. Hezekiah did not want to be like his father. As soon as he became king, he repaired the doors of God's Temple and opened the Temple again. He called all the men whose families had served in the Temple and told them to get ready to serve God again. They cleaned the Temple and got it ready for people to worship God again.

1. Draw Temple with broken doors. Blacken in and draw new open doors.

2. When the Temple was ready, Hezekiah sent letters and messengers to everyone in Judah and in Israel, too. He invited everyone to come to Jerusalem to celebrate the Passover. People began to get excited as they heard the news. On the day the Passover began, there was a large crowd of people in Jerusalem. For the first time in a LONG time, people from Israel and Judah worshiped God together in the way He told them to. Everyone was happy; they enjoyed celebrating God's goodness so much that they celebrated for another whole week!

2. Sideways "C"s for crowd.

3. Then a wonderful thing happened. After this great celebration, the people of Israel and Judah decided to get rid of the idols and false gods they had been worshiping. They cleaned up the places where people worshiped false gods. The people were going to worship ONLY the one true God!

3. Draw idol; add "no" slash.

4. Because Hezekiah led his people in doing what was right, God made life peaceful and good for the people of Judah. The Bible tells that King Hezekiah rebuilt many walls and towers in Jerusalem. He built a long tunnel system to bring water into the city and built buildings for storing the extra food from the good harvests.

4. Draw walls, towers from rectangles. Add canal with water.

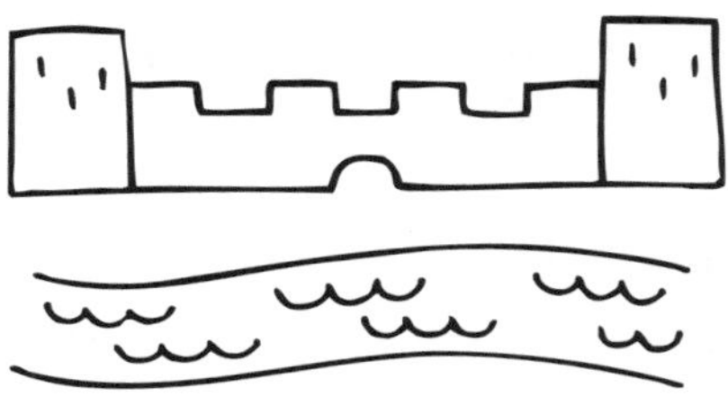

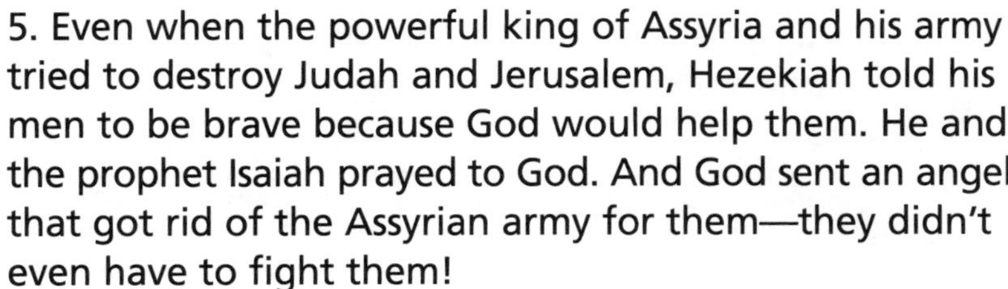

5. Even when the powerful king of Assyria and his army tried to destroy Judah and Jerusalem, Hezekiah told his men to be brave because God would help them. He and the prophet Isaiah prayed to God. And God sent an angel that got rid of the Assyrian army for them—they didn't even have to fight them!

5. Praying face: 3 "7"s, 4 "U"s.

6. Hezekiah obeyed God—most of his life. But even a good king like Hezekiah can do something wrong. Hezekiah became proud of all the good things he had. He enjoyed showing visitors all the fine things he owned. Hezekiah began to depend on his riches instead of trusting God.

6. Write a large "I." Add letters for "pride." Add arrows.

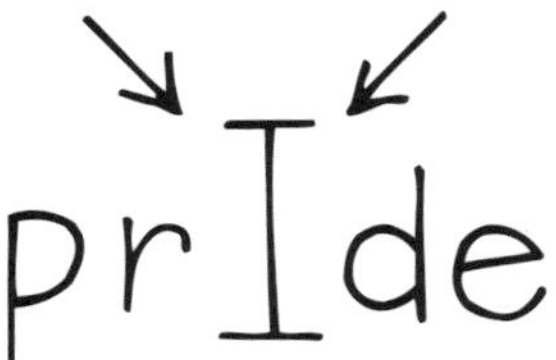


7. God's prophet Isaiah warned Hezekiah that all his riches would one day be taken away. That got Hezekiah's attention! He realized he had been proud—and he asked God to forgive him. He turned away from being proud and all the people of Judah and Jerusalem asked God to forgive them, too. God brought peaceful, happy times again for the rest of the years of Hezekiah's rule.

7. Draw U-turn sign.

## Conclude the Story

**How did Hezekiah show he wanted to obey God?** (Repaired the Temple doors. Fixed the Temple. Invited people to come and worship God.) **How did the people show they wanted to obey God?** (Got rid of the idols.) **When Hezekiah became proud, how did God show Hezekiah that his actions were wrong?** (Warned of trouble.)

**God wants us to always admit it and ask forgiveness when we've done wrong. It never helps to keep doing wrong. It will only cause us more trouble!**

**2 Chronicles 34—35**

# Josiah, the Child King

## Materials

Drawing materials/equipment for teacher and each student.

## Tell the Story

As you tell each part of the story, draw each sketch. Students copy your sketches.

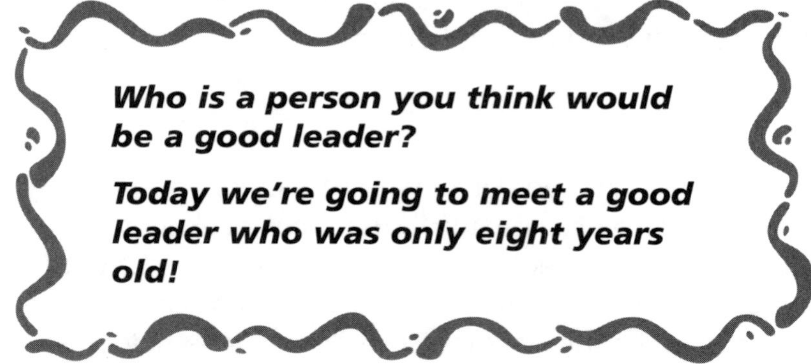


1. It had been many years since God's people had gone to the Temple to worship God. The Temple was empty and dirty. But when King Amon was killed, his son, Josiah, was crowned king. Now, Josiah was only eight years old! But Josiah learned quickly that his father's evil ways weren't what he wanted to follow. He began to pray to the God of Israel, whom his ancestor David loved. Josiah tore down the altars to the false gods.

1. Write "8." Add person details and crown.

2. Josiah also wanted to see God's Temple made beautiful again. He sent men to repair the Temple. They brought workers together to fix broken walls, clean the floors, shine the candlesticks and sew new curtains.

2. Temple from rectangles.

3. While the workers were busy, Hilkiah, the high priest, saw something lying in a corner, covered with dust. He picked it up and blew off the dust. It was a scroll, a book written on one long piece of paper made from plants or animal skins and rolled up. Hilkiah unrolled the scroll and began to read. It was a scroll of God's Law! Hilkiah took the scroll to King Josiah's servant. He said, "Look! I found a scroll of God's Law! This is IMPORTANT. Show it to King Josiah!"

3. Scroll from "O"s and "I"s.

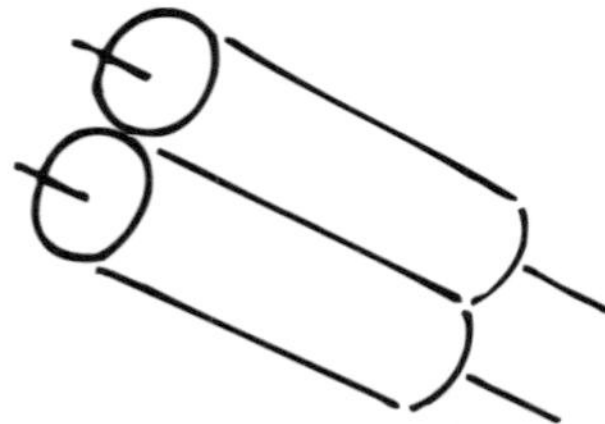

4. King Josiah's servant didn't waste any time. He ran to show King Josiah the scroll of God's Law! King Josiah saw that this scroll had not been read in a long, long time. Josiah asked his servant to please read it aloud.

4. Draw open scroll.

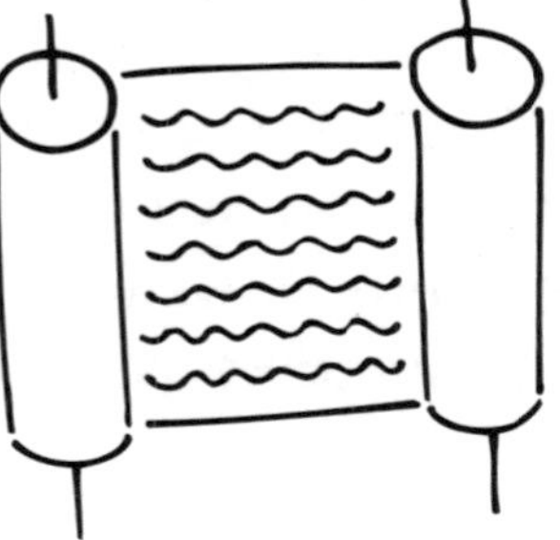

5. As the servant read, Josiah listened carefully. When Josiah heard the laws God gave to Moses, he felt so sad he tore his clothes. He realized that he and his people had not obeyed God! They had not even known what God had asked them to do, because they had not read God's Word. Josiah declared, "We must read God's words to all the people. Then EVERYONE will know how to obey God."

5. Face from "U," "7" for nose. Add details and crown.

6. King Josiah sent messengers to tell everyone to come to the Temple. Mothers, fathers, grandmothers, grandfathers, boys and girls came to hear God's words. King Josiah unrolled the Bible scroll and read it ALL. And all the people LISTENED! When King Josiah finished reading, he said, "I am going to follow the Lord and obey His words. And I want all of you to promise God that we ALL will obey His words." The people did. They promised to obey the God of Israel, the same Lord that Abraham, Moses and David had loved and worshiped.

6. Add open mouth and raised hand from "U"s.

Draw "C"s for crowd listening to king. Add faces.

7. After Josiah destroyed the idols, read God's Word and promised to obey God, THEN he was ready to open the Temple. It was time to celebrate the Passover, to celebrate and remember the time when God brought them out of slavery in Egypt. The people were glad to come and celebrate. King Josiah had everything prepared: the animals, the musicians, the priests—the Bible says there hadn't been such a big celebration of Passover since the days of Samuel! King Josiah was a good leader because he did EVERYTHING he knew how to do to obey God.

7. Music notes from "d"s and "p"s.

## Conclude the Story

**What did Hilkiah, the high priest, find in the Temple?** (Scroll of God's Law.) **What did Josiah do when he knew his people had not been obeying God's Law?** (Tore his clothes. Called people together to read the Law to them.) **Why do you think Josiah was a good leader?** (He helped others learn and obey God's Law.)

**Good leaders aren't always the strongest or biggest or smartest people. Josiah was only an eight-year-old when he became king! Good leaders do all they can to obey God and help others do what is right, too.**

**Nehemiah 1—4; 8—9**

# Nehemiah's Big Project

## Materials

Drawing materials/equipment for teacher and each student.

***What's a job you need someone else's help to do?***

***Today we're going to meet a man who showed his love for God by helping people work together to do great things!***

## Tell the Story

As you tell each part of the story, draw each sketch. Students copy your sketches.

1. Nehemiah lived in the country of Babylon, far from his real home in Jerusalem. Like Daniel, Nehemiah had been taken away from Jerusalem many years before. Nehemiah lived in the king's palace and worked for the king.

1. Draw Nehemiah from "N."

2. One day Nehemiah's brother came to visit him. His brother had been left behind when the Babylonians took so many people away. The brothers talked and talked, and Nehemiah wanted to know how things were in Jerusalem. Nehemiah's brother sadly told him that the walls around Jerusalem were broken down and the houses were falling down, too.

2. Falling walls from rectangles.

3. When Nehemiah heard this bad news, he was very sad for days and DAYS. He didn't even eat. But he did do something VERY important. He prayed! He asked God to help him find a way to get the king's permission to go and help rebuild the walls and the houses in Jerusalem.

3. Draw "U"s and "3" to make praying hands.

4. Nehemiah's sad face told the king that something was very wrong. The king asked, "Why are you so sad?" Before Nehemiah answered, he silently asked God to help him say the right words. "O King," Nehemiah said, "my brother has told me that the city where our family lived is ruined. The walls are broken down. I want VERY much to go and help the people rebuild the city."

4. Write "sad." Add "U"s for face and ears; "S"s for hair.

5. The king thought about Nehemiah's request. He told Nehemiah not only could he go, but also the king himself would help with supplies and people to do the job! Nehemiah must have been so excited! He thanked the king and soon he was on his way to Jerusalem with people and supplies to help do the job.

5. Write "help"; add facial details, "M"s for crown and "3"s for beard.

6. Nehemiah called all the people together. He announced that the king had sent him to help rebuild the city walls. Soon people were volunteering to repair a section of the wall. People were talking together about ways to help each other. Many families built the walls near their houses. Everyone worked together. There were people hammering and holding chisels to cut stone and people sawing wood to make gates. Every person worked hard.

6. Hammer from "I"s and "C"s; chisel from a long "V" and "C."

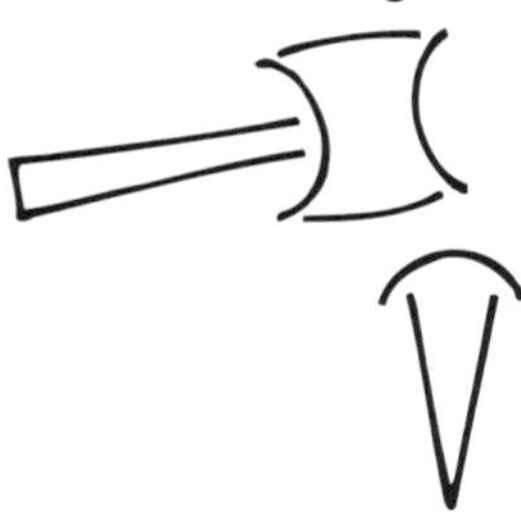

7. But there were enemies of the Jews who didn't want ANYONE to repair Jerusalem. They were angry that Jerusalem would be strong and safe again. They wanted to stop the workers. So they made fun of them. They tried to scare them. They said they would kill them! THEN they tried to make the king of Babylon angry at the workers!

7. Angry face from "U"s, "V."

8. But Nehemiah told the workers not to be afraid. The workers took turns guarding each other. Since they had to spend half their time guarding each other, it took a long time! But finally, the wall was finished. The heavy gates were hung in place. Everyone was glad to see the wall high and strong around the city.

8. Wall from straight lines; gate from "U."

9. The people came together to celebrate the rebuilt walls. Ezra, the priest, read the scroll of God's Law aloud. The people listened. They were very sad that they had not known God's commands earlier, but Nehemiah told them not to be sad—to celebrate. Now they had a city. Now they had heard God's laws and had worshiped God. Now they had worked together and a great thing had been done!

9. Draw sad face. Add arrow and happy face.

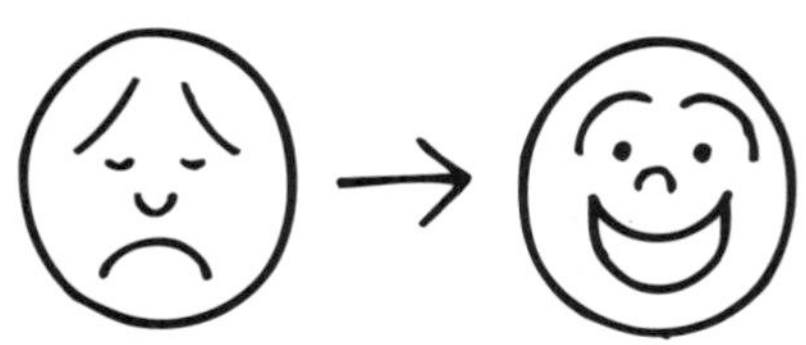

## Conclude the Story

**What did Nehemiah do first about the wall?** (Prayed.) **How did God help the people?** (Made them brave. Gave help from king.) **When we work together, we show love for God like Nehemiah did. And great things are done!**

## Nehemiah 8

# Ezra Reads God's Word

## Before the Story

Guide students to briefly practice signs for underlined words.

## Tell the Story

As you tell the story, lead students in responding as shown when you say the underlined words.

***When have you been in a really big crowd? What was the crowd doing?***

***Today we're going to find out how God's people worshiped God when they were all crowded together.***

1. For many years, God's people did not live the way God had wanted them to. They didn't remember God's Word. Because of their disobedience, God let them be taken from their homes and forced to live in another country. But God had told them that He would bring them back to Israel. And He did! By the time of today's story, many people had returned to Israel. But they still didn't remember God's Word.

1. Didn't remember: Right fist under chin, move forward; move right fist from brow to left fist and thumbs touch.

2. Nehemiah and Ezra were two leaders of the people who had come back to Israel. These men loved God and wanted to obey Him. But they had a problem because the people they had led back to Israel did not know much about God anymore. And since they did not know God's Word, they could not obey God.

2. Obey: Hold fists near forehead; bring down and palms up.

3. Nehemiah and Ezra had an idea. They sent word to everyone to come together. They were going to read God's Word out loud, so everyone could HEAR it! Soon, grandpas, grandmas, parents and children came to Jerusalem. Hundreds and hundreds of people crowded together in the big square and sat down.

3. Together: Place fists together; move in circle to the left.

4. Ezra climbed up to the high platform that had been built, so everyone could hear him. He unrolled a scroll of God's words. As he did, ALL the people stood up to worship God. Here was the book of God's words! Ezra and all the people praised the Lord. The people shouted, "Amen! Amen!" Then they bowed down and worshiped the Lord.

4. Worship: Left hand over right fist; move hands to body and bow head.

5. The people stood for hours and hours, listening to Ezra and his helpers. They heard how God had cared for their people through years and years and YEARS. The speakers explained the words to the people and helped them understand what God's Word said. The people learned that they had not been obeying Him and many cried as they listened. They had been disobeying God and hadn't even known it!

5. Listening, listened: Cup right ear; turn head to left.

6. When Ezra and his helpers were through reading God's words, Ezra said, "Don't cry! This is not a sad day but a day to celebrate! NOW you know what God says to you. You understand what He wants you to do! Be happy. Have a party. Share your food with people who don't have enough. Show God you love Him." So the people stopped crying. Instead, they began to celebrate!

6. Celebrate: Right index finger and thumb touching, make small circles.

7. The next day the people gathered again to hear more of God's Word. It was then that they heard God's command to celebrate the Feast of Tabernacles by building little houses. The little houses, called booths, would remind the people of God's care for their ancestors as they traveled to the Promised Land. Everyone went out into the countryside and gathered branches to build the booths.

7. Houses, booths: Hands outline roof and sides of house.

8. The people lived in their leafy booths and celebrated for a whole week of joy! They ate special foods and prayed to God. The Bible says that there had never been such a big celebration for hundreds and hundreds of years! Everyone was full of joy!

8. Joy: Move hands in forward circles, palms touching chest.

## Conclude the Story

**Why did the Israelites need to hear God's Word?** (They had forgotten God's Word.) **What did the people do as they listened?** (They cried with sadness.) **What holiday did they celebrate?** (Feast of Tabernacles.) **Why?** (Because they heard God's Word and remembered God's goodness.)

**God's people celebrated when they heard God's Word and remembered His goodness in keeping His promises. When we look back to see how God has cared for us, even in hard times, it makes us want to celebrate, too!**

# Esther Saves God's People

## Materials

Drawing materials/equipment for teacher and each student.

## Tell the Story

As you tell each part of the story, draw each sketch. Students copy your sketches.

***What's one thing you did today to get ready to come here?***

***Today we're going to meet a young woman God got ready for a very important job!***

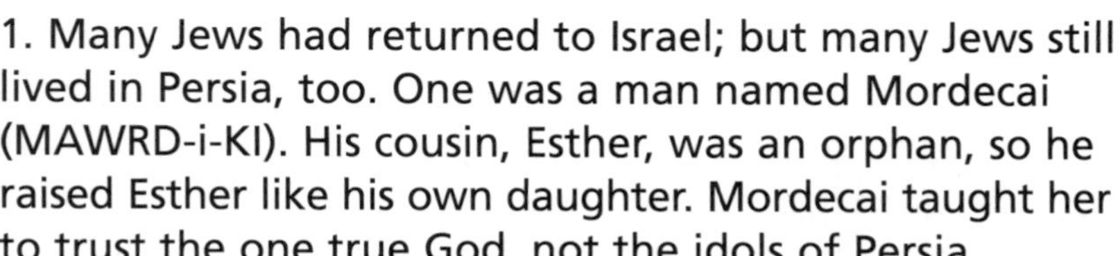

1. Many Jews had returned to Israel; but many Jews still lived in Persia, too. One was a man named Mordecai (MAWRD-i-KI). His cousin, Esther, was an orphan, so he raised Esther like his own daughter. Mordecai taught her to trust the one true God, not the idols of Persia.

1. Draw Esther from 3 "7s." Add hair.

2. When Esther was grown, the king of Persia wanted a new queen. He sent officers through the land to find beautiful young women who were taken to the palace. The king would choose one of them as his new queen. Esther was one of the girls chosen. When Esther was brought before the king, he liked her the best! Esther was crowned the new queen. God was preparing Esther to take part in some very big plans!

2. Draw elaborate crown from "O"s, "V"s and "C"s.

3. A man named Haman was the chief official of Persia, next to the king in power. And everyone in Persia BOWED before him—everyone except Mordecai, Esther's cousin! Mordecai bowed only before God. This made Haman ANGRY. He hated Mordecai and all the Jews. Haman told the king how much trouble all the Jews were. He asked the king to make a law that the Jews should all be KILLED!

3. Bowing person from 2 "L"s. Add details.

4. It doesn't seem that the king knew Esther was a Jew. He AGREED to let Haman write the law! And he gave Haman his signet ring to seal it. Haman's law ordered that all the Jews be killed on a certain day. With the king's seal on it, the law could never be changed. What an uproar! The Jews asked each other, "What have WE ever done to deserve THIS?"

4. Signet ring from "O"s and "C"s. Add crown.

5. Mordecai was VERY sad. When Esther heard that he was upset, she sent servants to find out why. Mordecai told Esther about the law. Esther would not escape being killed just because she was queen. Mordecai told her she HAD to talk to the king about this terrible law!

5. Draw teardrops and make into eyes. "U"s for facial features and hair.

6. BUT there was a problem: If a person went into the throne room without being invited and the king didn't hold out his scepter to that person, it meant DEATH! This made Esther afraid to go to the king at first. But Mordecai was sure she had become queen for this very reason! Only someone the king liked more than Haman could plead for the Jews!

6. Scepter from circle, rectangle and 2 triangles. Add hand.

7. Esther was willing to trust God even if it meant she had to die. Esther fasted for three days—instead of eating she spent time praying to God. Then Esther dressed up—maybe for the last time. She slipped into the throne room, her heart pounding. Would the king hold out his scepter to her? Her life and the lives of her people depended on his next move!!

7. Draw a beating heart.

8. The king held out his scepter! She touched it and invited the king and Haman to two feasts. At the second feast, Esther told the king that an enemy wanted to kill her and her people. The king wanted to know who this enemy was. Esther pointed to Haman and said, "The enemy is Haman!" So the king got rid of Haman and put Mordecai in his place. The king made a new law saying that on the day the Jews were to be killed, they could defend themselves! The Jews' enemies were quickly defeated, and the Jews living in Persia were saved because Esther was ready to obey God!

8. Add hand with finger touching the scepter .

## Conclude the Story

**What did Esther do?** (Saved her people.) **How did God prepare her for this event?** (Made her queen.)

**Queen Esther was ready because she knew how to rely on God. God used her to save all the Jewish people living in Persia. God gets us ready to do good things, too. We may not do the same job Esther did, but God has important work for each of us to do. He will get us ready as we trust Him and obey Him.**

## Job 1—2:10; 42

# Job Trusts God

## Materials

Play dough (1/4 cup, or 2 oz.) for each student.

## Tell the Story

**Follow along with me as we use our dough to tell today's story.**

***What do kids your age usually do when something bad or sad happens?***

***Today we're going to hear what a man said and did when some really TERRIBLE things happened to him.***

1. **Make a ball for the earth.** Things were going very badly for a man named Job. A terrible storm had killed his children; his animals had been stolen; he had become very sick. And he wondered why. In fact, Job wondered if God had forgotten all about him.

God had not forgotten about Job. Even though sad, terrible things had happened to Job, God still loved and cared for him. So God talked to Job to help him understand how great God is and how much He cared for Job.

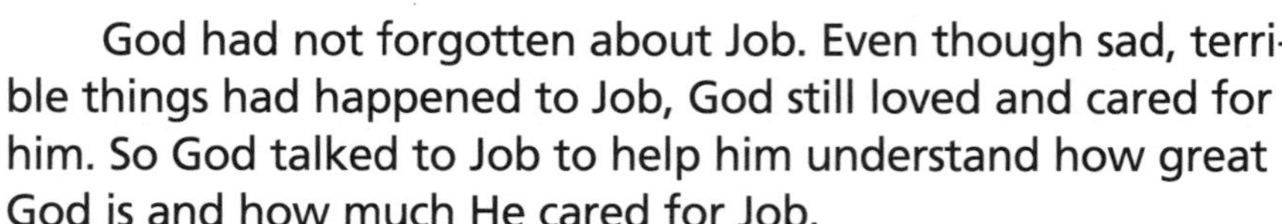

"Tell me, Job, do you know how I made the earth? And do you know how I control the oceans and keep their waters from washing all over the land?"

Job must have thought about the beautiful world. He knew that God made the sweet-smelling flowers and the roaring waterfalls, the puffy clouds and the blue sky. Job KNEW God made the earth and everything in it.

2. **Pinch out rays on the earth to turn it into the sun.** God wasn't finished asking Job questions. "Job, can you make the sun rise? Or can you make the rain fall and the grass grow?"

Job didn't know HOW God made the clouds or the rain. He didn't know exactly what God did to make it possible for the little grass seeds to sprout and grow. But there was one thing Job did know for sure—he didn't make the sun and he couldn't make it rain and he couldn't make the grass grow. Only God can do that!

3. **Flatten sun to make a star.** God had MORE questions to ask Job. "Do you know how to control the stars?" Job couldn't even count all the stars, much less control them!

"And Job, can you give food to the birds and the lions? Can you help the mother deer teach their babies to live on their own in the forests? Do you make horses to run SO FAST that the ground flashes by underneath them?"

Job knew God had made all the stars, created all the animals and made many of them strong and fast.

4. **Make a bird's nest.** "And Job," God continued, "does the eagle fly at your command? Are you the one who tells him to build his nest on rocky ledges high above the ground?"

Job must have thought of the strong eagles he had seen. He remembered how an eagle perched on the edge of its nest, carefully watching for food. Then the eagle flew off the nest, swooped down and caught the food. That's the way God planned for an eagle to get the food it needs. Job knew that God made eagles able to do all those things.

5. **Make a heart for love and a lightning bolt for power.** Job must have thought some more about his troubles. Then he must have thought about God's love and power.

Job said to God, "Now I know that you can do all things. All that you have planned will happen. Before I had heard of You, but I did not understand Your power or Your love. Now I know all that You can do. I'm sorry that I did not trust You."

Even though Job still had all of his troubles, he now trusted God to do what was best. Later, God gave Job twice as many sheep and cows and donkeys as he had ever had before. God also gave Job seven sons and three daughters. Job lived for a long, long time, enjoying all that God had given him.

Most important of all, God taught Job about His greatness. And Job learned that he could trust God's love and power when things were going well AND when things were going badly. Job waited patiently for God to answer him. God helped Job learn that people can depend on Him ALL the time.

## Conclude the Story

**What are some of the things God reminded Job He had made?** (The whole earth. The sun and stars. Deer. Horses. Eagles.) **When bad things happened to him, what did Job do?** (He talked to God.) **What did Job learn?** (That he could always depend on God's love and power.) **God gave Job the patience he needed to wait for good things to happen again.**

**When we're members of God's family, God doesn't promise that nothing bad will ever happen to us. But He does promise us that we can always trust in His love, power and wisdom. When we depend on God, He helps us have patience.**

**Jeremiah 1:4-10; 36—40**

# Jeremiah Writes God's Word

## Materials

Drawing materials/equipment for teacher and each student.

## Tell the Story

As you tell each part of the story, draw each sketch. Students copy your sketches.

***What's the most valuable thing you own?***

***Today we're going to talk about one of the most valuable things in the world.***

1. The time of the kings ruling over Israel and Judah was almost over. Because most of the kings had led the people away from obeying God, God had warned that their nation would be destroyed. God called a man named Jeremiah to be a prophet like Isaiah, Elijah and Elisha. God told him exactly what messages to tell the people. Jeremiah warned the people to love and obey only God and to stop worshiping idols. But the people of Jerusalem did NOT listen. They no longer cared about loving and obeying God.

1. Draw stop sign.

2. But God still loved the people! He wanted to warn them of the terrible things that would happen to them, so they would stop doing what was wrong. God told Jeremiah, "Take a scroll. Write My words on it." Jeremiah sent for his helper, Baruch (BER-uhk). As Jeremiah spoke God's message, Baruch wrote the words on a scroll.

2. Draw scroll from "O"s and "I"s.

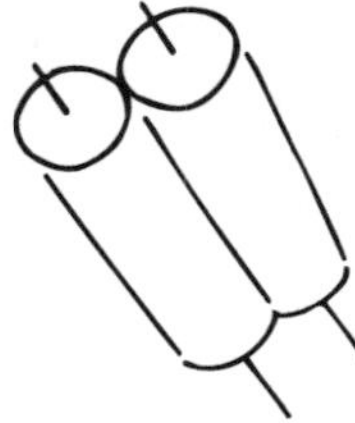

3. When the scroll was finally finished, Jeremiah told Baruch to take it to the Temple and read it to the people. Baruch went to the Temple and read God's words in a loud, clear voice. And this time, some people listened VERY carefully to God's messages.

3. Draw ears from "C"s, add face.

4. One person who listened was a man who went and told the king all about this scroll! The king ordered one of his leaders to bring it to him. The leader read God's words to the king. The king did not like what he heard. In fact, he was so angry that he grabbed a KNIFE.

4. Angry king: "3"s for beard, "C" for ear, "7" for nose.

5. Every time the leader finished reading part of the scroll, the king took the scroll from his hand. He took his knife and sliced off that part of the scroll and threw it into the FIRE! The king didn't care AT ALL about what God said! He wanted to forget about it and didn't want anyone else to read God's message!

5. Knife from 2 "D"s and scroll from "O" and "I"s.

6. But God's words are important and valuable. God loved these people. They needed to know that trouble was coming unless they changed! So God told Jeremiah to write out the same scroll again. The new scroll was to have all the words that were on the first scroll and more besides. Jeremiah and Baruch followed God's instructions and wrote another scroll. But the king and his people still did not listen.

6. Draw larger closed scroll.

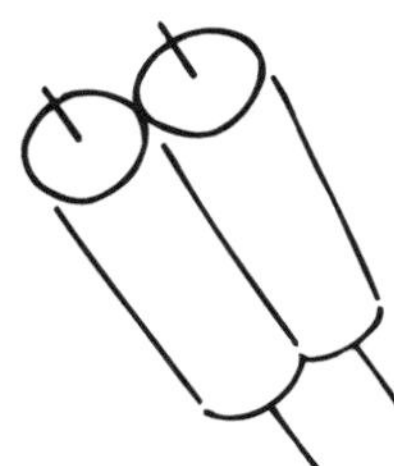

7. Then there was a new king. Did he listen? NO! First, Jeremiah was put in jail. THEN the king's officials had Jeremiah thrown into a cistern—a hole deep in the ground where rain water is stored. No one was listening to what God told Jeremiah to say.

7. Write "Jail"; add face and details.

8. The sad part of this story is that all the terrible things that Jeremiah had told the people would happen DID happen, just like God said they would. Their country was destroyed. Soon, an enemy army attacked them and their city burned, just as God had said. The enemies took most of the people away as slaves. The trouble that God said would come DID come. God's words are true and valuable.

8. Draw sad faces.

## Conclude the Story

**What does a prophet do?** (Tells God's messages to people.) **What did the king do with the scroll of God's words?** (Sliced it into pieces; burned the pieces.) **What did God tell Jeremiah to do next?** (Write the scroll again. Keep warning the people.) **What happened because the people did not listen to God's important words?** (Trouble did come. People were taken as slaves. The city was burned.)

**God's words are still just as important today as they were in Jeremiah's day. They are always true, and they are more valuable than anything in the world. God's words show us the best way to live.**

## Daniel 1; 5—6

# Daniel Loves God

### Before the Story

Guide students to briefly practice signs for underlined words.

### Tell the Story

As you tell the story, lead students in responding as shown when you say the underlined words.

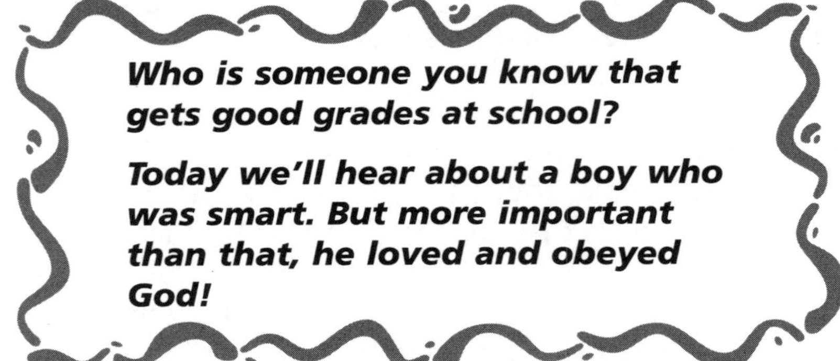

***Who is someone you know that gets good grades at school?***

***Today we'll hear about a boy who was smart. But more important than that, he loved and obeyed God!***

1. Daniel was a teenager who lived in Jerusalem about 600 years before Jesus was born. At that time, people from the country of Babylon had taken over most of that area of the WORLD! Daniel and other people from Jerusalem were taken to Babylon as captives. Daniel and some of his friends were chosen to be trained as workers for the king of Babylon.

2. Daniel and his friends were given Babylonian names. They were given Babylonian food to eat that was supposed to make them strong. BUT if they ate that food, Daniel and his friends would have to break God's laws about some things they weren't allowed to eat. So Daniel asked the king's servant if he and his friends could eat only vegetables for 10 days. The king's servant agreed, even though he was afraid he would get into trouble if eating the vegetables made Daniel and his friends weaker than the others.

3. When 10 days were up, the king's servant could see that they looked healthier than everyone else. Later, at the end of their years of training, the king thought Daniel and his friends were wiser than anyone in the kingdom! Daniel worked hard for that king for many years. Everyone knew Daniel was wise and honest.

4. Many years later when Daniel had grown up, another king was in charge. A VERY strange thing happened. This king was holding a banquet, eating and making offerings to the idols he worshiped. Suddenly, a HAND appeared out of NOWHERE! It wrote some words on the wall that no one understood. But someone remembered how WISE Daniel was. The king called for Daniel to come and tell what the words meant.

1. World: With first three fingers extended, right hand circles left, ending on top of left.

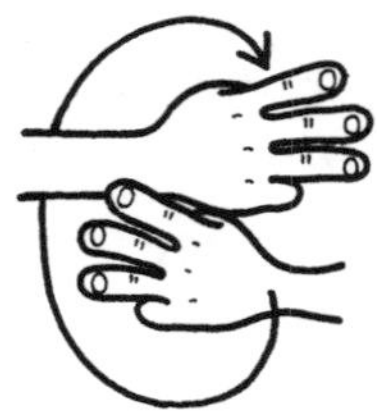

2. Eat, ate: Fingertips touching, move right hand to mouth a few times.

3. Wise: Bend right index finger; move up and down on forehead.

4. Word: Place right thumb and index finger against left index finger.

5. Daniel told the king exactly what the words said and what they meant: because the king had ignored God and had worshiped idols, this king's time to rule had come to an end. Everything Daniel said would happen came true! That very night, another king sneaked into Babylon with his armies. He took over the whole kingdom of Babylon and became the new king!

5. King: Right thumb between index and middle fingers; move from shoulder to waist.

6. The new king was named Darius and he must have heard all about Daniel because he made Daniel a very high official in HIS kingdom, too! By this time, Daniel was a very old man. He had loved and obeyed God his whole life!

Daniel did such a good job serving King Darius that the other officials were jealous. They tried to find something wrong that Daniel had done, so they could say bad things to King Darius about him. But they couldn't find ANYTHING! Daniel was a wise, honest and trustworthy man! Daniel showed his love for God by praying three times a day by his open window.

6. Praying: Touch palms in front; move hands to body and bow head.

7. Daniel's prayers gave the jealous officials an idea. They had the king sign a law that no one could pray to ANYONE but the king for 30 days! The king signed the law. And Daniel prayed—to GOD—as he always did. The other officials brought Daniel to the king and insisted that Daniel be put in the lions' den to be EATEN, because he had broken the king's law. The king did NOT want to do this, but even he couldn't change the law! Daniel had to be thrown into the lions' den!

7. Lion: Shake right curved open hand over head; move hand backward.

8. That night, King Darius didn't sleep. In the morning, he went out to the lions' den to see if Daniel was still alive. He was! Daniel called out and told the king that God had sent an angel who shut the lions' mouths. God had saved Daniel!

Daniel obeyed and loved God his whole life. Daniel lived wisely by loving and obeying God all of his life!

8. God: Point right index finger; lower and open hand at chest.

## Conclude the Story

**Why was Daniel in Babylon?** (The Babylonians took over Jerusalem and took Daniel as a captive.) **What are some ways Daniel showed God's wisdom?** (Obeyed God's laws. Acted wisely. Was honest and trustworthy.) **What are some ways God took care of Daniel?** (Gave Daniel wisdom. Kept him safe from the lions.)

**Every day, from the time we are very young to the time we are very old, we can choose to love and obey God. We can talk to God and ask His help in living wisely!**

## Daniel 1; 6

# Daniel and the Lions' Den

## Materials

Drawing materials/equipment for teacher and each student.

***What's something you like to do every day?***

***Today we're going to talk about a man who prayed to God every day, no matter what happened!***

## Tell the Story

As you tell each part of the story, draw each sketch. Students copy your sketches.

1. The king of Babylon had attacked Jerusalem. He took many people to Babylon as captives, just as the prophets had warned. Daniel was a young man who was taken to the king's palace to serve the king. Daniel served so well that he worked as an official for several kings. He was very honest; he loved and obeyed God; and every day, three times a day, Daniel knelt in front of his open window and prayed to God.

1. Draw a "3." Add details for praying Daniel and window.

2. Darius (duh-RI-uhs), the king of Babylon, was very pleased with Daniel's work. He decided to put Daniel in charge over EVERYONE in the government. When some other government officials heard about the king's plan, they were very jealous that the king liked Daniel so much.

2. Draw jealous faces.

3. These jealous officials spied on Daniel day and night, trying to think of a way to get rid of him or make the king not like him. But they found nothing wrong! When they saw that Daniel knelt in front of his window and prayed to God three times every day, they got an idea.

3. Add light bulbs over heads.

4. The officials tricked King Darius into making a new law. The law said that for 30 days, nobody could pray to ANYONE except to King Darius. Whoever disobeyed would be thrown to hungry lions! And no one lived through that! The jealous officials were sure Daniel would be eaten by lions, or would Daniel stop praying?

4. Scroll from "S"s.

5. Daniel soon heard about the new law! Now, Daniel COULD have hidden in the dark and prayed to God. He could have NOT prayed for 30 days. But praying to God was SO important to Daniel that he kept on praying in front of the window three times every day, just as he had always done. The minute the jealous officials saw Daniel praying, they ran to the king to tell him Daniel had broken the law!

5. Draw second praying Daniel figure. Add surprised face.

6. King Darius was very upset—not because Daniel had disobeyed his law but because he realized the leaders had tricked him into making this silly law to get rid of Daniel. In Babylon, once a king made a law, he could never change it. King Darius knew the silly law had to be obeyed. He sadly walked with Daniel—to the LIONS' DEN.

6. Lion from "5," "C"s, "3"s. Teeth from "V"s.

7. King Darius sighed. "You have been very faithful to your God. I hope He can save you from the hungry lions," he said. And with that, Daniel was put into a pit filled with hungry lions. A stone was rolled over the opening to the pit and King Darius had it sealed, so NO ONE could move it.

That night King Darius worried about Daniel. He walked back and forth, wondering if Daniel's God would save him. Early next morning, the king ran to the lion's den. He called, "Daniel! Did your God save you?"

7. Draw worried face. Add details for king.

8. Daniel called back, "Yes, God saved me from the lions. He sent an angel who shut the lions' mouths. God knew I had done nothing wrong." The king ordered his soldiers to pull Daniel out of the den. He sent a message to EVERYONE in his country that Daniel's God was the REAL God. And the jealous leaders were punished.

8. Lion with closed mouth from "E," "C"s and "3"s.

## Conclude the Story

**Why did the officials get the king to make the law?** (They were jealous of Daniel.) **What did Daniel do?** (Prayed anyway.) **What did God do when Daniel was with the lions?** (Protected Daniel. Sent an angel.)

**God wants us to pray to Him every day. If things are happy or sad, good or bad, He wants us to come to Him and talk with Him! When we pray, we get to know God better. He always wants to hear us pray to Him!**

Daniel 2

# Daniel Interprets a King's Dream

## Before the Story

Guide students to briefly practice signs for underlined words.

## Tell the Story

As you tell the story, lead students in responding as shown when you say the underlined words.

***Who do you like to talk to? What do you talk about?***

***Today we'll hear what a man talked to God about and what the man did when God answered his prayer.***

1. Nebuchadnezzar (NEHB-uh-kuhd-NEHZ-uhr) was the king of the rich and powerful Babylonian empire. There was no king on earth more powerful than him. But Nebuchadnezzar was afraid. He was afraid to go to sleep! He had dreams that he didn't understand and that frightened him.

1. Afraid, frightened: Fingertips touching, open hands and cover chest.

2. Nebuchadnezzar didn't believe in the one true God. He believed that his wise men could help him. Nebuchadnezzar called all his wise men in before him and said, "I had a dream that frightened me. I want you to tell me what the dream was AND what the dream means. If you can do this, I will reward you with fabulous gifts and great honor. If you can't tell me, I'll have you all KILLED."

2. Dream: Right index finger at forehead; move up and out, repeatedly bending finger.

3. The wise men must have thought to themselves, *If only he'd tell us what the dream was, we could make up some lie about what it means.* They asked for more time. But Nebuchadnezzar knew they were just stalling to make up a lie. The wise men pleaded with Nebuchadnezzar, "No one can do what you've asked us to do!" Well, Nebuchadnezzar was so angry, he ordered that all the wise men in Babylon be KILLED!

3. Lie: Move right index finger left across lips.

4. Daniel and his friends Shadrach, Meshach and Abednego were among the men to be killed. When Daniel heard what was going on, he asked the king to give him a little time so that he could interpret the dream. Nebuchadnezzar still wanted to know about his dream, so he decided to give Daniel the time he had asked for.

4. Time: With right index finger, tap top of left wrist a few times.

5. Daniel asked his friends to pray with him, asking God to tell about and explain the mysterious dream. Long into the night, the four men praised God and prayed for His help. God answered their prayers and the dream was explained to Daniel. "Praise be to the name of God for ever and ever!" Daniel said. Daniel praised God for His wisdom and power, and thanked Him for revealing the secrets of the king's dream.

5. Pray: Touch palms in front; move hands to body and bow head.

6. The next day, Daniel went right to Nebuchadnezzar. "No man on earth, no matter how wise, could tell you your dream or what it means. But God is wiser and more powerful than any man, and He has shown me your dream and what it means."

6. Wise: Bend right index finger; move up and down on forehead.

7. Daniel said the king had dreamed of a huge statue. The head was made of gold; the chest and arms were silver; the belly and thighs were bronze; the legs were iron and the feet were a mixture of clay and iron. A huge rock came and smashed the statue, breaking it into pieces that blew away in the wind. Then the huge rock turned into a mountain that filled the whole earth.

Daniel then explained that the golden head stood for Nebuchadnezzar and the other parts of the statue stood for different kingdoms after Nebuchadnezzar's reign. "The rock smashing the statue and turning into a mountain means that the God of heaven will destroy all these kingdoms and establish a kingdom that will last forever!" Daniel finished.

7. Statue: With thumbs in front of fists, move hands down in two arcing motions.

8. Nebuchadnezzar was amazed! Daniel, with God's help, had done the impossible. The king fell down on the floor at Daniel's feet and praised God, "Surely your God is THE God of gods and the Lord of kings."

Then Nebuchadnezzar gave Daniel and his friends fabulous gifts, positions in the government and great honor. But the real honor and praise belonged to God for His great power!

8. Praise: Clap hands a few times.

## Conclude the Story

**Why was Nebuchadnezzar afraid?** (He had dreams that he didn't understand and that scared him.) **Why was Daniel the only wise man who could help Nebuchadnezzar?** (Daniel is the only one who believed in the one true God and asked for God's help.)

**Just as Daniel prayed to God and praised Him for revealing the mystery of the king's dream, we can worship God for both who He is and all the wonderful things He has done.**

**Daniel 3**

# Shadrach, Meshach and Abednego

## Materials

Play dough (¼ cup, or 2 oz.) and paper clip for each student.

***What's the tallest thing you have ever seen?***

***Today we'll hear about something very tall that was built for a very interesting reason!***

## Tell the Story

**Follow along with me as we use our dough to tell today's story.**

1. **Use part of your dough to make three small figures.** Near the end of Old Testament times, many of God's people were taken to the country of Babylon. Three of these people were young men who were given the Babylonian names of Shadrach (SHAD-rak), Meshach (MEE-shak) and Abednego (uh-BED-nee-goh). These three had been trained to serve King Nebuchadnezzar, and now they were officials in his court.

2. **Make a big figure like a statue and another figure like a king from the rest of your dough. Use a paper clip to make a pattern on the statue.** One day, King Nebuchadnezzar decided to have a statue built. It wasn't any ordinary statue. It was going to be HUGE—90 feet (27 m) high! It was going to be covered with gold; and besides that, it had a very interesting purpose: King Nebuchadnezzar expected everyone to BOW and PRAY to the statue!

When the statue was finished, the king called all the officials of his kingdom to come to see it. Shadrach, Meshach and Abednego were part of the crowd. A royal messenger stood up and told the crowd: "This is what you are commanded to do: As soon as you hear the music, you must bow down and WORSHIP the statue that the king has set up. Whoever does not fall down and worship will be thrown into a blazing furnace!"

WELL! Bow down and worship a statue of gold? Shadrach, Meshach and Abednego could hardly believe their ears! If they obeyed the king and worshiped the statue, they would be disobeying God. God had told His people to worship ONLY Him and NOTHING ELSE! But if they did NOT worship the statue, they would be thrown into the fire.

3. **Use your figures to act out the story.** The music began. Everyone around Shadrach, Meshach and Abednego bowed low and worshiped the golden statue. But the three friends stood tall. When the king heard that the men had not bowed to his statue, he flew into a rage!

When the three men were brought to the king, he asked angrily, "Is it true you refused to worship the statue? I'll give you one more chance. Bow down before my statue or you will be thrown into the furnace. THEN who can save you?"

Shadrach, Meshach and Abednego looked up at the king. "O king," they said, "if we're thrown into the furnace, our God is able to rescue us. But even if He does not, we want you to know, O king, that we will NOT worship your image of gold!"

4. **Make your statue into a "7."** When King Nebuchadnezzar heard their words, he was FURIOUS! "Make the furnace SEVEN times hotter than normal. Then tie up these three and THROW them in!"

The furnace was SO hot that the soldiers who threw the friends into the furnace DIED just from the heat! Shadrach, Meshach and Abednego fell, tied up, into the flames. The king and his officers watched. Suddenly, the king leaped to his feet. "Didn't we tie up THREE men and throw them into the furnace? Look!" he exclaimed. "I see FOUR. They are not tied. They are walking around! They don't look like they are being burned at all. And the fourth man looks like a . . . a GOD!"

King Nebuchadnezzar called out, "Shadrach, Meshach and Abednego, servants of the true God, come out!"

And out they walked, cool and calm! Not only were they alive and well; but their hair was not burnt, their clothes weren't scorched, and they didn't even SMELL like smoke!

King Nebuchadnezzar praised God and declared, "From this day forward, NO ONE may speak evil about the God of Shadrach, Meshach and Abednego!"

The three friends obeyed God, no matter what! Their faithful actions caused everyone in Babylon to honor God!

## Conclude the Story

**Why did the king have the statue made?** (For people to bow to it and worship it.) **What did the three friends do?** (Stayed standing.) **How would you describe these three men?** (They wanted to love and obey God, no matter what.)

**Every day we can make choices that will show how much we love and obey God. When we show our love and obedience to God, it helps others see our belief in Him.**

# Jonah Preaches in Nineveh

## Before the Story

Guide students to briefly practice signs for underlined words.

***When have you not wanted to listen to your parents or your teacher? What did you want to do instead?***

***Today we'll meet a person who decided to say no to God! And we'll find out how God helped that person change and obey Him!***

## Tell the Story

As you tell the story, lead students in responding as shown when you say the underlined words.

1. There was once a man named Jonah who was a prophet of God; he told people messages from God. One day, God said to Jonah, "Go to Nineveh right away! Tell the people there to stop their wickedness or I will have to punish them!" But Jonah didn't like the people of Nineveh and didn't WANT to warn them. He wanted God to DESTROY them.

1. Told, said: With right index finger, make circular movement from mouth.

2. So Jonah got up and went, but instead of going to Nineveh, he got on board a ship that was going the OTHER way. Jonah thought he could hide from God! He went down into the bottom of the ship and fell asleep.

2. Hide: Touch lips with right fist; move right fist under cupped left hand.

3. While Jonah slept, God sent a storm! The wind began to blow and the ship began to rock back and forth! The waves got higher and HIGHER! And soon the sailors were praying to their false gods to help them. Then they remembered Jonah, asleep in the bottom of the rocking ship.

3. Ship: Right hand with first three fingers extended on left palm; move both hands in a forward wavy motion.

4. The sailors didn't waste any time! They hurried to Jonah and shook him awake. "Help us!" they said. Jonah knew GOD had sent the storm because of Jonah's disobedience. "You'll have to throw me overboard," he said. "Then the storm will stop."

So the sailors took Jonah and THREW him over the side. SPLASH!

4. Throw: Raise right fist beside head; move hand forward while opening.

5. Jonah went down, down, down—sinking like a stone. But then, a HUGE fish came by. The fish opened wide and swallowed Jonah whole! Jonah was in the smelly belly of the great big fish.

5. Fish: Place left fingertips on right wrist; swing right hand from wrist.

6. Soon Jonah began to think about how he had disobeyed God. And he began to pray. He asked God to give him another chance to obey by going to warn the people of Nineveh. He prayed some more. And he waited. And the great big fish kept right on swimming!

6. Pray: Touch palms in front; move hands to body and bow head.

7. Can you guess what happened? God sent that fish close to the shore. And he coughed Jonah right out onto the beach—not too far from the city! Then God called to Jonah AGAIN, "Go to Nineveh! Warn those people like I told you to do!" And this time Jonah obeyed.

7. Obeyed: Hold fists near forehead; bring down and palms up.

8. Jonah marched right into Nineveh. He must have looked very strange after three days in the big fish's belly. He may have smelled funny, too! But Jonah was going to tell these people God's message, no matter what! He began to warn everyone he saw. "Change your ways," he called out, "or God will destroy this city in 40 days!"

And the people of Nineveh listened! They didn't want to keep on with their wicked ways! And God forgave them and did not punish them. Because Jonah obeyed God, the Ninevites heard God's message and had the opportunity to ask His forgiveness.

8. Forgave, forgiveness: Stroke edge of left palm with right fingertips.

## Conclude the Story

**What did Jonah do when God told him to warn the people of Nineveh? Why?** (He wanted God to punish the Ninevites.) **How did God help Jonah to change his mind and obey?** (Sent a storm.) **Jonah learned that God loves all people!**

**God will forgive anyone who asks. He will make us part of His family when we are sorry for our sin and we believe that Jesus died on the cross to pay for our sin. God loves all people!**

## Isaiah 9:1-7; Micah 1; 5:2-4

# Prophets Tell of the Promised Messiah

## Before the Story

Guide students to briefly practice signs for underlined words.

***What is something you were promised but had to wait for?***

***Today we'll find out about some promises that took a long time to come true.***

## Tell the Story

As you tell the story, lead students in responding as shown when you say the underlined words.

1. Many years after Solomon built the Temple in Jerusalem, there lived a man named Isaiah. Isaiah was a prophet, a person who told the people messages from God. God spoke to Isaiah about many things and Isaiah wrote them down. Isaiah wrote about things that would happen in the countries around Israel. He also wrote about terrible things that would happen to the people of Israel because they had not obeyed God.

1. Wrote: Touch thumb and right index finger; make wavy line across left palm.

2. Isaiah's book could have been a very sad book, but it wasn't. Here's why: In that book, God made wonderful promises! God promised that a baby would be born who would make everyone glad. This baby would be the Savior—the One who would save people from the punishment their sins deserved!

2. Promises: Right index finger on lips; move to open hand on left fist.

3. This Savior sent by God would be the greatest King of all time. His kingdom would never come to an end! This King would be known by many names. One name was the Wonderful Counselor, because He would teach His people how to follow God and He would give them wisdom.

3. King: Right thumb between index and middle fingers; move from shoulder to waist.

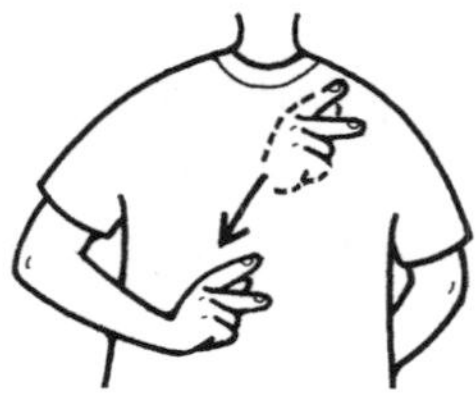

4. Isaiah also called this Savior the Mighty God, the Everlasting Father and the Prince of Peace. All these names meant that the Savior would not be an ordinary man. He would be God's own Son. And He would be the One who would bring peace to those people who would let Him rule their lives.

4. God: Point right index finger; lower and open hand at chest.

5. About the same time that Isaiah was telling God's messages, God sent another prophet to warn the people of Israel. Micah told the people that God wanted them to stop cheating each other and stop hurting the poor people. Micah also warned the people about terrible things that were going to happen very soon—things that really did happen, just as God said they would. But the most important thing Micah told about didn't happen until 700 years later.

5. Stop: Hit open left hand with edge of right open hand.

6. Micah told the people God's promise that a ruler would be born in Bethlehem, even though Bethlehem was a little town and didn't seem very important. Micah said that this ruler would be different from any other ruler they had ever known. When the people heard about this ruler, they knew that He would not be an ordinary man. He would be specially sent by God. It was another promise about the coming Savior!

6. Ruler: Move hands as though holding reins.

7. In many places in the Old Testament, God told His people things about the future and made promises about the coming Savior. Even at the very beginning of the Bible, when Adam and Eve had sinned, God had promised them that a Savior would come—a Savior who would make it possible for Adam and Eve and everyone in the world to be rescued from the punishment their sins deserved.

7. Promises: Right index finger on lips; move to open hand on left fist.

8. When the people heard God's promises to send a Savior, they were happy at the news. It wasn't long, however, before many people forgot to obey God. The sad things that God had said would happen, happened. But God did not forget His people. The GLAD things God promised happened, too! For 700 years later, in a little, unimportant town called Bethlehem, a great King WAS born. He is still the greatest King of all time! Do you know His name?

8. Forget: Move open hand on forehead to closed hand on the right.

## Conclude the Story

**What do prophets do?** (Tell God's messages to people.) **What are some of the things Isaiah told God's people?** (That God would send a Savior.) **What things did Micah tell the people?** (To obey God. That a ruler would be born in Bethlehem.)

**For hundreds of years after these prophets lived, God's people waited for God to keep His promise to send a Savior. And He did! While we get ready to celebrate Christmas, we can also get our minds and hearts ready to celebrate the birth of the King—Jesus!**

**Luke 1:26-56**

# An Angel Visits Mary

## Before the Story

Guide students to briefly practice signs for underlined words.

***What's something that makes you feel really happy?***

***Today we'll hear about a young woman who got a VERY big surprise that made her feel VERY glad!***

## Tell the Story

As you tell the story (or invite students to help tell the details of this familiar story), lead students in responding as shown when you say the underlined words.

1. In the dusty little town of Nazareth lived a young woman named Mary. She had promised to marry a man named Joseph. Maybe Mary was sweeping, brushing little clouds of dust, or weaving, sitting at the loom. But whatever she was doing, suddenly she STOPPED. The angel GABRIEL stood before her. Gabriel said, "Greetings! You are highly favored! The Lord is with you!" That meant that God loved Mary and wanted to honor her.

1. Angel: Fingertips on shoulders; draw away and out, waving up and down.

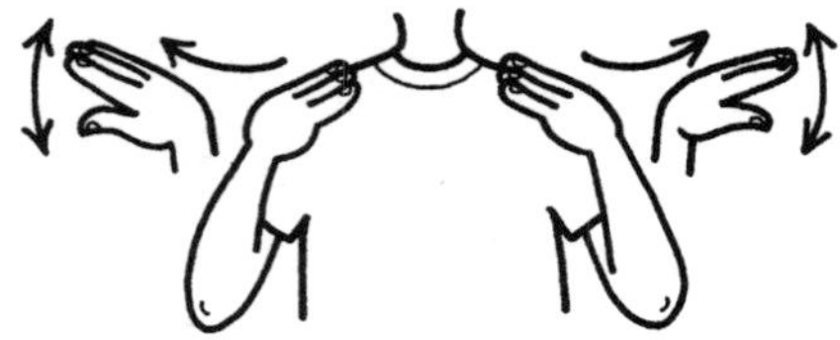

2. Mary must have DROPPED whatever she was doing! She was amazed and afraid and glad all at once! Then Gabriel said gently, "Do not be afraid! God is very pleased with you! You will have a son and will name Him Jesus. He will be great and will be called the Son of the Most High. He will rule forever!"

2. God: Point right index finger; lower and open hand at chest.

3. WELL! That was certainly a lot to take in! Perhaps Mary sat down, PLUNK, all at once. *A baby? The Son of the Most High . . . rule forever . . . ? How can such a wonderful thing happen?* she must have wondered. She finally asked, "How will I have a baby?"

3. Baby: Rock crossed arms.

4. The angel answered, "God's Spirit will come to you. God's power will make it happen. That's the reason this baby will be called the Son of God." Mary listened carefully to the angel's words. The angel told Mary some other news: Mary's relative Elizabeth, who had NEVER had a child and was quite old, was going to have a baby, too—in only three more months! Mary listened as the angel said, "For NOTHING is impossible with God!" God can do anything!

4. Listened: Cup right ear; turn head to left.

5. WOW! Mary must have felt excited and scared! But she knew God had honored her and chosen her for the most important job a person had ever had. She looked up at the angel, took a deep breath and said, "I am the Lord's servant. May this happen just as you have said it will." Then the angel left.

5. Servant: Face palms up, moving back and forth alternately; move hands down sides.

6. Soon after this, Mary traveled to visit her relative Elizabeth. As Mary walked into Elizabeth's house, Elizabeth said, "God has shown His love to you in a special way—you are blessed. And blessed is your baby, too! When I heard your voice, my baby jumped inside me for joy. You are blessed and honored for believing that God will do what He has promised!"

6. Blessed: Fists at mouth; open hands and move forward and down.

7. Mary answered Elizabeth's greeting with beautiful words that were like a song. She was so full of joy and amazement at the great things God had done for her, she just couldn't keep quiet! "My spirit rejoices in God, my Savior. The Mighty One has done great things for me," she said. Mary talked about what God had done for her and what wonderful things God was going to do to help His people. Mary talked about how God kept His promises and how He would make things right. It was a beautiful song.

7. Song: Move right hand back and forth in front of left palm.

8. Mary stayed with Elizabeth for about three months, probably until Elizabeth's baby John was born. Mary may not have wanted to go back to Nazareth. It could be very hard to face people who didn't understand why she was having a baby. But Mary knew what the angel had said. She knew that God can always be trusted. And she knew that NOTHING is impossible with Him!

8. Baby: Rock crossed arms.

## Conclude the Story

**Who visited Mary?** (The angel Gabriel.) **What did the angel tell Mary?** (God was pleased with her. She would have a son and name Him Jesus. Jesus would be great.) **What else did Mary learn?** (That nothing is impossible with God.) **What happened when Mary visited Elizabeth?** (Mary sang a beautiful song.)

**Mary said those beautiful words as a way to worship and honor God. We can worship and honor God, too, for His love and for keeping His promise to send a Savior.**

**Matthew 1:18—2:23; Luke 1:26-56; 2**

# Jesus Is Born

## Materials

Drawing materials/equipment for teacher and each student.

***What have you heard about the time when you were born?***

***In our Bible story today we'll hear about what it was like when Jesus was born and grew into a boy.***

## Tell the Story

As you tell each part of the story, draw each sketch. Students copy your sketches.

1. Hundreds of years had passed since any prophet in Israel told God's words to the people. But the people still read the scrolls written by the prophets many years earlier. These scrolls told of God's promise to send a great King.

1. Draw open scroll from "O"s and "I"s.

2. One day, a young lady named Mary ESPECIALLY remembered God's promise. She was visited by an ANGEL! The angel told her that she was going to be the mother of God's very special Son, the King whom God had promised. An angel also came to Joseph, the man Mary was going to marry. The angel told Joseph about this special child who was to be born.

2. Angel from "A." Add wings and head.

3. Not long after the angels' visits, the ruler of all the countries in that part of the world wanted to count everyone to keep track of the people he could tax. All the men had to return to the towns where their families were from. Joseph and Mary went to Bethlehem because he belonged to the family of David, the famous king of long, long ago.

3. Draw Bethlehem from squares and "C"s.

4. It was terribly crowded in Bethlehem and Mary's baby was about to be born. The only place Mary and Joseph could find to stay was a stable for animals. It wasn't very fancy, but it was warm and better than being outside.

4. Stable from "C." Add animals from "C"s, "U"s, "V"s and "I"s.

5. That night God's special Son was born. Joseph and Mary named Him Jesus, just as the angels had told them. Baby Jesus slept on hay in an animal feedbox, called a manger.

5. Manger from "X" and lines. Baby from "C"s.

6. That very same night, some shepherds were nearby with their sheep in the fields. SUDDENLY an angel came to them and the glory of God came shining all around! The shepherds were afraid. But the angel said not to be afraid. There was good news: the Savior, Christ the Lord, was born! A crowd of angels sang in the sky, praising God!

6. Sheep from curly lines. Add face from "U" and ears from "D"s. Add angel as in #2.

7. After the angels went back to heaven, the shepherds hurried off to find the baby Jesus. After they had seen the baby, the shepherds were so excited, they told everyone they met about the wonderful baby! At last the shepherds returned to their sheep in the fields, praising God for everything that they had seen and heard that night.

7. Running shepherd from "O" and "N." Add staff and conversation balloon.

8. Jesus grew and grew. Soon He was sitting up and crawling and then walking. When He was still little, some wise men traveled from far away to worship Him, bringing Him wonderful gifts. When King Herod heard that these men had come to see a child who was to become a great king, Herod wanted to get rid of Jesus. Because of an angel's warning, Joseph took Mary and Jesus and went away one night. They traveled to a country called Egypt and lived there.

8. Draw angry king from "V"s and "C"s.

9. When it was safe to return home, an angel told Joseph he could bring Mary and Jesus back to Nazareth, where they had lived before Jesus was born. Jesus grew up in Nazareth, just as the prophets had said He would. And as Jesus grew, God loved Him and many people did, too!

9. Series of stick figures in larger and larger sizes. Add heart.

## Conclude the Story

**Who was glad to know that Jesus was born?** (Angels. Shepherds. Wise men.) **What made the birth of Jesus so special? What had God promised that Jesus would do?**

**God had said that Jesus would be born in Bethlehem. He had made this promise through His prophets hundreds of years before. God's promise to send a Savior came true. And more things God had said about Jesus were yet to come true!**

**This story of Jesus' birth is so important that now people all over the world celebrate His birthday. They remember the good news about Jesus the Savior.**

**Matthew 3; John 1:19-34**

# John Announces the Savior

## Materials

Drawing materials/equipment for teacher and each student.

***What words would you use to describe Jesus to someone?***

***Today we'll find out how a man named John described Jesus.***

## Tell the Story

As you tell each part of the story, draw each sketch. Students copy your sketches.

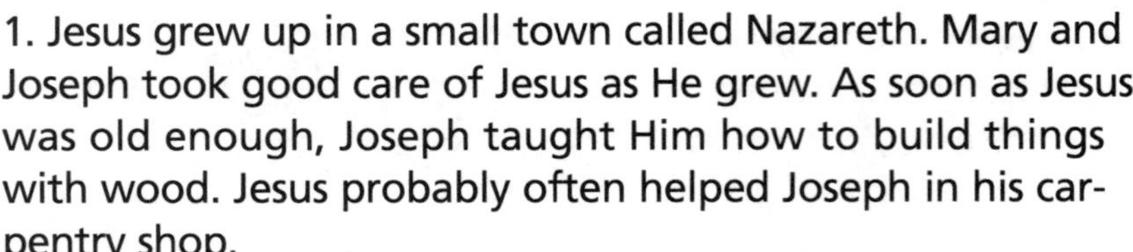

1. Jesus grew up in a small town called Nazareth. Mary and Joseph took good care of Jesus as He grew. As soon as Jesus was old enough, Joseph taught Him how to build things with wood. Jesus probably often helped Joseph in his carpentry shop.

1. Draw saw and hammer from "D"s, "V"s and lines.

2. The years passed, and Jesus grew up. Now Jesus was 30 years old. He knew it was time to begin His work as God's Son. So Jesus went to find a preacher named John. John had been preaching to many people, telling them that God's kingdom was coming. He was telling people to stop doing wrong and start obeying God. Jesus knew that John was helping people get ready for the time when Jesus would come.

2. "Wrong" with "no" slash.

3. John spent most days in the desert by a river, talking to crowds of people. He warned the people to turn away from all the wrong things they had done. Many of the people who listened believed what John told them. They wanted to show God they were sorry for doing wrong. They wanted to live the way God wanted them to live. John took them into the river where he baptized them with water to show that God had forgiven them, making them clean from the wrong things they had done. John also told the people that someone great would come to show God's great power.

3. River from "S"s. Add stick figures by river.

4. One day, who should come to John but Jesus! Jesus told John, "I want you to baptize Me." John was surprised. He said, "But Jesus, YOU haven't done ANY wrong things. YOU should baptize ME!"

Jesus told John that God wanted Him to be baptized by John. Jesus wanted to show He would always do what God wanted. John wanted to obey God, so he baptized Jesus.

4. Two faces from "7"s, "C"s. Add names.

5. As Jesus was coming up out of the water, something happened that had NEVER happened before! A dove flew down from the sky and rested on Jesus. And God spoke from heaven saying, "This is My Son, whom I love. I am pleased with Him."

5. Dove from "7"s, "V" and "C"s.

6. After Jesus was baptized, He went alone to the desert while John stayed by the river and kept telling people to obey God. Some people asked John if HE was God's Son.

"No," John answered. "I am helping people get ready for His coming. He is so great that I am not even good enough to untie His sandals."

6. Foot and sandal from 2 "L"s, 5 "C"s and 1 "X." Add sole and ties.

7. The next day Jesus came to where John was talking. John stopped and turned to point at Jesus. He said, "Look, there is the One who will take away the sin of the world! This is the One I told you about!" John wanted the people to know that Jesus is God's Son. Because of what John said about Jesus, many people believed that Jesus is God's Son and started following Jesus and listening to Him. John had done his job well.

7. Write "Look" and add eyes.

## Conclude the Story

**What was the message John wanted everyone to know?** (Stop doing wrong things. Jesus is God's Son who will take away our sins—the wrong things we do.) **How did God show that Jesus was His Son, the promised Savior?** (Sent dove. Said Jesus was His Son.)

**As we read in the Bible what John said about Jesus and what happened as Jesus was baptized, we discover that Jesus is truly the Savior!** Talk with interested students about salvation. (See "Leading a Child to Christ" on p. 13.)

**Matthew 4:1-11; Luke 4:1-13**

# Jesus Is Tempted in the Desert

## Materials

Drawing materials/equipment for teacher and each student.

***When is a time you have had to say no to something you wanted to do?***

***Today we're going to find out how Jesus was able to say no to the devil.***

## Tell the Story

As you tell each part of the story, draw each sketch. Students copy your sketches.

1. After John baptized Jesus in the Jordan River, Jesus went to the desert where He could be alone. Jesus spent 40 days in the desert, praying to God. This time was part of God's plan to prepare Jesus for teaching and healing people.

1. Draw number 40 and add details for praying figure.

2. While Jesus was in the desert, He didn't eat anything. After 40 days without any food, Jesus was very hungry! He was probably tired as well. That's when Satan, God's enemy, came to Jesus. Satan said, "Since You are the Son of God, why don't You make some of these stones into bread?" Satan wanted to see if Jesus would do a miracle just to get Himself something He wanted very badly—food!

2. Stones from "D"s.

3. But Jesus was not going to take any suggestions from Satan! Jesus knew God's Word. And Jesus used God's Word to answer the devil. He said, "It is written: 'Man does not live on bread alone, but on every word that comes from the mouth of God.'" Jesus meant that knowing and obeying what God said was far more important to Him than eating, even when He was very hungry.

3. Open scroll from "O"s and "I"s.

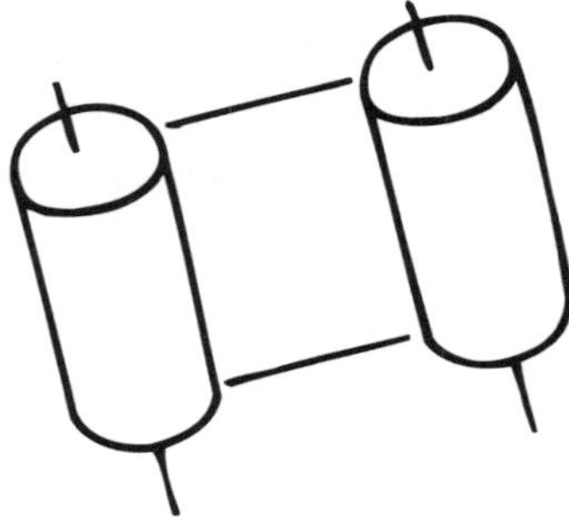

4. Satan had another idea. He took Jesus up to the highest point of the Temple in Jerusalem. He said, "Since You are the Son of God, why don't You throw Yourself off this high place?" The devil even quoted a Bible verse to make his idea sound good! He said a verse about God sending angels to protect people. But Jesus also answered Satan from God's Word. He said, "It is also written: 'Do not put the Lord your God to the test.'" Jesus meant that He wouldn't do a miracle just to show off or prove He was from God. He didn't come to earth to entertain or impress people. He came to teach them about God and bring forgiveness for their sins!

4. Temple from "7"s. Add 2 small stick figures.

5. Satan couldn't argue with Jesus' words, so he just tried again to get Jesus to disobey God. Satan took Jesus up to a very high mountain. Looking out from there, Satan showed all the beautiful kingdoms of the world. Satan said to Jesus, "I will give you all of this—everything in the world!—if you will bow down and worship me!"

5. Draw mountain and add 2 figures.

6. Jesus knew that Satan would do ANYTHING to get Him to do wrong! He would give Jesus ANYTHING if it meant he could get Jesus to sin. And once more, Jesus answered Satan with God's Word. He said, "Get away, Satan! For it is written: 'Worship the Lord your God and serve him ONLY.'" Jesus knew He had not come to earth to show off or do tricks or get things for Himself. He had come to obey God. And God's Word helped Jesus escape from Satan's temptations!

6. Write "ONLY"; add "GOD" to make acrostic.

## Conclude the Story

**What did Jesus say was the most important thing to do?** (Obey God.) **What helped Jesus obey God when Satan wanted Him to do wrong?** (Knowing and remembering God's Word.)

**When the devil tried to tempt Him into doing wrong, Jesus knew what to say because He knew God's Word. He was able to use God's Word to send Satan away. Knowing God's Word will help us know what to do when we are tempted to disobey God.**

# Jesus Chooses Disciples

## Materials

Drawing materials/equipment for teacher and each student.

## Tell the Story

As you tell each part of the story, draw each sketch. Students copy your sketches.

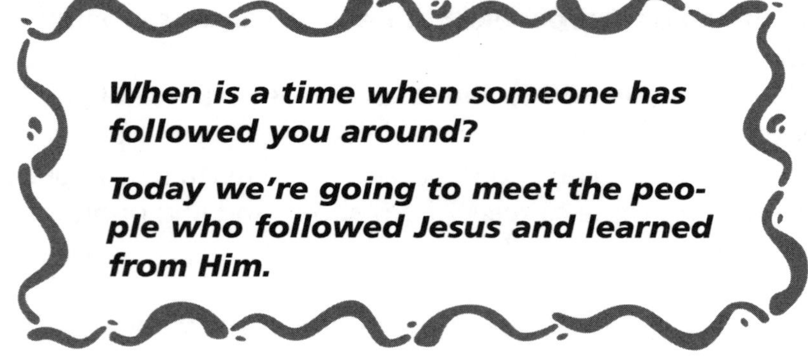

***When is a time when someone has followed you around?***

***Today we're going to meet the people who followed Jesus and learned from Him.***

1. One day, John the Baptist was talking with two of his friends. Suddenly, John stopped. He pointed at Jesus, who was walking by. "Look," he said, "the Lamb of God!" John was saying that Jesus was the special person God had sent to take the punishment for the wrong things people do. John's friends wanted to know more about Jesus! So they walked quickly after Him. "Where are You staying?" they asked Jesus. Jesus invited them to come along with Him and see.

1. Draw a walking stick figure, followed by two others.

2. One of John's friends, named Andrew, grew more and more excited as he listened to Jesus! He decided, *I must go and tell my brother about Jesus!* Andrew hurried to find his brother, Peter. He told Peter, "We have found the special person God has sent!" Peter hurried back with Andrew to meet Jesus.

2. Running figures with legs from "Z"s.

3. The next day, Jesus asked a man named Philip to come along with Him, too. As Philip listened to Jesus, he could hardly WAIT to tell his friend Nathanael! Philip looked for Nathanael and found him under a fig tree. Philip called, "We have found the promised One, Jesus! Come and see!"

3. Tree from "l"s, "3"s.

4. Nathanael was surprised, but he went with Philip. As Nathanael walked up, Jesus said, "Here is a truthful man! I saw you sitting under the fig tree!" Jesus knew where Nathanael had been! Now Nathanael realized that Jesus truly was the special person God had sent!

4. Surprised face and hair from "U"s and "C"s.

5. Later, Jesus was walking along the edge of the Sea of Galilee, watching fishermen throw their big fishing nets out into the water and pull them in again. Jesus saw Peter and Andrew there and called to them. They looked up, pulled in their nets and hurried to see what Jesus wanted. Jesus invited them to follow Him. Jesus said they would help Him tell people about God and bring people into God's family instead of bringing in fish! Peter and Andrew were glad to leave their boats and go with Jesus right away.

5. Draw a net from "X"s.

6. As Jesus, Peter and Andrew walked along, they saw two other fishermen in a boat, helping their father prepare the fishing nets. Jesus called to them, too. He invited them to follow Him. And so James and John put down their nets and went with Jesus, too.

6. Boat from "C" and upside-down "T."

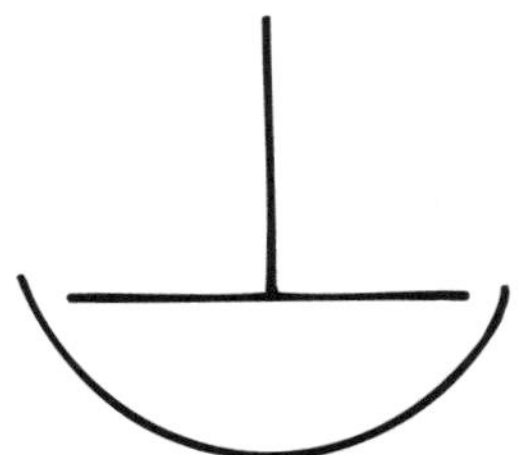

7. On another day, Jesus saw a man named Matthew sitting at his tax collector's table. "Come with Me, Matthew," said Jesus. Matthew looked up at Jesus, got right up and left his money box and all his work! Now Jesus had fishermen and a tax collector to help Him.

7. Money box from rectangles. Add coins.

8. Jesus invited more people to be His helpers until He had 12 friends to help Him. Each one was different, but they were all the same in one way: they loved Jesus and wanted to learn from Him. Jesus told His friends many wonderful things about God and about Himself. Then Jesus sent His helpers to cities and towns all around to tell other people what Jesus had taught them.

8. Draw 12 "O"s for helpers. Add details to make different faces.

## Conclude the Story

**What kinds of people decided to follow Jesus? What do you think Jesus' disciples learned about Jesus?** (How to tell people about God. How to help others learn about Jesus. Who Jesus is.)

**Jesus wanted all kinds of people to know Him and learn from Him. Then they could help all kinds of other people know Jesus! Even today, God chooses all kinds of people to learn from Him. God wants us all to be part of His family because He loves us all.**

## John 4:4-42

# The Woman at the Well

## Before the Story

Guide students to briefly practice signs for underlined words.

***Have you ever been really surprised by what someone did? What happened?***

***Today we'll hear about a woman who was surprised by something Jesus did and something Jesus said.***

## Tell the Story

As you tell the story, lead students in responding as shown when you say the underlined words.

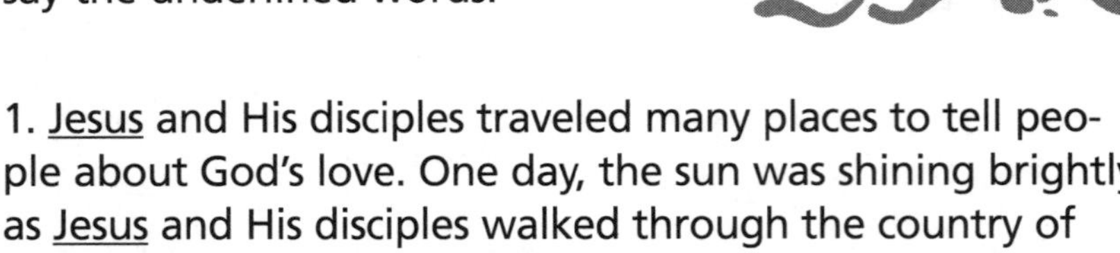

1. Jesus and His disciples traveled many places to tell people about God's love. One day, the sun was shining brightly as Jesus and His disciples walked through the country of Samaria. Now most Jewish people in Jesus' time would not go NEAR Samaria. You see, Jews and Samaritans had disliked each other for HUNDREDS of years.

1. Jesus: Touch palms with opposite middle fingers.

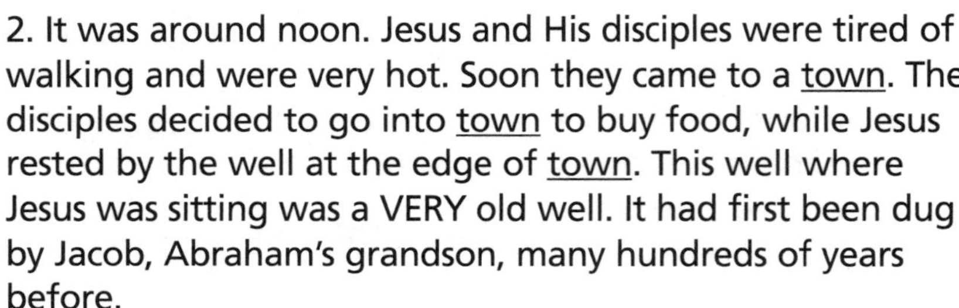

2. It was around noon. Jesus and His disciples were tired of walking and were very hot. Soon they came to a town. The disciples decided to go into town to buy food, while Jesus rested by the well at the edge of town. This well where Jesus was sitting was a VERY old well. It had first been dug by Jacob, Abraham's grandson, many hundreds of years before.

2. Town: Touch fingertips of flat hands; repeat, moving hands.

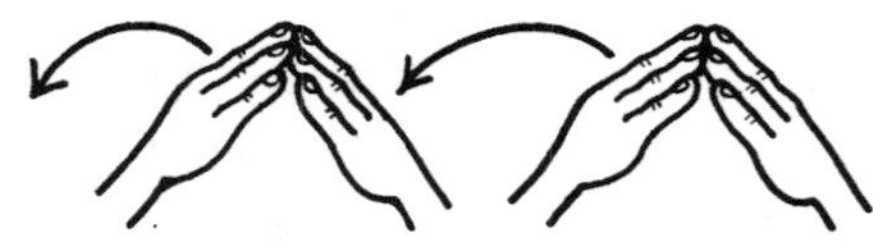

3. While Jesus sat by the well, He saw a woman coming with her jar to get water. Usually the well was deserted at this time of day, because people came to the well in the early morning when the day was cool. Anyone who came to get water in the hot part of the day probably wanted to be alone. This woman DID want to be alone, for the people in the town didn't like her or want to talk with her.

3. Woman: Thumb of open right hand touches chin and then chest.

4. When the woman set down her jar, Jesus asked her for a drink of water. The woman was VERY surprised! She wondered why Jesus talked to her AT ALL. You see, in Bible times, a man and woman did not speak to each other if they met on the street. And Jews and Samaritans usually NEVER talked to each other!

4. Surprise: Index fingers and thumbs touch at temples; flick up.

5. Jesus said to the woman, "If you knew who I am, you would ask Me for LIVING WATER!" The woman didn't understand. "How can You give me living water?" she asked. "You don't have a bucket or a rope. And this well is VERY deep. Where would You get this living water?"

"Anyone who drinks water from this well will become thirsty again," Jesus said. "But whoever drinks the water I give will NEVER be thirsty again. The water I give is like a flowing stream inside a person. It will last forever!"

5. Water: Extend three fingers; touch mouth a few times.

6. The woman thought about what Jesus said. "Give me some of this water!" she said. "Then I won't have to come to the well every day for water." She thought Jesus was talking about water she could drink. She didn't know that Jesus meant He could give her life from God that will last forever.

6. Drink: Move curved right hand in short arc to mouth.

7. The woman asked Jesus some questions about why the Samaritans worshiped God one place and why the Jews worshiped God in another place. Jesus told her that the place where people worshiped was not as important as what was in their minds and hearts as they worshiped. He said God wants people to worship Him with their whole hearts, not just pretend to be worshiping Him. Then Jesus told the woman some things that amazed her. She realized that Jesus knew EVERYTHING about her! She said, "I know that when the Messiah comes, He will tell us everything."

7. Worship: Left hand over right fist; move hands to body and bow head.

8. Jesus looked at her and said, "That's who I am!" Jesus had told HER, this woman no one else talked to, that He was the Messiah, the Savior God had promised to send! The woman was SO excited that she left her water jug at the well and hurried back to town. "Come and see a man who told me everything I have ever done!" the woman told the people in the town. "Could He be the Messiah?" People from the town followed her to Jesus. Many of them believed that Jesus was the Messiah because the woman told them about the GREAT things Jesus had done!

8. Messiah: With first three fingers folded over thumb, move right hand from left shoulder across chest to waist.

## Conclude the Story

**What people did Jews usually not talk to?** (Samaritans.) **Why do you think Jesus talked to the Samaritan woman?** (He cared about her and about the people in the town.) **What did the woman tell the townspeople?** (That Jesus was the Messiah. That He told her amazing things.)

**Jesus' actions showed love to the Samaritan woman. God has done great things for all of us. His actions show His love for us, every day.**

## John 4:43-54

# The Official's Son

## Materials

Play dough (¼ cup, or 2 oz.) for each student.

***What is something a kid your age might worry about?***

***Today we'll hear what a man did when he was very worried.***

## Tell the Story

**Follow along with me as we use our dough to tell today's story.**

1. **Divide your dough into five parts. With the first part, make a little bed.** Jesus had been busy helping people in the big city of Jerusalem. Besides teaching them about God, Jesus made sick people well and made blind people see. He made lame people walk and deaf people hear. He helped sad people to be happy, too. Many people heard about this wonderful man who could do these special miracles. So when Jesus came back to the area where He had grown up, all the people crowded around Him to welcome Him.

2. **With the second part of your dough, make a person to lay on your bed.** In the meantime, an important official had a problem. It was a problem that his important position could not help. This man's little boy was terribly sick. In fact, the little boy was SO sick that he was about to die! The official must have been VERY worried about his little son.

So when this official heard that Jesus was in a town nearby and heard that Jesus made sick people well, what do you think he did? He hurried off to find Jesus!

3. **Use the rest of the dough to make three people: the father, Jesus and servant. Act out the story.** The father walked and walked. The journey must have seemed even longer than usual because he was so worried! When he got to the town where Jesus was, he walked and WALKED and looked and LOOKED until he found Jesus. There was Jesus, in the middle of a crowd! The father pushed his way through the crowd until finally, he was face-to-face with Jesus.

"Jesus, PLEASE come to my house," the official begged. "My son is dying. Only You can help him. He needs You!"

Jesus looked at the whole crowd and said, "Won't any of you believe in Me unless I do more and more miracles?"

The official DID believe that Jesus could help his son. He said to Jesus, "Please hurry to my home right away before my boy dies!"

Jesus looked at the official and said, "You may go home. Your son is HEALED!"

Even though the official couldn't see his son, he believed what Jesus said to him. So the official immediately began his long journey home. But he wasn't worried anymore. After talking to Jesus, the official was SURE his son was healed!

It was a long journey to get back home, but now the man's worry was gone. Jesus' words had given him peace. The next day while the official was still traveling home, some of his servants came running toward him, very excited and out of breath!

"Sir, sir!" they called.

"What is it?" the official asked.

"Your son. Your son is WELL!" they called out to him.

"I know—I know!" laughed the father. He hurried to join his servants. "When did my son begin to feel better?"

"Yesterday afternoon, at about one o'clock, his fever just disappeared!" a servant answered.

Then the official knew that his son was healed at the EXACT time that Jesus had said to him, "Your son will be well."

"Jesus made my boy well!" the official exclaimed.

When the official reached his home, who do you think came running out to meet him? There was his boy, healthy and happy again! The father must have told his family the story of finding Jesus and everything that Jesus had said. Everyone in the household knew that Jesus had healed the boy. And from that time on, this official and his whole family believed that Jesus is the Son of God. Jesus had given peace to the official when He told him his boy would be well. And now everyone in the official's household knew God's gift of peace.

## Conclude the Story

**What did this official want Jesus to do?** (Come to his house. Heal his son.) **Why do you think Jesus did not go with the man?** (Didn't need to go there to heal the boy.) **How did the official react to Jesus' words?** (Believed Jesus had healed his son. Had peace.)

**Sometimes when we are worried, it is hard to have peace. But God asks us to trust Him and believe He will keep His promises. When we trust Him, He gives us His peace.**

**Mark 2:1-12; Luke 5:17-26**

# A Paralyzed Man and Four Friends

## Materials

Drawing materials/equipment for teacher and each student.

## Tell the Story

As you tell each part of the story, draw each sketch. Students copy your sketches.

***What do people who can't walk use to get from place to place?***

***In our Bible story today, we'll meet a man who couldn't walk and who was carried to a very strange place!***

1. When Jesus lived on earth, He went from town to town, teaching people about God. Besides teaching, He also healed people. If they were sick, He made them well again. If they couldn't walk or hear or see, He made their feet or ears or eyes work the way they should. One day, Jesus was in the town of Capernaum. Crowds of people gathered around Him. They filled the house where He was, and they filled the front yard and the backyard, too! People stood in the doorways, leaned through the windows and sat or stood on every inch of the floor! People were everywhere!

1. Draw house from rectangles and stairs from "L"s. Add "C"s for people.

2. Nearby, there lived a man who was paralyzed. In this case, that means his legs didn't work at all. But this man had some wonderful friends. His friends decided, "We'll take our paralyzed friend to Jesus. Jesus can make his legs well!"

2. Lying man from "C"s, "7"s. Add face.

3. Each of four of the friends took a corner of the man's sleeping mat. They lifted the paralyzed man and his mat right up off the ground and started walking. It didn't matter how heavy he seemed or how tired they got. They were going to make SURE that their paralyzed friend got to Jesus! They knew Jesus could help their friend!

3. Add long "C" for mat under lying man. Add "U"s to corners for handles.

4. Finally, they came to the house where Jesus was. Well, they were ALMOST to the house! There were so many people, it was even hard to see the house! How could they carry their friend on his mat through ALL these PEOPLE?

4. Add 4 "C"s and rectangle to drawing of crowded house.

5. They looked at each other. *How could they get their friend to Jesus?!* One of them had an idea! Carefully, the friends carried the man on his mat up the outside steps to the roof. They gently laid their friend down.

5. Draw roof. Add 4 "C"s and mat.

6. The roof was made of mats of woven branches, plastered with clay. And what do you think those friends did? They pulled up some of these mats and laid them aside. Soon, they had made a HOLE in the roof! They made the hole bigger and BIGGER, until it was SO big they could lower their friend's mat right down through it!

6. Draw roof with hole.

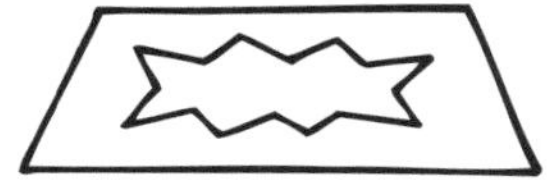

7. The friends slid ropes under the mat and lowered the paralyzed man down through that hole until he was right in front of Jesus! Jesus looked down at the paralyzed man. He knew the man needed two things: to have his sins forgiven and to be healed. So Jesus said to him, "Your sins are forgiven. And so that everyone will know I have the power to forgive sins, pick up your mat. You can walk!"

7. Add long "U" beneath hole. Add man and stick figure for Jesus.

8. Right there, in the middle of that crowd, the man stood. He picked up his mat. And he walked right out of that crowded house! His friends must have been VERY happy! They had known Jesus would be able to make their friend able to walk. And Jesus did! Even better, because He is God's Son, Jesus forgave the man's sins!

8. Draw "A"; add face, arms, feet and rolled mat.

## Conclude the Story

**What did the paralyzed man need?** (Healing. Forgiveness.) **Why were his friends so determined to bring him to Jesus?**

**When the paralyzed man's friends wanted to help their friend, they took him to Jesus. No matter what people need, Jesus is always able to help. He loves us and wants us to tell Him what we need. That's God's way of taking care of our problems!**

### Matthew 5—7; Luke 6

# The Sermon on the Mount

## Materials

Drawing materials/equipment for teacher and each student.

## Tell the Story

As you tell each part of the story, draw each sketch. Students copy your sketches.

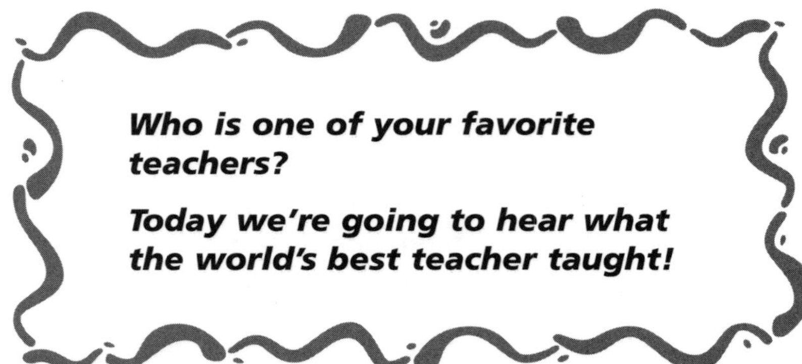

***Who is one of your favorite teachers?***

***Today we're going to hear what the world's best teacher taught!***

1. One day, Jesus saw a huge crowd of people coming toward Him. They wanted to listen to His teaching. Jesus had many important things to teach the people, so He went up on a mountainside and sat down to teach from there. Now, everyone could see and hear Him!

1. Draw mountain from upside-down "C." Add "C"s for crowd below.

2. First, Jesus told the people how to be happy the way God wanted them to be. He said, "Happy are those who know they need God. Happy are those who desire to do right. Happy are those who show kindness and make peace." Jesus told the people to show by their actions that they belonged to God, just like bright lights that shine in dark places.

2. Happy face. Add light rays around face.

3. Jesus went on to tell the people to obey God's law. "You have heard people say, 'Love your neighbor and hate your enemy.' But I tell you to forgive and love EVERYONE, even those who are enemies." That was a surprise!

3. Two faces: love and hate. Add "no" slash over "hate" face.

4. Jesus also said, "Don't worry about having enough food or clothes." He said that God takes care of the flowers and gives them beautiful clothes to wear. God takes care of the birds and makes sure they are fed. And to God, we are much more important than flowers or birds! So God's children don't need to worry. Instead, we can trust God and do what He wants; He will give us what we need!

4. Draw flower, bird from "Y"s, "V"s and "C"s.

5. Jesus also told the people that if they wanted to obey everything God had said about how to treat other people, there was a simple rule to follow: Treat other people the way you would like to be treated. Sometimes people call that teaching the Golden Rule.

5. Draw two faces smiling at each other.

6. As Jesus finished His long talk with the people, He told a story to help them learn to listen well to what He said and then DO what He taught them.

6. Draw face with big listening ears.

7. Jesus said, "A wise man always builds his house on a strong rock." A person who listens to Jesus' words and obeys them is like this wise builder.

7. Draw house on rock.

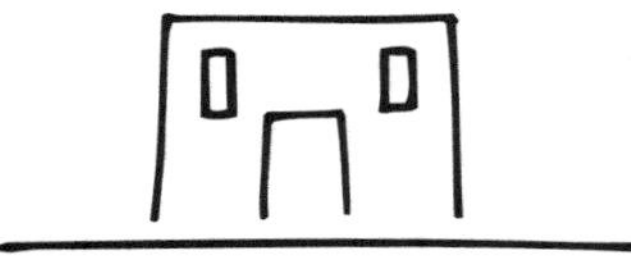

8. Jesus went on to say that anyone who hears Jesus' words and does NOT do what Jesus taught is like a man who built his house on sand. Jesus said this kind of person was foolish. Let's find out why.

8. House on sand.

9. Jesus explained that when a storm came, the water rose and the winds blew and the house built on sand fell down! But the house built on the rock stood firmly because it had a strong foundation. When the crowd of people heard all these teachings of Jesus, the Bible says they were amazed! They realized that Jesus' words were really true!

9. Add rain and wind; clouds from "C"s. Scribble over house on sand.

## Conclude the Story

**What are some of the things Jesus said we should do in order to build our lives on Him?** (Show kindness. Make peace. Love enemies. Treat other people the way we want to be treated.) **When we live in a way that shows we belong to and follow Jesus, we are like the man whose house was built on a rock. Our lives can handle troubles when they come, because we have built our lives on Jesus by trusting in Him and obeying Him every day.**

**Jesus wants us to live in ways that show we belong to Him and follow Him. When we are members of God's family, He will help us live in ways that show our love for Him and others.**

## Matthew 6:25-34

# The Birds and the Flowers

## Materials

A variety of small nature objects (twigs, shells, pebbles, etc.) and play dough (¼ cup, or 2 oz.) for each student.

***What are some of the things you need to live? How do you get these things?***

***Today we're going to hear what Jesus had to say about how we can get the things we need.***

## Tell the Story

**Follow along with me as we use our dough to tell today's story.**

1. **Make several people.** One day, moms and dads, grandparents, big kids and little kids were all walking out to a hillside where Jesus was going to teach. As the large crowd walked along, they must have talked to each other.

"Did we bring enough food?" one person might have asked. "We may be out here all day long!"

Someone else may have said quietly, "We didn't bring very much food. There wasn't much to eat at our house."

"Should we have brought our warm coats? It might get cold later," some people might have worried. Other people might have wished they even had warm coats at all!

But finally, all the people were out on the hillside where Jesus and His friends were. People were everywhere! They were sitting, standing, bumping and moving, trying to get a better view of Jesus.

Then Jesus began to talk. He told the people things about God. He talked about how God wanted them to live. Everyone listened carefully.

Jesus said, "Don't worry about things. Don't worry about having enough food to eat. And don't worry whether or not you will have enough to drink. Don't worry about what clothes you will wear. There are more important things in life than food and clothes!"

2. **Make one or two birds.** To show the people what He meant about worrying, Jesus talked about things they saw around them. Jesus pointed to the sky where birds were flying. "Look at the birds of the air!" Jesus told the people. "Think about what they do. Birds don't plant seeds to grow

crops. They don't gather up food like farmers do. But God makes SURE they will have enough food to eat. God takes care of them. He loves them. Now think. Aren't you even MORE important to God than birds in the sky? Of course you are! So remember, don't worry. Ask God for help and He will take care of you."

The people looked up to watch the birds for a moment. As they watched and thought about what Jesus said, they must have smiled. God loves the birds and feeds them. And Jesus said God loves us even more than He loves birds!

3. **Divide your dough in half. Make one or two flowers from half the dough. Add nature items to decorate the flowers.** Then Jesus said something else. Perhaps He picked a flower and held it up for everyone to see. He said, "Look at the way the flowers grow. They do not make cloth. They don't sew clothes!"

"But look!" He said. "I'm telling you, even the richest king in the world never had clothes as beautiful as these flowers have."

Jesus went on, "If God gives the flowers such beautiful clothes, don't you think He will take care of you?"

"So," Jesus said, "don't worry! Don't say, 'What are we going to eat?' or 'What are we going to wear?' That's what people who don't know God worry about. But God knows what you need. He will take care of you."

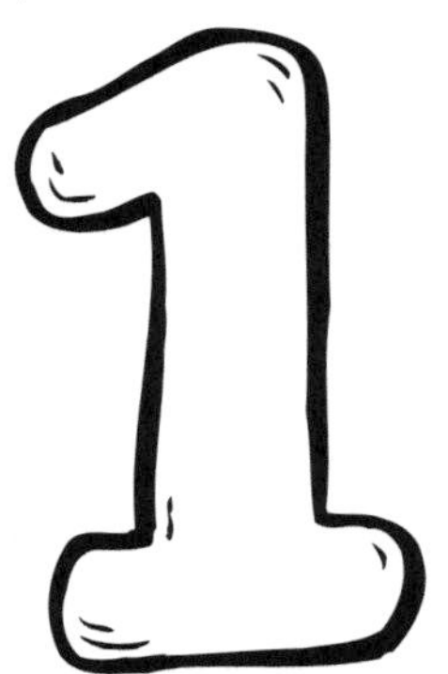

4. **Make a big number one from the other half of your dough.** "Instead of worrying about food or clothes," Jesus said, "the first and most important thing to care about is what God wants you to do. When you put God first and do what's right, all that you need will be given to you."

"And," said Jesus, "don't worry about tomorrow. Don't worry about how long you will live. After all, you won't make your life any longer by worrying about it! Every day has enough things for you to think about. God will take care of you today AND tomorrow!"

## Conclude the Story

**What did Jesus say about birds?** (God loves the birds and feeds them.) **About flowers?** (God gives them beautiful clothes.) **What did Jesus say about worrying?** (We do not need to worry about anything.) **What did Jesus want us to know about God's care for us?** (God will take care of us and give us everything we need.)

**Because we know that God loves us and will take care of us, we need never worry. We can have peace because God knows what we need and we can depend on God to keep His promises.**

**Mark 4:1-20**

# The Parable of the Sower

## Materials

Drawing materials/equipment for teacher and each student.

## Tell the Story

As you tell each part of the story, draw each sketch. Students copy your sketches.

***What kinds of seeds have you planted or watched grow?***

***Today we'll hear a story Jesus told about seeds and plants to help us learn that the very best way to live is found in God's Word.***

1. One day, Jesus began to tell a crowd this story: "A farmer went out to his field to plant some seeds. As the farmer walked up and down the field, he scattered seeds on the ground. Some of the seeds fell on a hard dirt path. The dirt was too hard for the seeds to put down any roots and grow. So the seeds just lay there on the path. Then birds swooped down and snatched up the seeds."

1. Draw straight line for hard soil; add seeds; add bird from "C"s and "V"s.

2. "Other seeds fell on rocky ground," Jesus said. "The plants sprang up quickly and grew for a little while. But then their roots couldn't get enough water and the plants died."

2. Rocky ground. Add plants; then cross them out.

3. Jesus continued, "As the farmer scattered more seeds, some of the seeds fell among thorny weeds." Jesus shook His head sadly. "The thorny weeds and the plants grew up together. But the thorny weeds grew stronger than the young plants. The weeds CHOKED the life out of the plants and they died."

3. Thorny weeds from lines. Add plants; then cross them out.

4. Some people must have wondered if that farmer was going to have any crop at all! But Jesus wasn't finished. He said, "Some of the seeds fell on good soil. They grew and became a huge crop! In fact, some plants produced 100 times MORE seeds than the farmer had planted."

4. Draw good soil and add growing plants from "V"s. Add "100."

5. Then Jesus ended His parable by saying, "He who has ears to hear, let him hear." The disciples looked at each other with puzzled faces. *What did Jesus mean?* they thought.

5. Question mark.

6. Jesus began to explain to His disciples. "The seeds are like God's Word. When someone hears God's Word, he or she may act in several different ways. People who hear God's Word but never believe it are like the hard dirt on the path where the seeds got eaten by birds." The disciples could tell Jesus felt very sad about these people who never let God's Word into their hearts and minds.

6. Next to the hard ground, add face from "U", "C"s and "V"s. Add "C"s and "I"s for hands over ears.

7. "Some other people hear the Word of God and gladly believe it," Jesus said. "But then, later, when it's too much trouble to do what God wants, they stop believing God's Word. They are like the shallow, rocky soil," Jesus said.

7. Next to rocky ground, draw happy face, arrow and sad face.

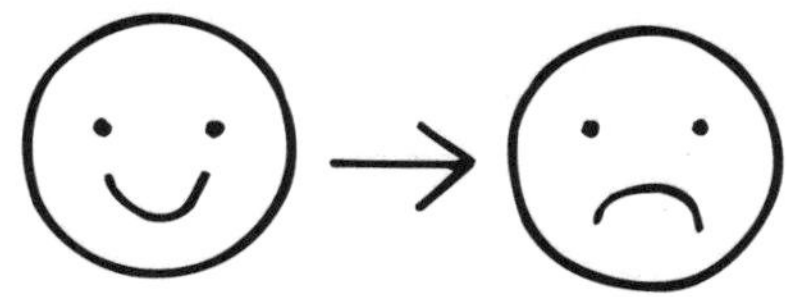

8. "What about the ground full of thorny weeds?" a disciple asked. "What kind of people are like that?"

Jesus explained, "The thorny, weed-filled ground is like people who have heard God's Word and believe it. They begin to grow, but then they let worries and their desires for other things keep them from growing. Soon they forget all about God. They're too busy with everything else." The disciples must have looked at each other uncomfortably. They knew what it was like to forget about God's Word.

8. Next to thorny weeds, draw worried face from "U"s, "C"s, "M"s; add thought balloon; then cross out "GOD."

9. Then Jesus finished His story by saying, "The good soil is like people who hear and believe the Word of God. They grow and their lives show that they've learned the way God wants them to live." The disciples knew they wanted to be people who were like the good ground, always ready to hear and believe God's Word.

9. Next to good soil, draw plant with happy face on top.

## Conclude the Story

**What were the four kinds of soil Jesus told about? What do the different kinds of soil remind us of?** (The soil reminds us of four ways people act when they hear God's Word.) **How do the people who are like the good soil act?** (They hear God's Word and obey it.)

**We want to be like the good soil, ready to hear how we can love and obey God. God's Word shows us the very best way to live!**

Mark 4:35-41

# Jesus Calms the Storm

## Materials

Drawing materials/equipment for teacher and each student.

***What would your face look like if you were in a boat being rocked by big waves?***

***Today we'll hear how Jesus' friends felt when they were in a storm.***

## Tell the Story

As you tell each part of the story, draw each sketch. Students copy your sketches.

1. When Jesus lived on earth, He could often be found teaching and healing people near the Sea of Galilee. One day, Jesus had been teaching and healing for a VERY long time. Jesus got VERY tired, but so many people who needed His help had come from all over that He and His disciples just stayed and stayed. As the sun set, Jesus and His friends got into a small boat and set out for the other side of the sea, so they could be alone and rest.

1. Draw boat from "C" and lines.

2. While His friends sailed the boat, Jesus lay down on a bench at the back of the boat and fell fast asleep. Suddenly, the wind began to blow. The wind began to knock the boat back and forth. And then, the waves came whooshing up! They slapped the boat so hard, it almost tipped over!

2. Add wind lines and then waves.

3. Jesus' friends began to be very afraid. Some of them rowed as hard as they could, fighting to keep the boat steady. Others began bailing out buckets of water as fast as their arms would go! But even those big, strong fishermen weren't fast enough or strong enough to beat this storm. As the boat began to fill with water, Jesus' friends became even MORE afraid. They knew that if the boat went down, they might all DROWN!

3. Draw bucket from "O" and "U"; add water.

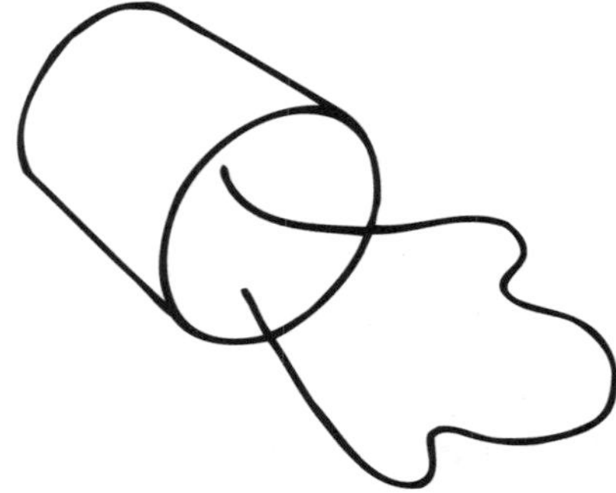

4. And guess who was sleeping through all of this! JESUS! Even with all the rocking and noise from the wind and the waves, He just kept on sleeping soundly! The storm didn't bother Him AT ALL! Finally Jesus' friends yelled, "Teacher, don't you care if we DROWN?!" They were scared and worried and wondered why Jesus didn't do something to HELP!

4. Draw scared face.

5. Maybe Jesus' friends expected Him to help bail the water or row the boat, but what do you think Jesus did? He got up and looked out over the wild, stormy water. Then He said, "Quiet! Be still!" And suddenly, the wind STOPPED! The waves went as flat as if there had never been a wind at all! Jesus' friends stood dripping wet, with buckets and oars in their hands, staring at Jesus. They were AMAZED!

5. "No" slash over stormy scene in #2. Draw new calm sea and boat.

6. Jesus looked from one amazed face to the next and said, "Why are you so afraid? Don't you have faith in Me yet? Don't you know you can trust Me to take care of you?" Jesus' friends had been very afraid of the storm. But what Jesus did to STOP it made them even MORE scared! They said to each other, "Just who IS Jesus? Even the wind and the waves obey Him!"

6. Draw amazed faces.

7. Jesus' friends didn't understand yet that Jesus is God's Son! They didn't know what great power He has and that they could depend on Him to help them in ANY situation, no matter how scary things looked! He is always in control, and we can always go to Him for help.

7. Add conversation balloon to one amazed face.

## Conclude the Story

**What did Jesus' friends do at first when they were afraid of the storm?** (Rowed hard. Bailed water.) **When they finally asked Jesus for help, what did they discover?**

**Jesus' friends learned that no matter how bad things looked, Jesus could always be trusted to help. He was never surprised by even the worst problem! We can always depend on Him, too.**

## Mark 5:21-43; Luke 8:40-56

# Jairus and His Daughter

### Before the Story

Guide students to briefly practice signs for underlined words.

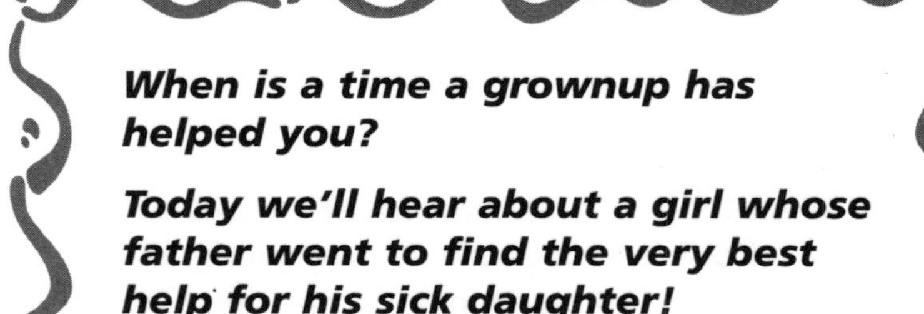

***When is a time a grownup has helped you?***

***Today we'll hear about a girl whose father went to find the very best help for his sick daughter!***

### Tell the Story

As you tell the story, lead students in responding as shown when you say the underlined words.

1. One day a large crowd of people watched as a boat came to the shore of the Sea of Galilee. As the boat came near, Jesus and some of His disciples got out. The crowd was excited. THIS was the person they were watching for! They pushed in eagerly around Jesus. They all wanted to see Him.

1. Watch: Move right two fingers away from eyes.

2. In this crowd was a very important man. His name was Jairus and he was a leader in the synagogue (the place where people met to worship God). This important leader pushed and pressed and SQUEEZED through the crowd, trying to get to Jesus. When he reached Jesus, he bowed down on the ground at Jesus' feet. Then he looked up at Jesus and said, "Jesus, my little girl is DYING. Please come quickly to my house. I know if you touch her, she will be healed and live."

2. Leader: Right hand pulls left forward; move hands down sides.

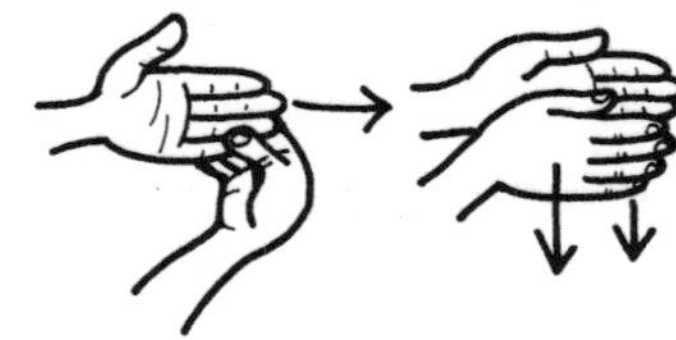

3. Jesus immediately turned to go with Jairus to his house. But as they went, people tried to get as close to Jesus as they could. In this crowd was ANOTHER person who needed Jesus, a woman who had been sick for 12 YEARS. She knew that if she could just get close enough to Jesus to touch His robe, she would not be sick. So when she got quite close, she reached out and touched His robe. And she was WELL!

3. Sick: Right middle finger on head; left middle finger on stomach.

4. Jesus stopped. "Who touched My clothes?" He asked.

One of His disciples answered, "There are LOTS of people here. MANY people have touched You!"

But Jesus kept looking to see who had touched Him. The woman who had touched Jesus finally, fearfully spoke up.

4. Touch: Touch left hand with right middle finger.

5. The woman told Jesus how she had touched Him because she believed she would be healed. Jesus kindly said, "Your faith has healed you. Be happy, you are well!"

Meanwhile, Jairus was waiting. While Jesus was still talking to the woman, some men came and told Jairus, "Don't bother Jesus anymore. Your daughter is dead."

DEAD? Poor Jairus! He had tried so hard to hurry. Now it was too late.

5. Healed, well: Curved hands on chest move forward to fists.

6. Jesus just kept walking toward Jairus's house. He looked at Jairus and said, "Don't be afraid. Just believe!"

When they got to the house, neighbors and friends had gathered there with the family and were crying loudly.

Jesus called out, "Why all this crying? The girl isn't dead; she's just asleep." Jesus meant that the girl would live again. But the people laughed at Him. They knew she was dead! They didn't believe Jesus could help this girl.

6. Believe: Touch right finger to forehead; clasp hands.

7. Jesus told the neighbors and friends to leave the room. Jesus, a few of His disciples and the girl's parents stood quietly by the bed where the dead girl was lying.

Jesus took her hand. He gently said to her, "Little girl, get up now."

The girl opened her eyes. She sat up. Then she got out of bed and walked around the room. She was ALIVE! Her parents were full of joy! Their little girl was not dead!

7. Tell, say: With right index finger, make circular movement from mouth.

8. Jesus told Jairus and his wife to get their girl some food. Imagine what all those people who had laughed at Jesus thought when the girl came laughing and running out of the house! Jesus loved the girl and her family. He had time to care about the woman on the way and still had plenty of time to bring this girl back to life. His love and power are greater than ANY bad thing that can ever happen to us—even greater than death itself!

8. Love: Cross fists over heart.

## Conclude the Story

**How did Jairus show love for his daughter?** (Went to get Jesus.) **Why didn't Jesus get there before the girl died?** (Crowd slowed Him down. A woman was healed.)

**Jairus was a loving dad. He cared for his daughter and found the BEST help for her ever! One way God shows His love to us is by giving us people who love us, too. And Jesus loves us more than ANYONE!**

**Mark 6:30-44; John 6:1-15**

# Jesus Feeds a Large Crowd

## Materials

Drawing materials/equipment for teacher and each student.

## Tell the Story

As you tell each part of the story, draw each sketch. Students copy your sketches.

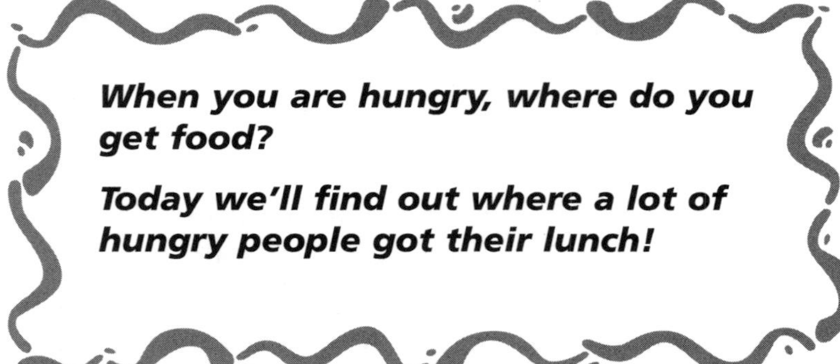


1. Jesus was a VERY famous teacher. Many people wanted to see Him. One day a big crowd gathered to see Jesus. Men and women stopped working and children stopped playing. They heard where Jesus was going to be and RAN to see Him. As Jesus started teaching about God, more and MORE people gathered. Soon hundreds and THOUSANDS of people sat around Jesus, quietly listening. They wanted to hear everything He had to say.

1. Draw stick figure Jesus and many "C"s for crowd.

2. As it got late in the day, Jesus' helpers were getting hungry! They knew the people who were listening to Jesus were probably hungry, too. One disciple said to Jesus, "Teacher, we are far from town. It is getting late. Send the people away, so they can go find something to eat." But Jesus just looked at the disciple and said, "YOU feed them!"

2. Draw setting sun.

3. Well, the disciple was very surprised. *Jesus must be joking,* he thought. "There are 5,000 people here!" said the disciple. "We'd have to work for eight months to earn enough money to buy food for all these people! We couldn't POSSIBLY buy enough bread for all these people!"

"Then go and see how much bread you can find," Jesus answered.

3. Disciple from "L"s and "O"s and "C"s.

4. The disciples searched and searched and searched through the crowd. Hadn't ANYONE brought food along? Finally Andrew found a young boy who had five loaves of bread and two fish for his lunch. Andrew took the boy to Jesus.

"This boy has five loaves of bread and two fish," said Andrew. "But what good will that do us? This little bit of food would not even feed a few of us. There is not enough here to feed all these people!" Jesus turned to the boy. We don't know what Jesus said to the boy, but we do know that the boy gave his small lunch to Jesus.

4. Basket from "O," "U" and "X"s. Add fish and bread.

5. Jesus asked everyone to sit down in groups. He took the bread in His hands, thanked God for it and divided the bread among the disciples. He told them to go and share it. The disciples gave the pieces to the groups of people. The people shared those pieces of bread, and where there had been five loaves of bread, now there was enough bread for EVERYONE to eat all they wanted!

5. Draw pieces of bread from "C"s and "V"s.

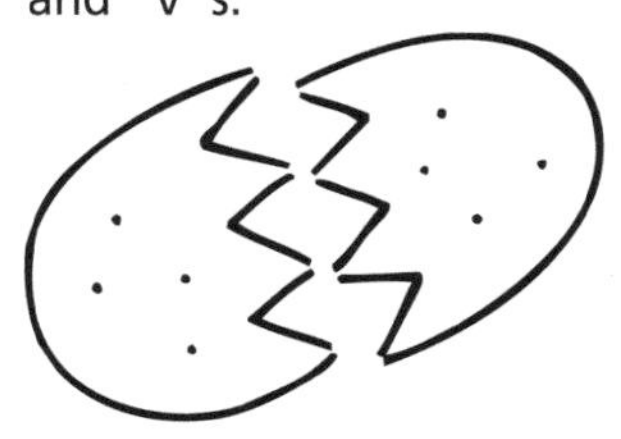

6. Jesus also took the two fish and divided them, giving pieces to the disciples. The disciples took the pieces of fish and shared them with every group of people. And everyone ate and ate and ate, until they were happy and full!

6. Draw happy face.

7. Jesus told His disciples, "Now go and pick up the leftovers and put them in baskets." How could there be LEFTOVERS from just five loaves of bread and two fish? But when they had gathered up the pieces, there were 12 baskets FULL of leftovers! Jesus had been able to feed more than 5,000 people from one little boy's lunch!

7. Twelve baskets from "U"s and "X"s. Add "3"s for leftovers.

## Conclude the Story

**What happened as a result of the little boy's gift to Jesus?** (Jesus made the lunch into enough food to feed over 5,000 people!) **Why do you think the little boy was willing to give his lunch to Jesus?**

**When we are willing to give what we have to God, God can do great things with our gifts to Him!**

## Matthew 17:1-13; Luke 9:28-36

# Jesus Prays on a Mountain

### Before the Story

Guide students to briefly practice signs for underlined words.

***When do you or people in your family pray?***

***Today we're going to hear about something surprising that happened when Jesus and three of His disciples were praying together.***

### Tell the Story

As you tell the story, lead students in responding as shown when you say the underlined words.

1. Jesus spent many days with His 12 disciples, teaching them about God and helping them learn how to love and obey God. Jesus told His disciples how important it was to talk to God. In fact, Jesus often went off by Himself to pray. But on one particular day, Jesus asked three of His disciples, Peter, James and John, to go with Him to a quiet mountain.

1. Disciples: Move left fist ahead of right; move open hands down sides.

2. Peter, James and John probably talked with Jesus as they climbed up the mountain. They may have talked about places they liked to fish or what they might see from the top of the mountain. When they finally reached the top of this mountain, they could see the farms and villages way off in the distance. But no one else seemed to be around.

2. Mountain: Strike right fist on left; move flat hands in wavy motion.

3. As they settled themselves on flat rock or maybe rested their backs against a tree trunk, Jesus and the three disciples began to pray. The disciples may have thought this prayer time was going to be just like all the other prayer times. The disciples were even feeling a little bit sleepy! This prayer time, however, turned out to be VERY different. The disciples were in for a BIG surprise which really woke them up!

3. Pray: Touch palms in front; move hands to body and bow head.

4. As Jesus prayed, talking to His Father in heaven, His face and even His clothes became brighter and brighter! It was as if a very bright light was shining inside of Jesus. The light was so bright, it was like a flash of lightning! Jesus' face became as bright as the sun! Peter, James and John were startled! *What was happening?* they must have wondered.

4. Bright: Open closed fists.

5. But the bright light wasn't all! As the three disciples looked at Jesus, they saw two men talking with Jesus. The three disciples recognized these two men as Moses, to whom God had given the Ten Commandments, and Elijah, who was one of God's prophets. NOW Peter, James and John were REALLY surprised!

5. Men: Touch right thumb to forehead and then to chest.

6. The three disciples may have been sleepy before, but now they were wide awake! Peter was so excited, he jumped up and said, "Lord, this is so wonderful. Let's build three shelters—one for each of you!" Peter was so excited he may have been hoping that building the shelters (like little houses) would cause Moses and Elijah to stay longer and to keep talking with Jesus.

6. Excited: With circular motion, strike chest alternately with bent middle fingers.

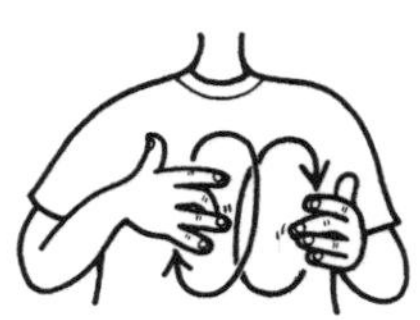

7. Just as Peter finished speaking, something else happened that not only surprised the three disciples but also made them VERY afraid. A cloud suddenly appeared all around them so that they could hardly see! Then booming out of the mountaintop air, a voice—God's voice—said, "This is My Son! I have chosen Him! Listen to what He says!"

After hearing these words, the disciples were so afraid that they fell down to the ground and buried their faces in their hands!

7. Afraid: Fingertips touching, open hands and cover chest.

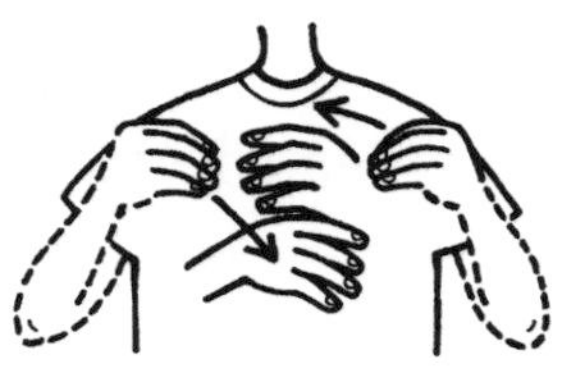

8. The next thing the disciples heard was Jesus' gentle voice. "Get up," He said quietly. "Don't be afraid." When the disciples looked up, Moses and Elijah were gone; Jesus was alone. The bright light and cloud were gone; the mountaintop was quiet and still once more; and it was time to climb down the mountain.

Even though the disciples didn't understand what had happened, they knew that Jesus was truly the mighty Son of God. The disciples must have remembered this special day for the rest of their lives!

8. Jesus: Touch palms with opposite middle fingers.

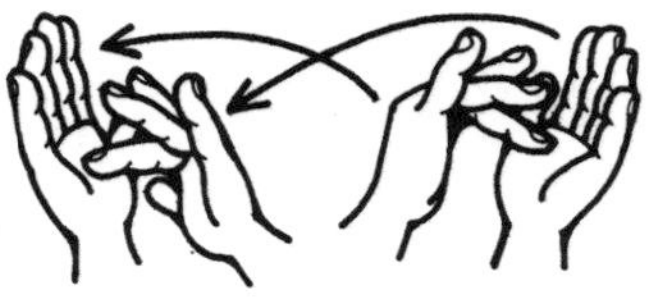

## Conclude the Story

**Why had Jesus and the three disciples climbed to the top of the mountain?** (To pray together.) **What surprised the disciples?** (A bright light. Jesus' face shone. A loud voice.) **What did the disciples hear God say about Jesus?** (He is God's Son.)

**When we pray, we get to know who Jesus is and what He is like. Praying reminds us that Jesus is God's Son and that He is always caring for us and ready to help us! Knowing that we can pray and get to know Jesus is something truly worth celebrating!**

**Matthew 18:21-35**

# The Forgiving King

## Before the Story

Guide students to briefly practice signs for underlined words.

## Tell the Story

As you tell the story, lead students in responding as shown when you say the underlined

***When have you forgiven someone for something wrong that was done?***

***Today we're going to hear a story Jesus told about two men who had to choose whether or not to forgive.***

1. Jesus wanted to teach His friends something very important. So He told them this story:

Once there was a king who had many servants. One of those servants had borrowed a lot of money from the king. One day the king noticed that this servant had never repaid ANY of the money. The king called for his servant to come to him.

2. The king said, "You must pay me what you owe!" Now this servant owed the king 10,000 talents. It was like owing millions of dollars! There was no way the servant could pay back so much money! So the king ordered that the servant and his family be sold as slaves. Everything they owned would be sold to repay the servant's debt.

3. "Oh, PLEASE, your majesty," the servant cried. "PLEASE be patient. I will pay back EVERYTHING I owe."

The king felt sorry for his servant, so the king said, "I will forgive and forget about your debt. You no longer owe me ANY money!" The servant must have been VERY happy. The king had forgiven him his whole ENORMOUS debt!

4. But that wasn't the end of the story. As the servant was walking home, he saw a friend. This friend had borrowed a small amount of money from him. He had borrowed a hundred denarii, which was like a few dollars. The servant grabbed his friend. "You owe me money," he growled. "Pay it NOW!"

1. King: Right thumb between index and middle fingers; move from shoulder to waist.

2. Servant: Face palms up, moving back and forth alternately; move hands down sides.

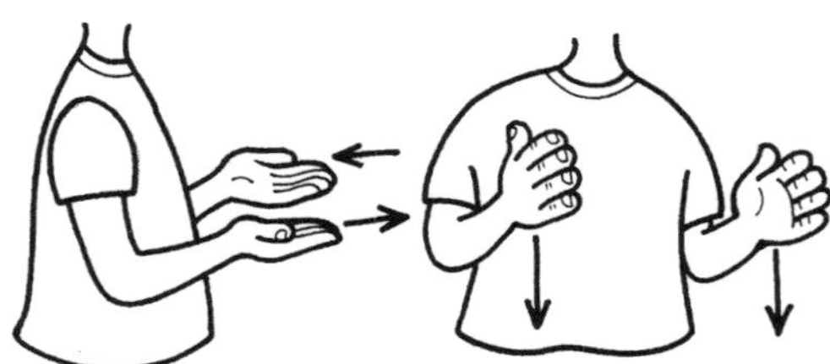

3. Forgive: Stroke edge of left palm with right fingertips.

4. Friend: Interlock index fingers; repeat in reverse.

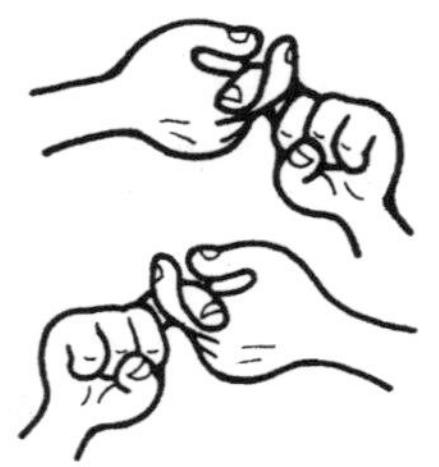

5. "I'm sorry," said the friend. "I don't have the money. Please be patient. I will pay back what I owe you."

But the servant would NOT be patient. He had his friend thrown in jail because the friend could not pay what he owed.

5. Jail: Face palms in, spread fingers crossing.

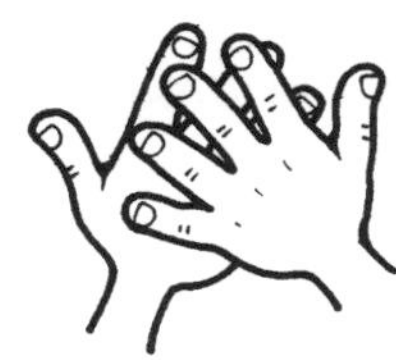

6. Other people saw what this servant did to his friend. They ran to the king. They reminded the king of ALL the money the king had forgiven. They told the king that the very same servant had put his friend in jail because the friend couldn't pay back a LITTLE bit of money he owed that mean servant!

6. Money: Touching, right fingertips strike left palm a few times.

7. "What?!" roared the king. "Bring that servant here IMMEDIATELY!"

The servant was brought to the king.

"I forgave you a LARGE amount of money. In the same way, you should have forgiven your friend for a small amount!" the king said. "Now YOU will be put in prison!"

7. King: Right thumb between index and middle fingers; move from shoulder to waist.

8. Then Jesus explained His story. "God is like the king. He will forgive you for all the wrong and unkind things you do, if you ask Him. You do not have to pay for your sins. In fact, you CANNOT pay for them. Your debt is TOO BIG to pay. But because God has forgiven you such a BIG debt, He wants you to forgive others when they do wrong things to you. In the same kind way God has forgiven you, you should forgive others."

8. God: Point right index finger; lower and open hand at chest.

## Conclude the Story

**Why didn't the servant have to pay back the large amount of money he owed?** (The king forgave his debt.) **How did the forgiven servant treat his friend who owed him money?** (Had him thrown into jail.)

**Jesus told this story so that we would know that because God has forgiven us such a big debt, He wants us to forgive people in the way He has forgiven us.** Talk with interested students about salvation (see "Leading a Child to Christ" on p. 13).

**John 9**

# Jesus Heals a Blind Man

## Materials

Drawing materials/equipment for teacher and each student.

## Tell the Story

As you tell each part of the story, draw each sketch. Students copy your sketches.

***How would you help a person who cannot see?***

***Today we'll hear how Jesus helped a man who couldn't see.***

1. One day a blind man moved slowly through the streets of Jerusalem. When he reached a familiar place, he sat down with his little bowl to beg for the coins people would drop in. In those days, all that most blind people did was wait for people who passed by to give them food or money.

1. Draw beggar's bowl from "U," "O". Add coins.

2. Suddenly the man heard a voice ask,"Teacher, why is that man blind? Did he do something wrong—or did his parents?"

*That man is talking about me!* the blind man thought. He strained to hear the answer. Jesus was the Teacher! He said, "This man did not sin, nor did his parents. He is blind, and now God's work can be shown in his life."

2. Draw face of blind man from "U," "C"s, "V"s and "7."

3. *What does Jesus mean?* the blind man wondered. He heard Jesus spit on the ground. Then he heard sounds of someone stirring up the dirt. Then the blind man felt gentle, wet hands touching his eyes as Jesus patted damp mud over them! Then Jesus said, "Go wash off the mud in the Pool of Siloam." The blind man slowly made his way to the pool.

3. Draw question mark; add details to make a face.

4. As he splashed cool water on his face, the man realized he could SEE his hands. He could SEE the water! He jumped up, eager to see his friends' faces as he told how Jesus had healed his eyes! He couldn't wait!

4. Draw two hands from "U"s, happy face and water drops.

5. But when the man told his story, not everyone believed him. Some people said he wasn't the same man who had been blind. But he insisted, "I AM the man!" "Then tell us again how your blindness was cured!" they said. "The One called Jesus healed me—and now I can SEE!" the man answered.

5. Suspicious face from "U" and "V"s.

6. The people took the man to the synagogue, the place where people met to pray. When he told the leaders how Jesus had healed him, an argument started! Some shouted that Jesus could not be from God because He had healed the man on the Sabbath (the holy day of rest). Healing on the Sabbath was against God's rules! But others wondered how someone not from God could do such amazing things!

6. Arguing face from "U"s and "V"s. Add fist from "U"s and lines.

7. "All I know is that I was blind, but now I see!" the man replied. When the leaders asked AGAIN how Jesus opened his eyes, the man answered, "I've told you over and over! Do you want to follow Him, too?"

7. Draw face with closed eyes; then change to open eyes.

8. That made the leaders FURIOUS! "WE don't follow Jesus!" they shouted. The man said, "If Jesus were not from God, He could not have healed me." That was IT! The leaders threw the man out of the synagogue!

8. Shut doors from rectangles and lines. Add stick figure.

9. Jesus soon found the man. "Do you believe in the Son of God?" Jesus asked. "Who is He?" the man wanted to know. Jesus said, "You have seen Him. He is talking to you!" The man looked up at Jesus. He knew that voice! The man said, "Lord, I believe in You!" And he worshiped Jesus, whose power had changed his life!

9. Draw smiling face.

## Conclude the Story

**What did Jesus do to show how powerful and great He is? What did the blind man learn about Jesus?** (That Jesus is God's Son.) **How did the man feel about Jesus?**

**Jesus still does wonderful things today! He can do anything and He is always ready to hear our prayers. When we see how great Jesus' power is, it makes us want to worship Him, just as the man did whose blindness had been healed! Worshiping Jesus means we show how much we love and respect Him.**

Luke 10:25-37

# The Good Samaritan

## Materials

Drawing materials/equipment for teacher and each student.

***Who has helped you when you have been hurt?***

***Today we'll hear about someone who was hurt and needed help.***

## Tell the Story

As you tell each part of the story, draw each sketch. Students copy your sketches.

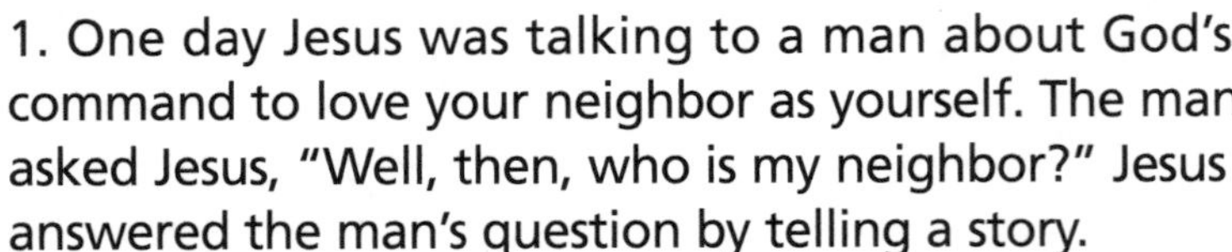

1. One day Jesus was talking to a man about God's command to love your neighbor as yourself. The man asked Jesus, "Well, then, who is my neighbor?" Jesus answered the man's question by telling a story.

1. Draw a question mark.

2. Jesus' story happened on the road to Jericho. This road went up and down and around many hills. People who traveled the road had to be very careful of robbers hiding in the hills. These robbers hurt people and took their money! Jesus said, "There was a man traveling from Jerusalem to Jericho. He hurried past one hill and another hill and another hill. And then it happened!

2. Draw a curvy road; add hills from "C"s.

3. "Some robbers jumped out and grabbed him. They tore off his clothes and beat him and took all his money. Then they left the man lying beside the road. The poor man was so badly hurt, he couldn't get up. All he could do was hope that someone would come by and help him.

3. Draw wounded man from "3" and "7"s.

4. "And THEN—he heard footsteps! Someone was coming! The man turned his head and saw a priest. *Oh good,* thought the man. He knew a priest taught the people about God. He was sure the priest would help him. But the priest looked at the hurt man, crossed to the other side of the road and WALKED AWAY.

4. Add "U"s for footprints walking away.

5. "The poor hurt man was all alone again. And THEN—he heard more footsteps. Someone else was coming! The man turned his head and saw a Levite! *Oh good!* the poor hurt man thought. He knew a Levite taught the people God's laws. He was sure the Levite would help him. But the Levite crossed to the other side of the road and WALKED AWAY! The poor hurt man was sad and all alone again. He must have wondered if ANYONE would ever help him!

5. Add another set of footprints beside the first.

6. "And THEN—he heard the clippety-clop of a donkey! The hoofbeats were getting closer. Someone was coming! *Maybe this person will help me,* thought the poor hurt man.

6. Draw donkey from 2 "U"s and 2 "V"s; add details.

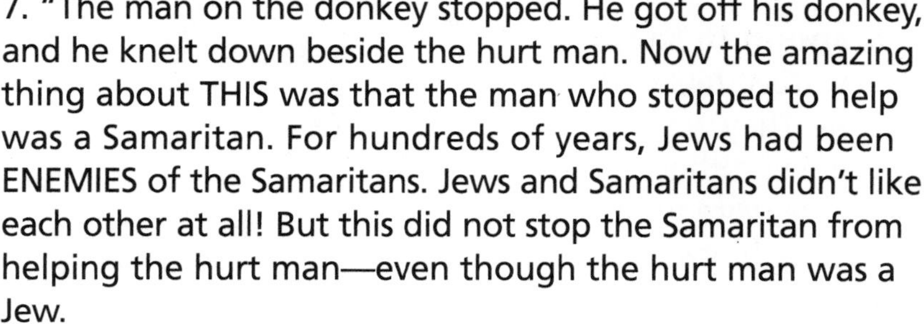

7. "The man on the donkey stopped. He got off his donkey, and he knelt down beside the hurt man. Now the amazing thing about THIS was that the man who stopped to help was a Samaritan. For hundreds of years, Jews had been ENEMIES of the Samaritans. Jews and Samaritans didn't like each other at all! But this did not stop the Samaritan from helping the hurt man—even though the hurt man was a Jew.

7. Write "ENEMY"; add "no" slash.

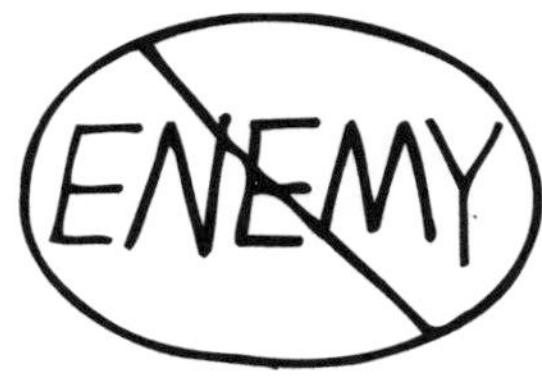


8. "The Samaritan put soothing medicine on the man's wounds. He bandaged all the hurts and gently helped the hurt man onto the donkey. At last they came to an inn, a place where travelers could stay. The Samaritan put the man to bed and tried to make the man comfortable. He even paid the owner of the inn to take care of the hurt man!"

8. Bottle from 2 "O"s and lines.

9. When Jesus finished the story He asked, "Which of the men was a neighbor to the hurt man?" Of course, it was the man who HELPED him! Then Jesus said, "Go and do he same. Be a good neighbor to ANYONE who needs your help!"

9. Draw heart.

## Conclude the Story

**Who showed God's love in this story? What would most people have expected the Samaritan to do?** (To walk away from the man who was his enemy.)

**The Samaritan acted as if the hurt man were his neighbor. Jesus told this story to help us understand that if we love God, we should show it by loving all kinds of people!**

Luke 10:38-42

# Mary and Martha

## Materials

Play dough (¼ cup, or 2 oz.) and plastic spoon for each student.

***When is a time a kid might think another person is being unfair?***

***A woman in today's story felt that her sister was being unfair. Let's find out what happened.***

## Tell the Story

**Follow along with me as we use our dough to tell today's story.**

1. **Divide your dough in half. With one half make bowls, plates and cups. Use a plastic spoon to shape the bowls and cups.** Mary and Martha were sisters who lived in Bethany with their brother, Lazarus. They were friends of Jesus, and they loved to have Him visit their home! Today Jesus was coming to visit. There were so many things to do to get ready—many of the same things your family does when company is coming. There were bowls and plates and cups to wash. There were floors to be scrubbed, meat to be roasted and vegetables to be picked from the garden.

"Hurry, Mary!" Martha might have said. "I've swept the floor, but everything needs dusting. Oh, and where are the spices for the fish?"

Mary and Martha must have made sure the house was spotless. But there was still work left to do. They probably had to fetch the water, bake the bread and wash the grapes! They hustled and bustled and hurried all over the house to finish the work before Jesus arrived.

Soon they saw a little cloud of dust rising over the horizon. Jesus and His friends were walking down the road! Mary probably shouted, "Jesus is here! He's here!" and ran out to meet Him. Martha probably stayed in the house because she saw that there still was work to be done. She wanted this dinner with Jesus to be PERFECT!

2. **Make a table with the other half of the dough.** As Jesus and the other guests came in, Martha continued to hurry around, making sure that everyone's feet were washed and that everyone was comfortable. She ran back and forth with bowls of water and plates of grapes and olives.

Suddenly Martha stopped and looked around. *Where is Mary?* she wondered. *Why isn't she helping me?*

Mary was sitting on the floor at Jesus' feet. She was watching Him and listening closely to every word He said. She didn't want to miss one second of Jesus' visit!

In Bible times, women were not usually in the room where a group of men sat. They usually came in and out with food and drink for the men, perhaps listening while they worked. But Mary stayed in the room with the men, as if she belonged there! It was so wonderful to her just to be near Jesus. She had forgotten EVERYTHING else but listening to Him.

3. **Set table with bowls, plates, cups.** Martha saw Mary sitting by Jesus—not working, not helping out, just sitting and listening to Jesus with a big smile on her face. Martha grumbled and complained to herself as she worked to finish getting dinner ready. Finally, Martha couldn't stand it any longer. She walked up to Jesus.

"Lord, don't You care that my sister has left me to do the work by myself? Tell her to help me!" Martha insisted.

Martha was thinking so much about the work and the fact that Mary wasn't helping that she couldn't enjoy being with Jesus—even though HE was the reason she was working so hard to make everything wonderful.

Jesus understood how Martha felt. "Martha, Martha," Jesus said. "You are worried and upset about many things, but only one thing is needed. Mary has chosen what is better, and it will not be taken away from her."

Martha had hurried and worked so hard to help make Jesus and the other guests comfortable. She was doing a very good, kind thing. The only problem was that Martha had forgotten that the BEST thing was that Jesus had come to talk with them and teach them. That's why Jesus said that Mary had chosen what was better—the wisdom she learned from Jesus was something that could never be taken away from her.

## Conclude the Story

**How were Mary and Martha the same? Different?** (Mary and Martha both loved Jesus. Mary wanted to listen to Jesus. Martha wanted to make a good dinner for Him.) **What did Jesus say about the choices Mary and Martha made?** (Mary had made a better choice than Martha because Mary would not lose the wisdom she learned from Jesus.)

**People who take the time to listen to God and others and learn from them show gentleness in their lives. Mary's gentle attitude caused her to want to spend time listening to Jesus. By having a gentle attitude, we can learn wisdom from God and others who love Him.**

Matthew 18:10-14; Luke 15:4-10

# The Lost Sheep and the Lost Coin

## Before the Story

Guide students to briefly practice signs for underlined words.

***Of all the things you have, what's your favorite? Have you ever lost it? What did you do?***

***Today we'll hear about two people who looked for what they had lost.***

## Tell the Story

As you tell the story, lead students in responding as shown when you say the underlined

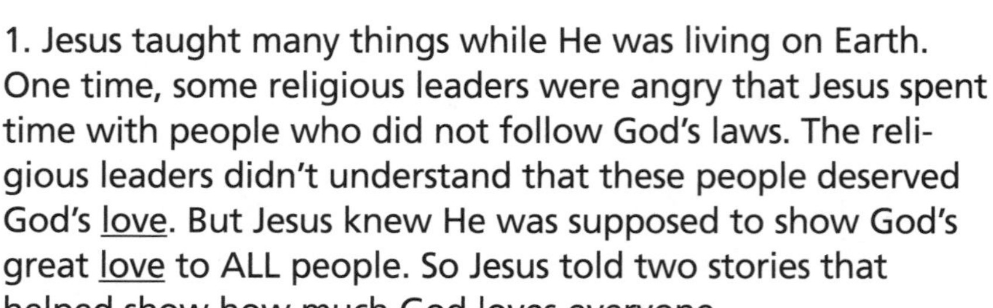

1. Jesus taught many things while He was living on Earth. One time, some religious leaders were angry that Jesus spent time with people who did not follow God's laws. The religious leaders didn't understand that these people deserved God's love. But Jesus knew He was supposed to show God's great love to ALL people. So Jesus told two stories that helped show how much God loves everyone.

1. Love: Cross fists over heart.

2. One story Jesus told was about a shepherd with 100 sheep. This shepherd took very good care of his sheep. Every day he took the sheep to places where they could find good things to eat and water to drink. Every night he gathered the sheep together and took them to a safe place where they could sleep. And he would count his sheep as they came to him, just to make sure that each sheep was there. The shepherd even had a special name for each sheep!

2. Sheep: Open and close right fingers, moving up left arm.

3. One night, the shepherd was counting his sheep—*95, 96, 97, 98, 99.* What? He counted only 99 sheep! The shepherd started over and counted again. But there were STILL only 99. One sheep was MISSING! What could the shepherd do? That one sheep was IMPORTANT to the shepherd. So he left the 99 sheep in a safe place and went to find the lost sheep.

3. Count: With thumb and index finger touching, move right hand up left palm.

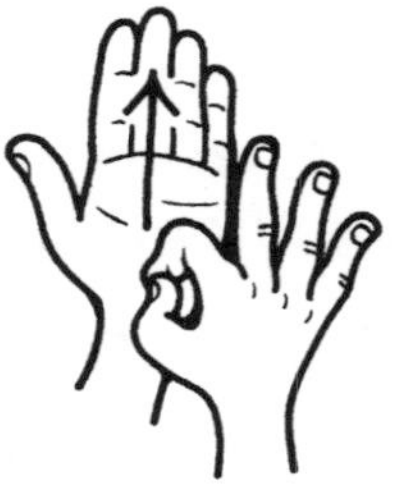

4. The shepherd probably looked down cliffs and in creek beds where the sheep might have fallen. He searched behind big rocks, up hills and along roads. He searched EVERYWHERE for his lost sheep. Every few minutes, he called for his sheep. He paused to listen, hoping he would hear his lost sheep bleating.

4. Search: Curved right hand circles in front of face while moving to the side.

5. Finally, the shepherd heard the bleating of the frightened lost sheep. He was SO happy! He found his sheep, picked it up and carried it back to the safe place. Then he called to his friends and neighbors, "Come and see! Come and see! My lost sheep has been FOUND!" Everyone came to see and to CELEBRATE! The lost sheep had been FOUND!

5. Celebrate: Right index finger and thumb touching, make small circles.

6. Then Jesus told another story about a woman who had 10 silver coins. These were special coins she had received when she got married. The coins were worth a lot of money and were very important to the woman. One day the woman noticed that one of her coins was MISSING! *Oh no,* she probably thought. *What will I do?* The woman lit a lamp, so she could see in every dark corner. Then she took her broom and carefully swept the floor. She probably swept under the furniture, looked inside all the jars, shook her clothes and turned over her cups and dishes and pots.

6. Coin: With right index finger, make a small circle in left palm.

7. The woman searched and searched. She was so worried! She looked and looked, high and low, under and over. Then SUDDENLY, there it WAS! She had FOUND her coin. She was SO happy! She ran to tell her friends, "I found my coin! I found my coin! Come help me CELEBRATE!" All of her friends and neighbors came to see and to celebrate!

7. Celebrate: Right index finger and thumb touching, make small circles.

8. Then Jesus explained that God is like the shepherd and the woman. All people are like the sheep or the coin. People want to do things their own way instead of God's way, and that separates us from God. It's as though we're lost. So God sent Jesus to bring us into God's loving family. Jesus did that by dying on the cross to take the punishment for the wrong things we've done. When people receive God's forgiveness and become part of God's family, God is SO happy that He and the angels and everyone in heaven CELEBRATE!

8. Cross: Move curved right hand down; then from left to right.

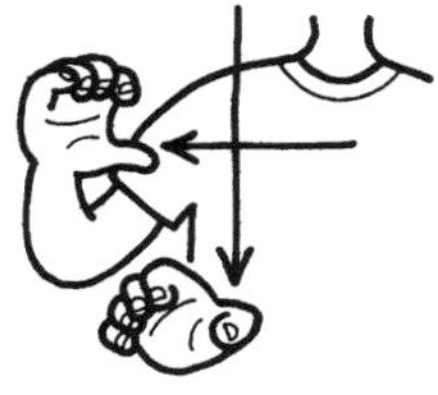

## Conclude the Story

**How many sheep were lost?** (Only one.) **Why do you think the shepherd looked for just one sheep?** (He cared about the sheep.) **Why did the woman look for her lost coin?** (It was very important to her.) **What did the shepherd and the woman both do when they found what was lost?** (Invited others to celebrate with them.)

**When someone becomes a member of God's family, what does God do?** (Celebrates!) **God's love is the greatest love of all.** Talk with interested students about becoming a member of God's family (see "Leading a Child to Christ" on p. 13).

**Luke 15:1-2,11-32**

# The Prodigal Son

## Materials

Drawing materials/equipment for teacher and each student.

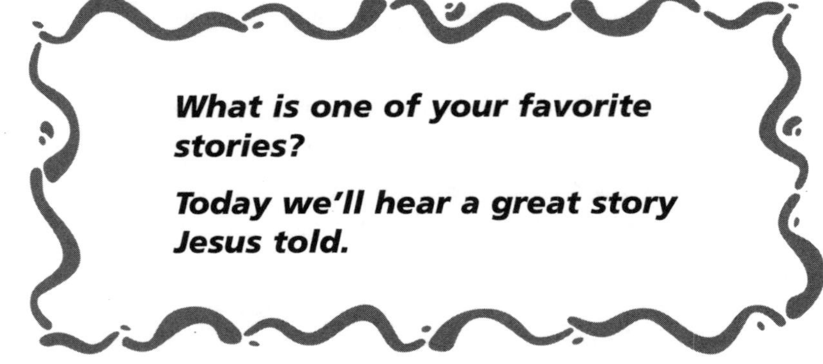


## Tell the Story

As you tell each part of the story, draw each sketch. Students copy your sketches.

1. Once Jesus went to a dinner where there were many people who were proud of the way they obeyed God. Some of them said Jesus was wrong to care about people who didn't follow God's laws as well as they did. They thought God only loved people who obeyed God. So after dinner, Jesus told a story to teach what God's love is really like.

1. Draw table; add "C"s for people.

2. The story went something like this: A man had two sons and owned a big farm. He loved both his sons very much and planned to divide his money between them when they were older. But the younger son didn't want to WAIT for his share of the money. He wanted it NOW! He was eager to leave home and do what he wanted, even if it was wrong.

2. Three "U"s; add details to make faces of father and sons.

3. So the father sadly gave the younger son his part of the money. The younger son said good-bye and headed to a faraway city. There, he started spending his money VERY foolishly—on wild parties and anything he thought would make him happy. He had lots of friends who enjoyed the parties he paid for!

3. Full money bag from "U" and "C"s.

4. But one day the younger son looked in his money bag. It was completely EMPTY! All of a sudden, people he thought were his friends didn't come to see him anymore. He was all alone. And he was in big TROUBLE. He had no money to buy food or to pay for a place to live. This was awful!

4. Empty money bag. Add details to make sad face.

5. At last he found a job taking care of pigs! And he was so HUNGRY all of the time, he started thinking about eating the pigs' food!

5. Pigs from "O"s, "C"s and "V"s.

6. One morning the younger son thought, *I am starving to death while the people who work for my father have plenty of food to eat. I'm going to go back home. I'll tell my father I was wrong. I'll tell him I don't deserve to be treated like his son anymore. But I'll ask him if I can please be his servant.*

6. Print word "DAD" in thought balloon.

7. Meanwhile, back on the farm, the father missed his younger son VERY much. Every day he looked down the road, just hoping his son might be coming home again. One day, he looked and someone was walking down the road! Could it be? YES! It was his son! The father was SO excited, he RAN to meet his son! He hugged him and kissed him. He couldn't hug him enough, even though his boy was smelly and dirty and ragged and didn't DESERVE to be kissed at all!

7. Draw 2 faces from "7"s and "C"s; add arms from "C"s and legs from lines.

8. The father told his servants to bring his son new clothes and sandals and a ring of his own. Then the father had a BIG party to celebrate! Even though the younger son had been foolish and selfish and wrong, his father still loved him and forgave him! But the older brother didn't think the father should welcome his foolish brother at all!

8. Ring from "O"s and triangle.

9. The people at the dinner who thought they were better than others were like that older brother. Jesus told this story because He wanted them to know that God is like that patient, loving father. God is so full of love for us, He wants us with Him and wants to forgive us when we do wrong!

9. Open-armed father from "L"s and "U"s; add details.

## Conclude the Story

**How would you describe the father? the younger son? What did the father do to show his love?** (Welcomed his son. Celebrated his return.)

**No matter what wrong things we do, God is patient and loving. He is eager to love and forgive us.**

**Luke 17:11-19**

# Jesus Heals 10 Lepers

## Materials

Play dough (¼ cup, or 2 oz.) and several 3-inch (7.5-cm) lengths of yarn for each student.

***When have you been sick? What did you do to get better?***

***Today we're going to meet some men who had a sickness even doctors couldn't help. But guess who could!***

## Tell the Story

**Follow along with me to use our dough to tell today's story.**

1. **Divide your dough in half. From one half, roll two ropes. Make the number 10.** Once there were 10 men who had a sickness called leprosy. Leprosy caused terrible sores. In Bible times, doctors couldn't help people with leprosy. The sickness got worse and worse until eventually people with leprosy died. And there was another reason it was awful, too—the law said that people with leprosy couldn't even go NEAR other people. They had to stay far away from healthy people for fear of making them sick, too.

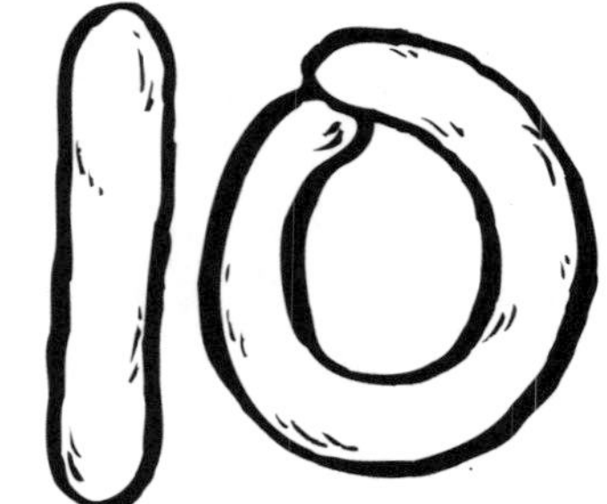

More than anything else in the whole world, those 10 sick men wanted to get WELL! They must have been very sad to have to live outside the city and stay far away from their families and friends. But these men had heard that Jesus could make people well.

2. **From the other half of your dough, make a heart. Use yarn to decorate your heart.** One day, these men heard that Jesus was coming past the place where they lived. So they went out to meet Him. When they saw Jesus, they stayed a distance away from Him, as the law required. They must have wondered if Jesus would walk past and ignore them the way other people did.

When they saw Jesus coming, the men with leprosy called, "JESUS, have pity on us! Jesus, please HELP us!"

Jesus saw these men. He didn't ignore them. He loved them and wanted to make them well!

He called to them, "Go and show yourselves to the priests." That sounds like a strange thing to say. But in those days, the law said any person who had been cured of leprosy had to be examined by a priest. That meant Jesus was saying they were CURED!

The 10 men hurried off in amazement. *Show themselves to the priests? They sure would. WOW!* As they jogged along, they looked at each other. Their sores were GONE. Their leprosy was HEALED! They COULD go to the priest. He would say they could go HOME. They could live with their families again!

3. **Take away the one from the number 10. Add eyes and mouth to the zero to make a happy face.** The Bible doesn't tell us what nine of these men did next, but it DOES tell what one man did. When this man saw that he was healed, he didn't keep jogging on his way to see the priest. He stopped. He turned around and ran back to Jesus. He threw himself down on the ground at Jesus' feet. And he said, "Jesus, wonderful teacher, THANK YOU! You have made me WELL!"

Jesus looked down at this happy, grateful man. He asked, "Weren't all 10 of you made well?"

"Yes, we were all HEALED!" the man answered.

"Where are the other nine?" Jesus asked. "Didn't they come with you to thank God for being healed?"

This man must have looked around in surprise. NONE of the others had come back to thank Jesus for healing him.

Jesus looked kindly at the man and said, "Get up now. You may go. Your faith in Me has made you well!"

Jesus was glad to see how thankful the man was. God's gift of making him well had filled him with joy! His thankfulness was OVERFLOWING! He was so grateful to Jesus for loving him and healing him that he had to come back and say thank-You. He didn't care what anyone else did. He was filled with JOY!

## Conclude the Story

**Why were the 10 men waiting for Jesus?** (They wanted Jesus to make them well.) **What did Jesus tell the men? What did it mean?** (Jesus told them to show themselves to the priest. That meant they were cured.) **What did one man do?** (Came back to thank Jesus.) **Why do you think the others didn't?**

**God has given us wonderful gifts, too. That's because He wants us to be filled with joy. When we are grateful to God for all He has done, it gives us so much joy we can't help showing it to others!**

Luke 18:9-14

# Jesus Teaches Us to Pray

## Materials

Play dough (¼ cup, or 2 oz.) for each student.

## Tell the Story

**Follow along with me as we use our dough to tell today's story.**

***When have you heard a grown-up pray?***

***Today we'll hear about two grown-ups who were both praying, but their prayers were VERY different!***

1. **Roll four ropes from your dough and make the word "LAWS."** One day, Jesus was talking with some men called Pharisees. These men were important religious leaders. Pharisees tried to obey every one of the Old Testament laws. They even obeyed MORE laws than were IN the Old Testament. They thought their obedience caused God to love them more than He loved anyone else. They were proud of all the things they did to make God love them.

But these men were WRONG—wrong about God's love and wrong about being proud. Jesus wanted these men to learn the truth, so He told them a story.

2. **Now make the word "PRAY."** Jesus' story was about two men who went to the Temple to pray. The first man Jesus talked about was a Pharisee. This Pharisee stood up in the Temple. He lifted his arms, so everyone could see him. He began to pray so loudly that everyone could hear him. He was proud of all he had done.

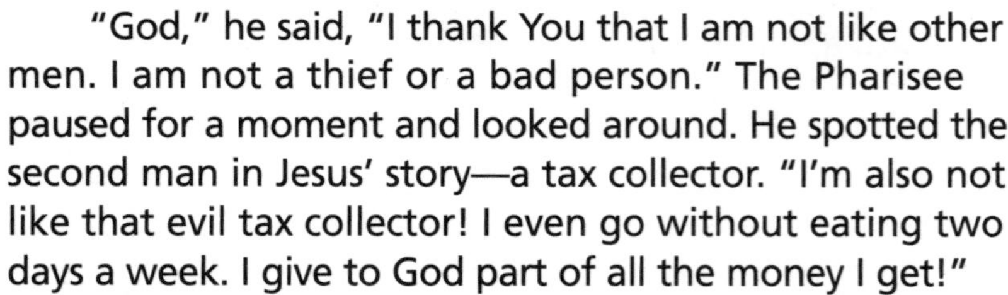

"God," he said, "I thank You that I am not like other men. I am not a thief or a bad person." The Pharisee paused for a moment and looked around. He spotted the second man in Jesus' story—a tax collector. "I'm also not like that evil tax collector! I even go without eating two days a week. I give to God part of all the money I get!"

Perhaps everyone in the Temple who heard this Pharisee might have been impressed. After all, he not only followed the rules, but he also did MORE than the rules said to do. He fasted (did not eat) twice a week, even though the Old Testament law said that everyone needed to fast only on one special day each year.

 

3. **Make the word "HATE."** Now in his prayer, the Pharisee mentioned he was glad he wasn't like the tax collector whom he saw in the Temple while he was praying. The Pharisee probably thought that a person like the tax collector should never even be allowed INTO the Temple!

Tax collectors were hated by the people of Israel. You see, when the Romans took control of the cities of Israel, they hired Jewish men to be tax collectors. The Romans allowed them to gather MORE money than Roman law said they should take for taxes. Tax collectors kept the extra money for themselves! The Pharisee was sure everyone hated the tax collector as much as he did.

4. **Make the word "SINS."** That tax collector also may have felt like he wasn't good enough to come into the Temple. But he hadn't come to impress people with his goodness. His prayer was very different from the prayer of the Pharisee. The tax collector stood by himself. He couldn't even look up.

Beating himself on the chest and sobbing, he prayed, "God, have mercy on me! I am a sinner." The tax collector remembered his sins—he knew he had disobeyed God. He understood that he didn't deserve anything good from God. He was humble, not proud. To be humble means we don't think we are better than others. The tax collector knew that the only way he could receive God's forgiveness was if God had mercy on him. He hadn't done ANYTHING good to try to make God love him!

5. **Make the word "LOVE."** Jesus said to the men listening, "God forgave the tax collector but NOT the Pharisee." He looked around at these people who were so proud of themselves. He wanted them to know the truth about God: God loves EVERYONE. And everyone should come to God with a humble attitude like the tax collector had. The Bible says God listens to people who have a humble spirit!

## Conclude the Story

**Who were the men who went to the Temple to pray in Jesus' story?** (Pharisee. Tax collector.) **Why did the Pharisee come to pray?** (To brag.) **Why did the tax collector come to pray?** (To ask mercy and forgiveness.) **Why did God forgive the tax collector?** (He was humble and knew he needed forgiveness.)

**Being gentle is not something people talk much about. But gentleness helps us to be humble and not to look down on anyone else. And as God helps our gentleness and humility grow, we treat others in ways that show God's love!**

**Matthew 19:13-15; Mark 10:13-16; Luke 18:15-17**

# Jesus and the Children

## Before the Story

Guide students to briefly practice signs for underlined words.

***Who's the most important person you have ever met?***

***Today we'll hear about some children who met a VERY important person who showed them that they were important, too!***

## Tell the Story

As you tell the story, lead students in responding as shown when you say the underlined

1. When Jesus lived on earth, many people followed Him. Some of them loved to listen to the things He said. Some people wanted to see the wonderful things He did. Some people came to argue with Him! On this particular day, however, some people came to see Jesus for a different reason. These people were moms and dads who wanted to bring their children to Jesus. These parents had heard about Jesus and the wonderful things He did and said. They wanted their children to meet Jesus.

1. People: With thumb and middle fingers touching, alternately make inward circles.

2. The children must have been VERY excited. Maybe they were noisy and silly, laughing and talking excitedly. Maybe they ran all the way! It must have been wonderful to be going to see JESUS, this amazing person their parents thought was so important.

2. Excite: With circular motion, alternately strike chest with bent middle fingers.

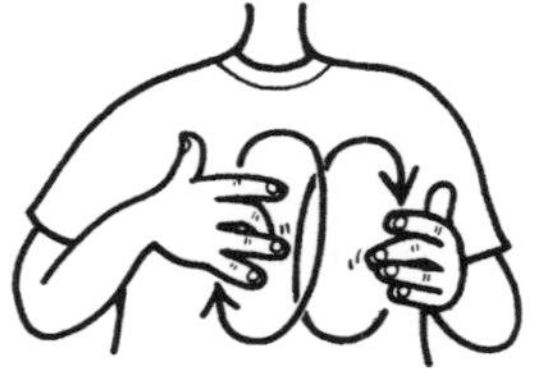

3. When the parents and children came to the place where Jesus was, He was talking to some grown-ups. The disciples saw the children coming, probably running and laughing. Perhaps the disciples thought, *How could these parents be so rude to bring noisy children? After all, wasn't Jesus talking about important things with these adults? He shouldn't be bothered.* The disciples did NOT like being interrupted by children.

3. Disciples: Move left fist ahead of right; move open hands down sides.

4. The disciples said to the parents, "Take the children and go away!" The disciples didn't think Jesus needed to bother with children. After all, He had more IMPORTANT things to do. The parents and the children were suddenly very sad. They turned around and began to go away.

4. Go away: Right hand moves forward as it closes.

5. But Jesus noticed what was going on. He looked past those grown-ups who were standing around Him. He watched the disciples fussing at the parents and sending the children away. He watched as the parents and children turned and began to walk away with their shoulders slumped and their heads bowed because now they wouldn't be able to see Jesus AT ALL.

5. Watch: Move right two fingers away from eyes.

6. Jesus was NOT happy! In fact, the Bible says He was INDIGNANT. (That means Jesus was ANGRY at the unfair way the disciples were treating the children.) He was ANGRY that the disciples were turning the children away. He called out, "Don't send those little children away! Let them come to Me!"

6. Angry: Bend right fingers and pull away from face.

7. The children and their parents stopped. They turned around because Jesus WANTED to see them! Now the children must have all had BIG smiles on their faces. Jesus WANTED to see them! Jesus opened His arms to welcome the children. He turned to the disciples and the other grown-ups. "The kingdom of God belongs to people who are like these little children," He said. Jesus meant that the way in which little children loved and trusted Him should be the way everyone loves and trusts God.

7. Want: Palms up, move curved hands toward self a few times.

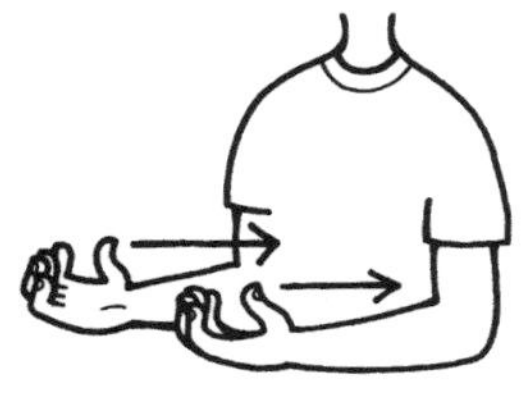

8. Then Jesus took the children in His arms. He laid His hands on their heads, saying loving words to every child. Some parents probably held out their babies to Jesus. Jesus took the babies, held them and smiled at them. Toddlers probably climbed up into His lap. Jesus hugged and touched each one. Then Jesus prayed for them. It was a day those children would NEVER forget. Jesus didn't think that only grown-ups were important. He thought every child was important, too!

8. Child: Move right hand up and then down in front of chest.

Children: Move hand in same manner several times.

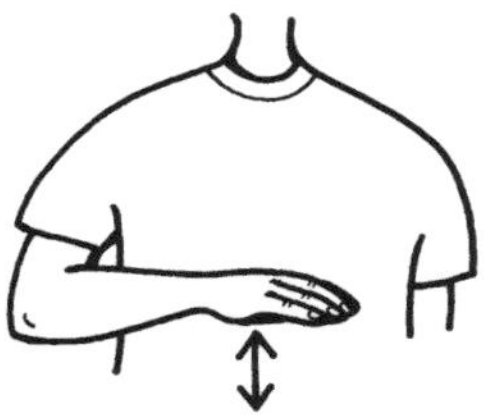

## Conclude the Story

**Why did the parents bring their children to Jesus?** (They wanted Jesus to see and bless them.) **What did the disciples tell the parents?** (Go away.) **How did Jesus feel about the disciples' actions?** (He was angry and indignant.) **What did Jesus say about children?** (That God's kingdom belongs to people who are like little children.)

**What are some times when kids your age may feel that adults don't think kids are important? The Bible tells us that EVERY person is important to God!**

**Mark 10:46-52**

# Blind Bartimaeus

## Materials

Play dough (¼ cup, or 2 oz.) for each student.

## Tell the Story

**Follow along with me as we use our dough to tell today's story.**

***When have you tried to get the attention of someone? Why? What did you do?***

***Today we'll hear about a man who really wanted to get Jesus' attention!***

1. **Divide your dough into three parts. With the first part, roll a rope and make the letter *B*.** One day a blind man named Bartimaeus (BAR-tih-MAY-uhs) was sitting at the gate of the town of Jericho. He was begging. Bartimaeus couldn't see to plant seeds and take care of plants like a farmer. He couldn't see to cut wood and build like a carpenter. In Bible times, the only way that a blind person got the money he needed was to beg. Beggars called out to people walking nearby, asking them for money or food. So Bartimaeus sat along the busy road and begged. Day after day all the people around would hear Bartimaeus calling out for people to help him.

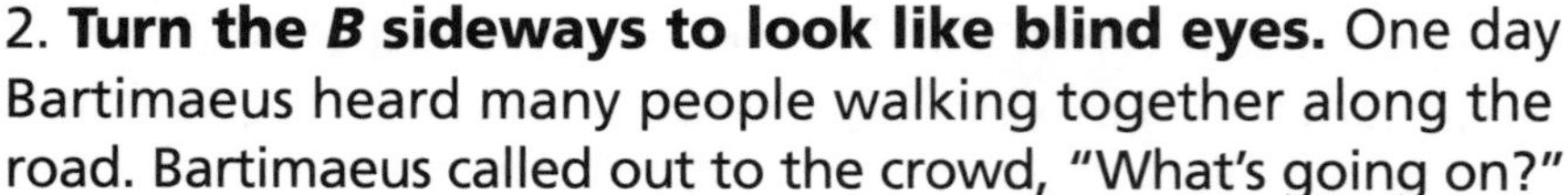

2. **Turn the *B* sideways to look like blind eyes.** One day Bartimaeus heard many people walking together along the road. Bartimaeus called out to the crowd, "What's going on?"

"Jesus of Nazareth is coming!" someone shouted back.

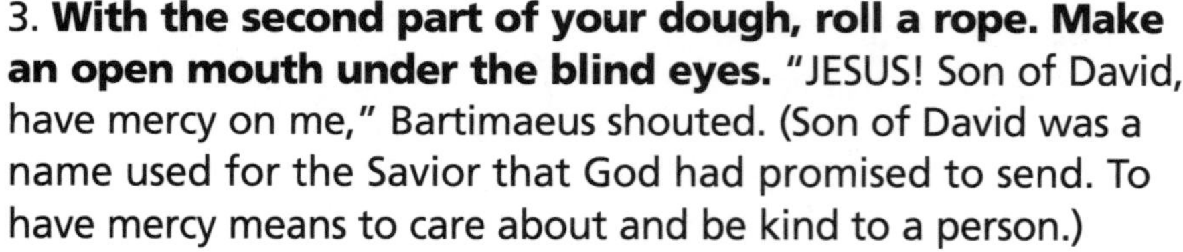

3. **With the second part of your dough, roll a rope. Make an open mouth under the blind eyes.** "JESUS! Son of David, have mercy on me," Bartimaeus shouted. (Son of David was a name used for the Savior that God had promised to send. To have mercy means to care about and be kind to a person.)

Bartimaeus was making a LOT of noise! The people around Bartimaeus told him, "BE QUIET!" These people had seen Bartimaeus begging every day. Perhaps they thought he was making too much noise. Or maybe they wanted to see what Jesus was going to do and didn't want Jesus to be interrupted.

But Bartimaeus didn't listen to the people who told him to be quiet. He wanted Jesus to HEAR him! So he shouted out louder still, "JESUS, HAVE MERCY ON ME!" Bartimaeus hoped that Jesus would hear him and care about him.

Jesus could have passed right on by this noisy man. He could have said, "Not now, Bartimaeus." But Jesus didn't ignore him. He didn't keep walking down the road. No, Jesus cared. He STOPPED! He said, "Bring Me that man who is shouting out My name."

Several people quickly came to Bartimaeus. "Cheer up! Get on your feet. JESUS is calling you!" they said. They pulled Bartimaeus up by the arms and guided him to Jesus.

When Bartimaeus came up to Jesus, Jesus asked, "What do you want Me to do for you?"

Bartimaeus said, "Wonderful Teacher, I want to SEE!"

4. **Add the third part of your dough to the *B* eyes so that they look open.** Jesus must have smiled when He heard what Bartimaeus wanted. This man was VERY sure Jesus could help him! Bartimaeus wouldn't be stopped, even though other people hadn't cared about him. He wouldn't be stopped, although they had said unkind words to him.

Jesus said to him, "Then open your eyes. Your faith in Me has healed you!"

5. **Change the open mouth to a smiling mouth.** Instantly Bartimaeus could SEE! Jesus' face was probably the first thing Bartimaeus ever saw! He was so happy that he began praising God for giving him sight!

Bartimaeus could SEE the crowd following Jesus. Now he could WALK by himself without bumping into things. He wanted to stay with Jesus, who had loved him and healed him. So Bartimaeus came right along with the crowd and followed Jesus, too! The crowd was AMAZED! They joined Bartimaeus in praising God. They had seen a MIRACLE—something only God can do. And it only happened because Jesus cared about this noisy blind man when others just wanted him to be quiet!

## Conclude the Story

**Why did Bartimaeus beg for a living?** (He was blind and couldn't earn money.) **What did people tell him to do when he began to call to Jesus?** (Be quiet.) **How did Jesus treat Bartimaeus?** (Paid attention to him. Helped him.)

**Sometimes we see people to whom others don't pay much attention. Jesus cared about all people, including people others didn't care much about. He wants us to act like that, too. We can show God's love to others by caring about them.**

**Luke 19:1-10**

# Jesus Forgives Zacchaeus

## Before the Story

Guide students to briefly practice signs for underlined words.

***What are some celebrations you've enjoyed?***

***Today we'll hear about a man who discovered the best reason of all to celebrate!***

## Tell the Story

As you tell the story, lead students in responding as shown when you say the underlined words.

1. When Jesus lived on earth, the people in Israel had to pay taxes to the Romans. The Israelites weren't happy about paying these taxes. First of all, they didn't LIKE the Romans. And second of all, paying taxes to Rome took money that they needed for buying food and clothes. And WORST of all, every time they paid taxes it just REMINDED them of how UNHAPPY they were that the Romans were in charge!

1. Tax: Move crooked right finger down left palm.

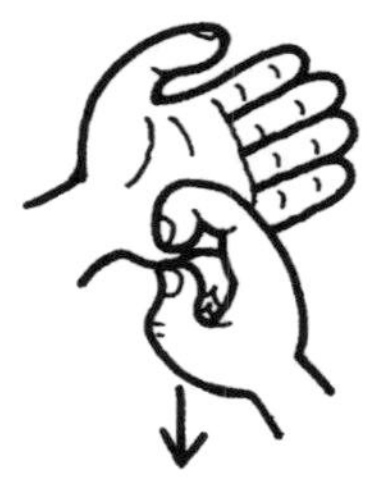

2. But one man WAS happy about people paying taxes to Rome. This man was the tax collector. His name was Zacchaeus; and not only was he a tax collector, but he was also RICH. He had a big house and nice clothes. But he had NO friends.

2. Rich: Put right hand in left palm; then lift up, curve open and face down.

3. Zacchaeus was rich because he took more money from people than they were supposed to pay in taxes to Rome. Then Zacchaeus kept the extra money for himself! Everyone in town could see that he had extra money because of his rich-looking house and clothes. NO one liked him!

3. Money: Touching, right fingertips strike left palm a few times.

4. But one day Jesus came to the town where Zacchaeus lived. People crowded along the road, waiting to see Jesus. Zacchaeus wanted to see Jesus, too. But Zacchaeus was so short that he couldn't see past all the people. And nobody would let him through the crowd! He couldn't see Jesus at all!

4. Jesus: Touch palms with opposite middle fingers.

5. Zacchaeus REALLY wanted to <u>see</u> Jesus. He had probably heard many wonderful things about Jesus. So he ran past the crowd. He could <u>see</u> a big tree up ahead! Quickly Zacchaeus climbed up the tree. NOW he could <u>see</u>! He could <u>see</u> Jesus—coming closer and closer!

5. See: Move two right fingers away from eyes.

6. When Jesus was right under the tree where Zacchaeus was sitting, Zacchaeus got a big <u>surprise</u>. Jesus looked up right at him! Then he got another <u>surprise</u>! Jesus called, "Zacchaeus, come down! I want to go to your house." The crowd was <u>surprised</u>, too. They were <u>surprised</u> that Jesus would want to be with that greedy, cheating tax collector! *Why would Jesus want to be friends with a man like that?* But Jesus did! And Jesus' love CHANGED Zacchaeus!

6. Surprise: Index fingers and thumbs touch at temples; flick up.

7. Zacchaeus said, "I want to <u>give</u> half of everything I have to poor people. And if I have cheated anyone, I will <u>give</u> back FOUR TIMES as much money as I took!" Zacchaeus wanted EVERYONE to know that Jesus was now his friend. Zacchaeus was different now. He wanted to <u>give</u>, not take!

7. Give: Hands down and fingertips touching, flip hands forward and open, palms up.

8. Jesus knew that Zacchaeus was sorry for cheating and stealing and doing other wrong things. Jesus <u>forgave</u> Zacchaeus. He was glad to <u>forgive</u> Zacchaeus and be his friend. And Zacchaeus was VERY glad Jesus had <u>forgiven</u> HIM! Now EVERYTHING would be so much better for Zacchaeus!!

8. Forgive: Stroke edge of left palm with right fingertips.

## Conclude the Story

**How did Jesus show He cared about Zacchaeus?** (By talking to him. By forgiving him.) **How did Zacchaeus show he was sorry for his cheating?** (Promised to give back more than he took.) **Jesus forgave Zacchaeus and because of Jesus' loving forgiveness, Zacchaeus had a reason to celebrate.**

**If you admit that you've disobeyed God and if you believe that Jesus died for you, God will forgive all your sins. That's a great reason to celebrate!** Invite children to talk with you about becoming members of God's family (see "Leading a Child to Christ" on p. 13).

**Mark 11:1-10; Luke 19:28-40**

# Jesus Enters Jerusalem

## Materials

Drawing materials/equipment for teacher and each student.

## Tell the Story

As you tell each part of the story, draw each sketch. Students copy your sketches.

***What kinds of parades have you seen?***

***Today we're going to hear about a very important parade!***

1. For three years, Jesus had traveled around the country of Israel, teaching people about God. He had fed hungry people and made sick people well. Wherever Jesus went, people came from all over to see Him!

1. Draw a "3" and details for Jesus. Add "C"s for people.

2. Now Jesus was going to Jerusalem, where God's Temple was. He was going to celebrate the holiday of Passover in Jerusalem. But Jesus wasn't ONLY going to Jerusalem to celebrate Passover. He knew that it was time to show people that He was the Savior (called the Messiah) God had promised to send.

2. Sideways "J"; add lines to make city gate and wall.

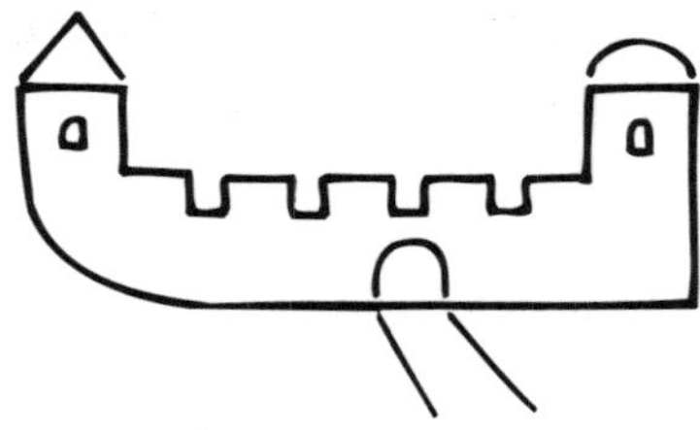

3. As Jesus and His friends walked toward Jerusalem, Jesus sent two of His disciples to bring Him a donkey. Soon the disciples returned with the donkey. They threw their coats over the donkey's back, and Jesus sat on the donkey and rode it up the road to Jerusalem. The world's most important parade had begun!

3. Donkey from "U"s, "I"s and "V"s.

4. As Jesus rode toward Jerusalem, the news spread quickly: "Jesus is coming!" Crowds gathered along the road, shouting, singing and waving palm branches. Some spread their coats and lay palm branches on the roadway like a beautiful carpet! This was the way the people welcomed a great king! They called out, "Hosanna! Hosanna! Blessed is He who comes in the name of the Lord! Hosanna in the highest!"

4. Add road to donkey; palm branches from lines.

5. Some people thought that Jesus the Messiah would be a mighty king—a fierce warrior to save them from the Romans, who had taken over their country. Whatever their reasons, people came from EVERYWHERE to join the shouting, singing crowd!

5. Crown from "O" and "V"s.

6. Soon the people in Jerusalem heard the noise. "What is going on? Who is coming?" they asked. Now many more people ran from their houses into the streets of Jerusalem. Jesus rode through the shouting, singing crowds. It seemed that EVERYONE had come to greet the King!

6. Draw faces over wall in #2.

7. When He got to the Temple, Jesus got off the donkey and went into the Temple. Some children walked with Him, waving their palm branches and singing, "Hosanna! Hosanna!" The Temple leaders growled to Jesus, "Do You hear what they are SINGING to You? Make them be quiet!"

Jesus told the leaders, "These children are right to sing praises to Me. In fact, if they were not praising Me, the rocks would shout out praise to Me!"

7. Temple from rectangles and "M"s.

8. Jesus showed the people that He is the Messiah sent from God. But He would not become the kind of king some people expected. Instead, Jesus knew it was almost time for Him to show how very much He loves everyone. Jesus was going to die on a cross to pay for all the wrong things people had done. Then all people could become part of God's family! Jesus knew this was God's good plan. But for now, Jesus waited.

8. Draw a cross.

## Conclude the Story

**What are some reasons people had for praising Jesus as He entered Jerusalem?** (Jesus had done many miracles. Jesus had helped them.) **What are some reasons we can praise Him?** (He loves us. He forgives our sins.)

**Jesus is the great King of all kings. He loves us so much, He was willing to die so that we could be part of God's family. The more we know about Jesus, the more reasons we have to praise Him!** Talk more with interested students about becoming members of God's family (see "Leading a Child to Christ" on p. 13).

**Mark 12:41-44; Luke 20:45-47; 21:1-4**

# A Poor Woman's Offering

## Materials

Drawing materials/equipment for teacher and each student.

## Tell the Story

As you tell each part of the story, draw each sketch. Students copy your sketches.

***What's a valuable gift you have given to someone?***

***Today we'll hear how a woman gave a gift that was very valuable.***

1. In Bible times many people worshiped God at the Temple in Jerusalem. Jesus worshiped there, too. Often when Jesus was at the Temple, people crowded around Him to hear everything He said. One thing Jesus said on this day was to watch out for people who do good things just to impress others.

1. Letter "WATCH OUT"; turn "O" and "U" into eyes.

2. After teaching all day, Jesus and His friends sat down near a row of big offering boxes. People brought gifts of money to the Temple and put the money in these boxes. Some of the people were very rich, throwing in handfuls of gold coins from their big money bags. Sometimes the rich people looked around to smile and nod when others noticed how much money they were giving. The sound of many big, valuable coins made it obvious when a rich person had given a lot of money.

2. Offering box from rectangle, "O", "V." Add coins, smiling face.

3. Jesus and His friends watched person after person put money in the boxes. Jesus' friends may have been amazed at how much money some people gave! Perhaps they wondered why Jesus had warned them to be careful of people who do good things to impress others! *Weren't these rich people doing a good thing by giving God so much money?*

3. Add more coins and a question mark.

4. Then Jesus and His friends saw a very poor woman walk to an offering box. She didn't have to carry a big bag. She had only two little coins in her hand. They were so TINY that both of them together were worth less than one of our smallest coins. The poor woman quietly dropped those two tiny coins into the offering box and then walked away. If the two little coins made any sound, no one seemed to notice.

4. Add two tiny coins to others.

5. Of course, Jesus knew all about the poor woman. He knew that she had to work very hard to get money for food. He knew that those two little coins were ALL the money she had in the world!

5. Circle two coins; add "ALL."

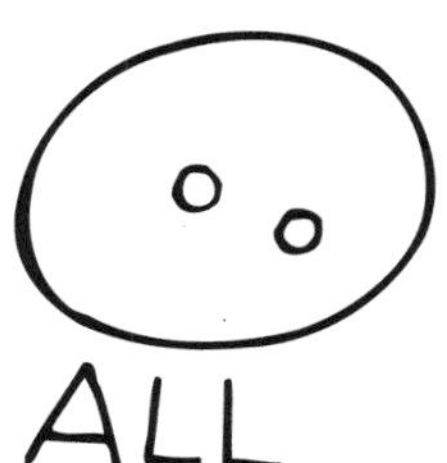


6. Jesus told His friends, "This poor woman has given MORE than all the others." *What on earth could Jesus mean by that? How could the poor woman's two tiny coins be worth MORE than all the gold coins the others put in?* Jesus explained, "After they have given to God, those other people still have plenty of money left for themselves. But THIS woman has no more. She gave ALL she had."

6. Draw two empty hands from "U"s and lines.

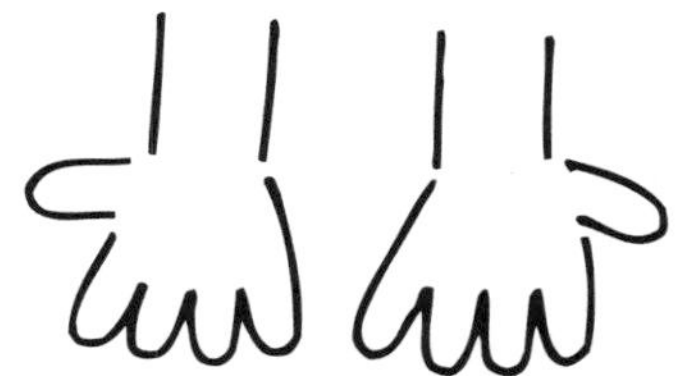

7. As the disciples thought about what Jesus said, they must have begun to understand. The poor woman didn't give her two little coins because she HAD to. She certainly wasn't trying to IMPRESS anyone by what she gave. She gave her gift to God ONLY because she loved God VERY much. She trusted Him, too. She knew that God loved and cared for her. And she wanted to show her thankfulness to Him. Jesus' explanation helped His friends understand that the poor woman's gift really was the biggest gift of all!

7. Draw gift box. Add heart around gift.

## Conclude the Story

**How did the woman show her love for God? How were the other people who gave money different from the woman?**

**It's good to give money to God, but what's most important to God is that we love Him first and most of all! When we love God most, we give generously. We may think we don't have much to give to God. But how much we give is less important than whether or not we give it gladly and out of love.**

## Matthew 25:14-30

# The Parable of the Talents

## Materials

Play dough (¼ cup, or 2 oz.) and coin for each student.

***What would you do if someone gave you a lot of money? How would you use the money?***

***Let's hear a story Jesus told about how three men used large amounts of money they'd been given.***

## Tell the Story

**Follow along with me as we use our dough to tell today's story.**

1. **Pinch off eight small pieces of your dough, leaving some dough for later. Use a coin to make coin shape in each piece of dough.** Once there was a man who had three servants that he really trusted. The master had to go on a long trip. While he was gone, he wanted his servants to use his money to make more money for him. They could use the money to buy a piece of cloth and then sew it into clothes and sell them. They could buy and plant vegetable seeds and sell the vegetables for money.

2. **Separate coins into three piles: five coins, two coins, one coin.** The master went to his servants and gave each of them some of his money to use. He gave the first servant five talents. In those days, the word "talent" did not mean an ability. It meant a huge amount of money. The master gave the second servant two talents. And he gave the third servant one talent. Then the master left on his trip.

3. **Make five more coins and add to pile of five coins.** At once the servant with five talents went to work. He used the money to make more money. While his master was gone, this hardworking servant earned five MORE talents. He had been given five talents to begin with, and now he had 10! His hard work had certainly paid off!

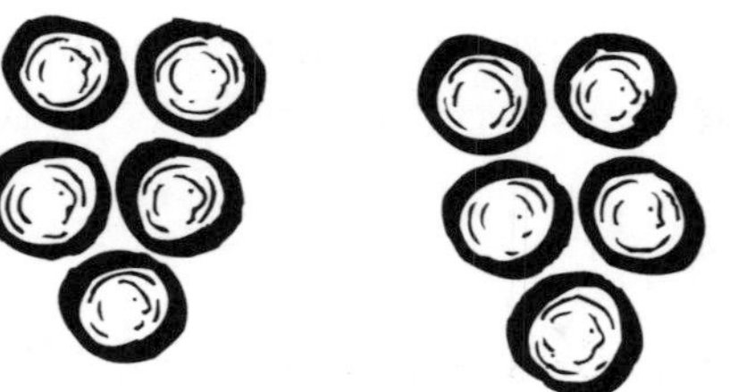

4. **Make two more coins and add to pile of two coins.** The servant with two talents also got right to work. He took his master's money and increased it as well. Perhaps he bought and sold some animals. Whatever he did certainly increased his money. Now he had four talents, twice what he had started with!

5. **Make a shovel with remaining dough.** The third servant could have taken his one talent and bought and sold some sheep. But he was afraid. The money might get lost or stolen. So instead of using it to make more money for his master, he dug a hole in the ground and buried the money, hiding it in the dirt!

After a time the master returned. He called the servants together to see what they had done with his money. The servant who had earned five more talents gave the 10 talents to his master and said, "You gave me five talents and see—I have earned five more for you!"

"Good work!" the master told him. "You were faithful to use what I gave you! Now I will give you MUCH MORE to take care of. I'm happy with what you have done for me."

6. **Add pile of four coins to pile of ten coins.** The second servant gave the money he had earned to his master and said, "Master, you gave me two talents. Now here are two more talents for you."

"You have been faithful and did what I said to do!" the master smiled. "I will put you in charge of more, too. You've pleased me!"

7. **Add single coin to large pile of coins.** Then the third servant who had buried his money said, "I knew you would be angry if I lost your money. I was afraid! So I hid your money in the ground. Here is the one talent you gave me."

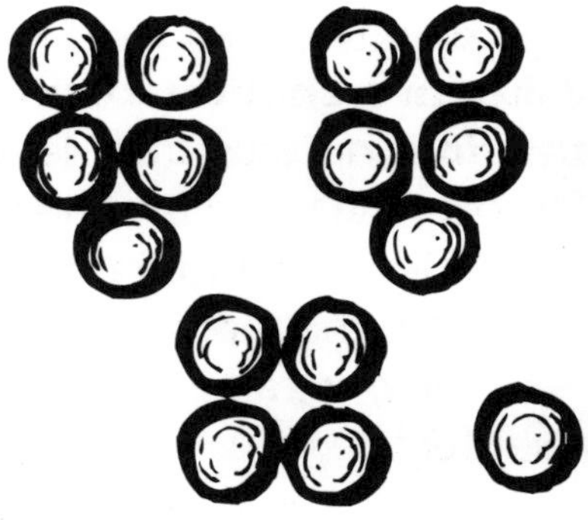

"WHAT?" roared the master. "You did NOTHING with my money? At least you could have put it in the bank! It would have earned interest there." (Interest is the money a bank pays for being able to use the money stored there.)

The master said, "I'll give your money to my servant who earned the most money!" The master had wanted his money to be USED, not hidden away. Jesus told this story so that we would all know that God expects us to USE the abilities and gifts He has given us. It doesn't matter how much we have to start with. What's important to God is that we are faithful to use what He gives us to help others. That pleases Him!

## Conclude the Story

**Why was the master angry with the servant he'd given one talent?** (The servant did nothing to earn more money for the master.) **What do you think Jesus wanted people to learn from this story?** (To use the gifts God gives us. To be faithful and dependable. To do our best.)

**God has made each of us with special gifts, or abilities. We never have to feel afraid or nervous about using a gift from God. And by using these gifts, we show God and others that we are growing the fruit of faithfulness!**

John 13:1-17

# Jesus Washes His Disciples' Feet

## Materials

Play dough (¼ cup, or 2 oz.) and coin for each student.

## Tell the Story

**Follow along with me as we use our dough to tell today's story.**

***Tell me about someone you know who teaches you. What kinds of things does that person use to teach you?***

***Today we'll find out what Jesus used one day to teach His friends.***

1. **Divide your dough into two parts.** It was Passover, the biggest celebration of the year in Israel. Big crowds of people were coming to Jerusalem to worship at the Temple, eat special meals with relatives and visit with friends. The streets were full of people!

2. **Make a shallow bowl from one part of the dough.** Jesus' disciples came together to eat a Passover meal as well. They all gathered in a room where Jesus had told them to go. But when they came into the room, all dressed and ready for the feast, no one came with a bowl and towel to wash their feet.

You see, usually when anyone came in from the outdoors, that person's feet were washed immediately because the roads were dirty, dusty and filled with animal droppings. In wealthy houses, a servant removed the person's sandals and washed and dried the person's feet.

Since no servant was there to wash their feet, Jesus' friends just sat down around the table with their feet still dirty. Perhaps they all thought that they were too good for a messy job like washing someone's feet. Whatever the reason, Jesus wanted to teach them how to show love to each other.

3. **From the remaining dough, make two feet to go in the bowl.** Jesus got up from the table where they were all ready to begin eating. He wrapped a towel around His waist and poured water into a shallow bowl. He began to wash the feet of the nearest disciple.

He finished washing His first friend's feet and dried them with the towel He had around His waist. Then He moved to the next pair of dirty feet. When Jesus came to Peter, Peter tried to stop Him.

"Lord," Peter said, "are You going to wash MY feet?" It must have seemed very strange to Peter that Jesus was doing a SERVANT'S job! It was embarrassing!

Jesus answered Peter, "You don't fully understand what I'm doing now, but you'll understand later on."

Peter said, "No! You will never wash MY feet!"

Jesus must have smiled on the inside. Peter wanted Jesus to act important, to act like the person in charge, not the lowly servant who washed feet! But Jesus did wash Peter's feet. He washed the feet of each of His friends—even the feet of Judas, who would later walk out with his clean feet and help Jesus' enemies arrest Him.

Finally, Jesus put away the bowl and towel and sat down at the table. He looked around at His friends. "Do you understand what I have done? You all call Me teacher and Lord. But if your Lord and teacher washes your feet, you also should be willing to wash each other's feet. I did this for an example. Treat each other the way I have treated you."

Jesus' friends must have looked at each other and felt a little embarrassed. Jesus had been a gentle servant. Without saying a word, He had taught them how to treat each other. They realized they needed to treat each other as if the other person was more important. It was all right to be a servant. In fact, it was what Jesus wanted them to be!

## Conclude the Story

**What did people usually do when they came into a house in Bible times?** (Had their feet washed.) **Why do you think the disciples hadn't washed their feet?** (Didn't want to act like a servant.) **How did Jesus teach His friends?** (He washed their feet.) **What did Jesus want His friends to learn?** (To serve and care for each other.)

**It's not easy to treat people the way Jesus treated His friends. It takes God's help to show gentleness. But Jesus said that if we want to be great in His kingdom, we need to be gentle servants like He was. We can follow Jesus' example.**

 

**Matthew 26:17-30; Mark 14:12-26; Luke 22:7-20; John 13:1-17**

# The Last Supper

## Before the Story

Guide students to briefly practice signs for underlined words.

## Tell the Story

As you tell the story, lead students in responding as shown when you say the underlined words.

***What does your family eat when you have a special meal? What other things does your family do when you have a celebration?***

***Today we'll hear about what Jesus and His friends did at a special meal they ate together.***

1. The roads to Jerusalem were full of people. Everyone was coming into the city to celebrate Passover, when all the Israelites remembered how God freed their ancestors from slavery in Egypt. Passover was one of the three times every year when people came from all over the country to celebrate, feast, sing and pray at the Temple.

1. Celebrate: Right index finger and thumb touching, make small circles.

2. Jesus and His friends were coming to celebrate Passover, too. Jesus told Peter and John to get everything ready for the special Passover meal, called the *seder*, they would eat together. This was to be the last time the disciples would eat with Jesus before He died on the cross. (That's why many people call this Passover meal the Last Supper.)

2. Eat: Fingertips touching, move right hand to mouth a few times.

3. Toward evening, Jesus and the rest of the disciples gathered around the low table. But no servant was there to wash their dusty, dirty feet. Much to everyone's surprise, Jesus got up from the table, poured water into a bowl and began to wash their feet. At first, Peter didn't want Jesus to wash his feet. But Jesus explained that letting Him wash Peter's feet meant that Peter wanted to follow Jesus. Washing the dirty feet of His friends was an example of Jesus' love and caring.

3. Wash: Rub knuckles together in circles.

4. Soon after, Jesus and the disciples began to eat and sing together and to listen once again to the story of how God had freed the Israelites. While He ate with His disciples, Jesus told them that He would die soon. He said that one of them would betray Him to the men who would kill Him. Jesus knew that Judas would be the one to betray Him by leading soldiers to arrest Him later that night.

4. Betray: With thumbs, index and little fingers extended, slide right hand back and forth over left.

5. The disciples were horrified and sad. One of them would BETRAY Jesus? Eleven of them thought, *I wouldn't do such a thing—would I?!* But Judas got up and left. Jesus told His disciples that even this sad thing was part of God's plan. It was going to happen in just the way the prophets in Old Testament times had said it would so that salvation from sin could be offered to all people.

5. Sad: Palms in, drop hands down face.

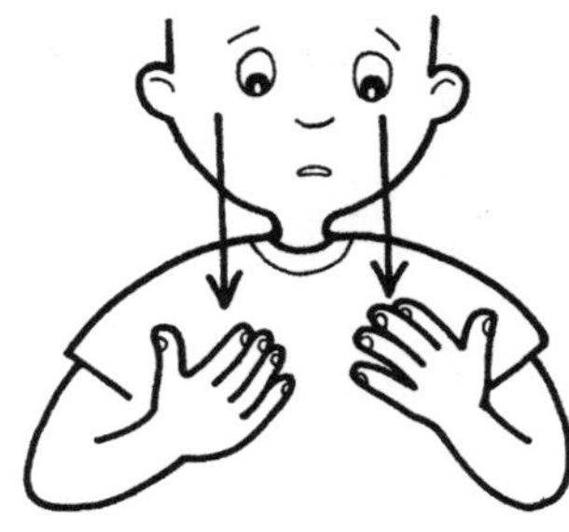

6. As Jesus and the disciples finished the special meal and its story, Jesus tried to help the disciples understand why He would die on the cross. As He spoke, Jesus broke off the unleavened bread used for the seder and shared the wine from one of the Passover cups with His disciples. From now on, Jesus wanted His followers to celebrate the Passover meal in a new way. It was now more than a reminder of God freeing the Israelites from Egypt. It would always remind Jesus' followers of His death.

6. Meal: Fingertips touching, move right hand to mouth a few times.

7. Jesus also explained how much He loved His disciples. He promised to send the Holy Spirit to help them after He died and rose again. The disciples listened carefully. They listened so that they would remember the words Jesus spoke that night.

7. Listen: Cup right ear; turn head to left.

8. When they finished the meal, they sang together. At the end of the seder it was traditional to sing a song that began, "Blessed is the One who comes in the name of the Lord . . ." They had sung it at the end of Passover meals for years. But now as they sang, they must have begun to understand that those words meant even more. That song was about Jesus! Quietly, they went out to pray in a garden on the Mount of Olives. It was the beginning of the end of Jesus' time on earth with His disciples.

8. Sing: Move right hand back and forth in front of left palm.

## Conclude the Story

**What meal did Jesus and His disciples eat?** (The Passover meal.) **What did Jesus tell His friends?** (That He was going to die.) **What did Jesus want His friends to remember when they ate the unleavened bread and shared the cup?** (Jesus' death.)

**Jesus' love for us is so great, He was willing to die on the cross to take the punishment for our sins. That's great love. And it's a BIG reason to celebrate!** Talk with students about becoming Christians (see "Leading a Child to Christ" on p. 13).

**Luke 22:39-48; John 13:1-30; 18:1-14,19-24,28—19:16**

# The Last Supper and Jesus' Arrest

## Materials

Drawing materials/equipment for teacher and each student.

***What are some things a servant does?***

***Today we'll find out how Jesus acted like a servant to His friends.***

## Tell the Story

As you tell each part of the story, draw each sketch. Students copy your sketches.

1. Everyone in Jerusalem was looking forward to the Passover celebration and eating a special dinner as well as singing and praying to God. But this Passover time would be different, especially for Jesus and His friends.

1. Draw stick figures; music notes from "d"s and lines.

2. Jesus and His friends gathered for their special meal, but no servant came to wash everyone's feet. So Jesus washed the feet of each of His friends. He talked about the ways He had shown love to them and how He wanted them to show love to each other. Then, while they ate, Jesus said, "One of you will give Me to My enemies. They will kill Me on a cross."

2. Foot from "L"s and "C"s; add bowl and water.

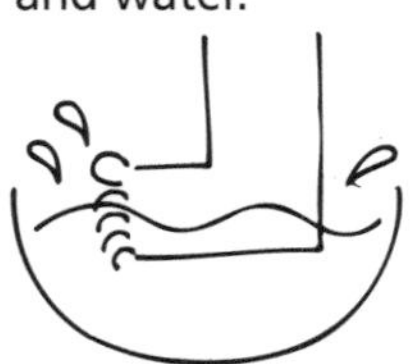

3. *How could this be?* Jesus' friends wondered. When Jesus had ridden into town four days earlier, the people had called Him their KING! But even though many people loved Jesus, some of the leaders HATED Him. They said, "We must STOP Jesus. If we don't get RID of Him soon, WE won't be in charge anymore!" They made a mean plan to KILL Him.

3. Draw crown from "V"s and "O"; add "no" slash.

4. Jesus knew their plan and that His friend Judas had been paid with 30 coins to lead them to Jesus when there weren't many people around. But Jesus also knew that He had come to earth to take the punishment for all the wrong things people had ever done—or ever would do. God was in charge of what was happening. And God was going to use the leaders' evil plan to do something VERY GOOD!

4. Coins; turn into "GOOD."

5. After their meal, Jesus and His friends walked to the nearby Mount of Olives together. He asked His friends to wait for Him while He went off by Himself to pray. Jesus asked God to help Him as He followed this plan to take the punishment for all the wrong things people had done.

5. Ridge from "C"; trees from "3"s and lines.

6. When Jesus finished praying, He woke His sleeping friends. Judas was coming. But Judas wasn't alone. A crowd of men, armed with swords and clubs, had come with Judas to take Jesus away! Judas kissed Jesus to show the men whom they should arrest. Jesus could have stopped the men, but He quietly let them take Him.

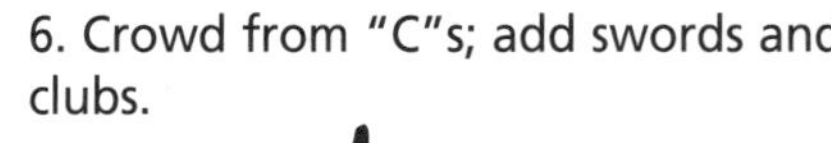

6. Crowd from "C"s; add swords and clubs.

7. Many, many years before, the prophets of God had said that Jesus would be as quiet as a sheep when all this happened. They had said Jesus would let people hurt Him and never say anything to defend Himself or hurt them in return. God's prophets had also said that all of Jesus' friends would run away and leave Him alone. And they did!

7. Running stick figure from "N."

8. The men with the swords and clubs took Jesus to the house of the high priest. There the leaders told lies about Him. People slapped Him and hurt Him. And He let them.

Then they took Jesus to the Roman ruler named Pilate. They wanted to get permission to KILL Jesus on a cross. Pilate knew Jesus had not done anything wrong, but he gave permission, just so the other leaders wouldn't cause any trouble for him. The Roman soldiers took Jesus. They hurt Him and put a crown of hard, sharp thorns on His head. They made fun of Him. And Jesus let them. He was willing to do this because He loved us.

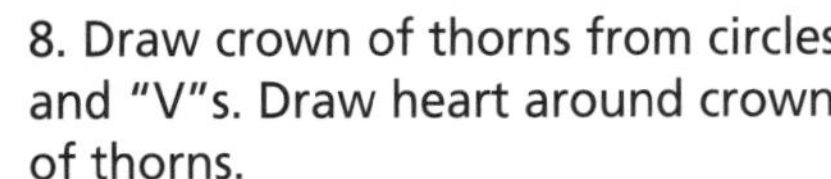

8. Draw crown of thorns from circles and "V"s. Draw heart around crown of thorns.

## Conclude the Story

**How did Jesus show His love for us?** (He died for us.) **What are some ways we can show our love for Him?** (Tell other people about Him. Obey His Word.)

**Jesus had come to earth to take the punishment for all the sins people had ever done—or would do. Jesus was willing to do this because He loves us. And Jesus knew that even when He died, He wouldn't STAY dead! God would turn this very BAD event into a very GOOD thing!**

**Mark 15:21—16:8; John 20:10-18**

# Jesus' Death and Resurrection

## Materials

Drawing materials/equipment for teacher and each student.

## Tell the Story

As you tell each part of the story, draw each sketch. Students copy your sketches.

***What are some ways people celebrate Easter?***

***Today we'll talk about why a time that started out so sad became something to celebrate!***

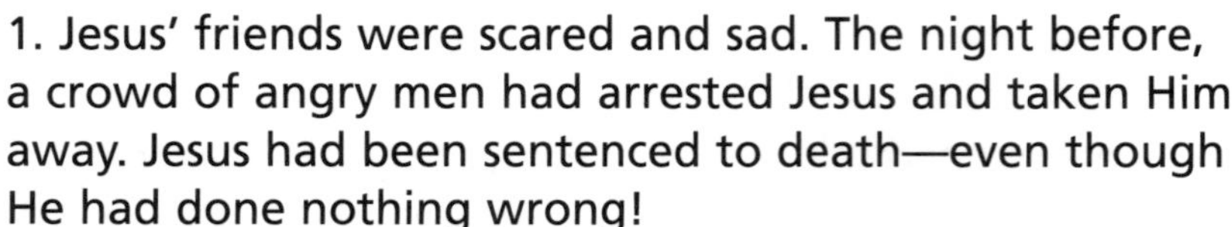

1. Jesus' friends were scared and sad. The night before, a crowd of angry men had arrested Jesus and taken Him away. Jesus had been sentenced to death—even though He had done nothing wrong!

1. Draw scared face, moon and star.

2. Late in the morning, Roman soldiers made Jesus carry a heavy cross on His back. Jesus had been so badly beaten that He could hardly walk. So the soldiers made another man help Jesus. When they arrived at the place of crucifixion, the soldiers nailed Jesus to His cross and placed the cross into the ground. People came up to Jesus and spit on Him. They said terrible things to Him. Jesus let them. He could have stopped them, but He loved us so much He was willing to be hurt and killed to take the punishment for our sins.

2. Draw sun and hill; add cross.

3. Soon it got very dark, even though it was the middle of the day! Suddenly there was a huge EARTHQUAKE! And then, Jesus died. It was a horrible, scary time!

3. Color over sun. "W"s for earthquake.

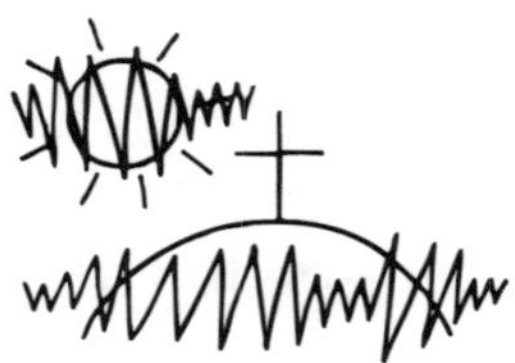

4. After Jesus was dead, two of His friends laid His body in a tomb in a garden. (A tomb is a little room usually made in the side of a hill.) A HUGE rock was rolled in front of the doorway, so no one could get inside. Jesus' friends went home feeling very sad. It looked like EVERYTHING had gone wrong! But what they didn't understand was that this day, as awful and horrible as it was, would turn out to be a BIG part of God's GOOD plan!

4. Tomb from "U"s, "O".

5. On the third day after Jesus died, several women who had been Jesus' friends got up very early. They wanted to get to the tomb by the time the sun was rising. But when they got to the garden where the tomb was, they could see that the big rock that had been in front of the tomb doorway had been ROLLED AWAY!

5. Add rising sun behind tomb. Change rock to open door.

6. One of the women, Mary, didn't know what to think! She ran to get Peter and John, two more of Jesus' friends. Peter and John ran back to the tomb. And when they went inside, they could see that Jesus' body was GONE! Peter and John went home, wondering what was going on!

6. Tomb interior from "U"s. Add question mark.

7. But Mary, who had followed them back to the garden, stayed there, crying. When she looked into the tomb again, it WASN'T empty. Now she saw two ANGELS!

One angel asked, "Why are you sad?"

Mary said, "Because Jesus' body is gone. I don't know where He is!" She turned away from the tomb and almost bumped into someone. *Is this the gardener?* she wondered. But then the person spoke.

7. Angels from "O"s and triangles.

8. "Mary!" He said. Mary knew that voice—it was JESUS! Jesus was there in front of her. And He was ALIVE! She was so very HAPPY! Jesus said to her, "Go and tell the others."

And Mary DID! She must have run like the wind! Coming through the door to the house where Jesus' friends were, she said, "Jesus is ALIVE! I've SEEN Him!" Jesus' friends were amazed! What Jesus had said was true! God's plan was GOOD! Soon Jesus came to see His friends. And they began to tell everyone the GOOD NEWS: Jesus is alive! And He is STILL alive!

8. Ears from question marks. Add happy face from "U"s.

## Conclude the Story

**How did Jesus' friends feel at the beginning of the story?** (Sad. Scared.) **How did they feel at the end?** (Happy. Surprised.)

**Jesus died to take the punishment for our sins, as God had promised He would. And because He is alive, all people everywhere can have salvation and eternal life. When we believe that Jesus is God's Son and that He died for us, our sins are forgiven and we can be part of God's family!**

**John 20:19-31**

# Jesus Appears to Thomas

## Before the Story

Guide students to briefly practice signs for underlined words.

***Have you ever heard about something and wondered whether it was true or not?***

***Today we're going to hear about someone who didn't believe what his friends told him.***

## Tell the Story

As you tell the story, lead students in responding as shown when you say the underlined words.

1. There was a time when most of Jesus' disciples and friends were very <u>scared</u>. The Romans had killed Jesus, and His friends were <u>afraid</u> they might be killed, too. They didn't know what to do. So Jesus' friends were hiding in an upstairs room of someone's house. They locked all the doors, so no one could get in.

1. Scared, afraid: Fingertips touching, open hands and cover chest.

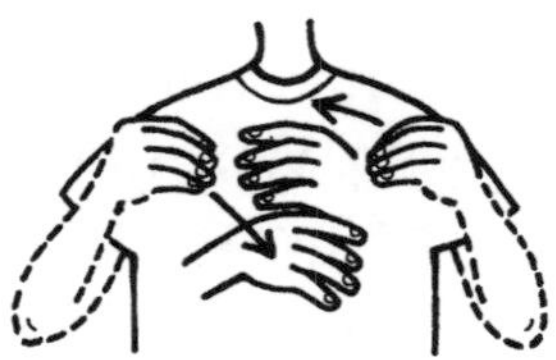

2. Ever since morning on this third day after Jesus died, Jesus' friends had been hearing exciting but confusing reports about Jesus. First, they had heard that His tomb was empty. Then some people actually claimed to have seen Jesus. They said He was <u>alive</u> again! But most of the people who were hiding weren't at all sure they could believe that Jesus was <u>ALIVE</u>.

2. Alive: Thumbs and index fingers extended, move hands up body.

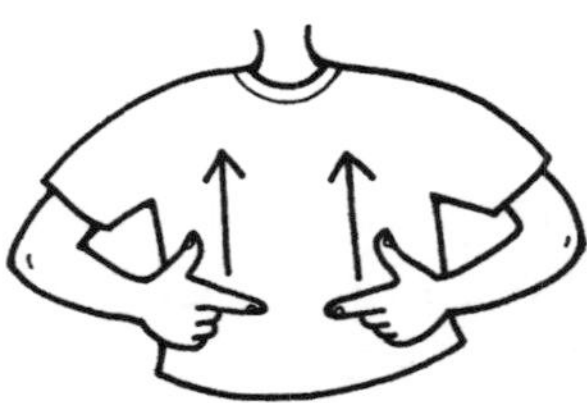

3. SUDDENLY, there was Jesus standing in the room with them! He didn't come through the door. He was just THERE!

"Peace be with you," He said. Jesus' friends thought they were seeing a ghost! They couldn't believe their eyes!

"I am not a ghost," said Jesus. "Come and <u>touch</u> Me. I'll show you that I am alive." His friends <u>touched</u> Him.

3. Touch: Touch left hand with right middle finger.

4. Then just to be sure His friends knew it was really Him and not a ghost, Jesus asked them to bring Him some <u>food</u>. One of His friends gave Jesus some fish. Jesus <u>ate</u> it right there in front of them. Jesus' friends were amazed. Since only living people could <u>eat</u>, they knew that Jesus was really ALIVE!

4. Food, eat: Fingertips touching, move right hand to mouth a few times.

5. Jesus' friends looked at each other. It really WAS Jesus! The room began to buzz with excited questions. Jesus explained to them again how it had been God's plan for Him to die and come back to life so that people could be forgiven for their sins and become part of God's family. Then Jesus was gone, just as quickly as He had appeared.

5. Jesus: Touch palms with opposite middle fingers.

6. One of Jesus' friends named Thomas was not there when Jesus visited. The other disciples could hardly wait to see Thomas and tell him, "WE HAVE SEEN JESUS!"

Thomas didn't believe them. It sounded too good to be true! "Until I put my fingers in the nail prints in Jesus' hands and touch the place where the sword pierced His side," Thomas said, "I will not believe!"

6. Believe: Touch right finger to forehead; clasp hands.

7. Nothing anyone said could change Thomas's mind. But Jesus loved Thomas and wanted him to know He was alive. A full week later, Jesus' friends were meeting in the same house. This time, Thomas was with them. Just like before, the doors were all locked. And SUDDENLY, just like before, there was Jesus, RIGHT there with them in the room!

7. With: Touch fists together.

8. Jesus turned to Thomas first.

"Thomas!" said Jesus. "Come and touch Me. I want you to believe that I am really alive." All of Thomas's doubts suddenly were gone. Thomas knelt down and said, "MY LORD AND MY GOD!"

Now Thomas truly believed that Jesus was alive!

Jesus said to Thomas, "You believe now that you have seen me." Then Jesus said something about all of us who weren't there that night. Jesus said, "Imagine the happiness of those who believe without being able to see Me." When we believe that Jesus truly is alive, we share in the same happiness Jesus' friends enjoyed that night they saw Jesus.

8. Alive: Thumbs and index fingers extended, move hands up body.

## Conclude the Story

**What did Jesus' friends tell Thomas?** (That Jesus was alive. That they had seen Him.) **Why didn't Thomas believe his friends?** (He said he wanted to touch Jesus.) **What did Thomas say when Jesus invited him to touch Him?** ("My Lord and my God!")

**Jesus will help us believe He is alive and accept His love for us. He showed that love by dying for us and rising again.** Talk with students about salvation (see "Leading a Child to Christ" on p. 13).

**Matthew 26:31-35,69-75; John 21:1-24**

# Jesus Forgives Peter

## Before the Story

Guide students to briefly practice signs for underlined words.

***What is something you've done that you wished you could do over again?***

***Today we'll meet a man who wished he could go back and change something he did. And we'll hear what Jesus did about it!***

## Tell the Story

As you tell the story, lead students in responding as shown when you say the underlined words.

1. When Jesus lived on earth, He had many friends. But from them, He chose 12 men, called <u>disciples</u>, to follow Him and learn from Him. Jesus said to these men, "Come and follow Me!" One <u>disciple</u> was named Peter. Peter loved Jesus very much. Peter was one of the first people to tell Jesus, "You are the Son of God!"

1. Disciple: Move left fist ahead of right; move open hands down sides.

2. After Jesus had been with His friends for three years, He told them that He would be arrested and sent to die. Jesus also told His disciples that they were going to run away and say they did not know Him. Well, Peter spoke right up. He said, "I will <u>NEVER</u> say I don't know You!" And each of Jesus' other disciples said the same thing: "I will <u>NEVER</u> say I don't know you!"

2. Never: Move right hand in half circle; then drop to right.

3. Things happened just as Jesus said they would. Soldiers came and arrested Him. All His friends DID run away. But Peter followed at a distance. While Jesus was being questioned inside the high priest's house, Peter stood outside. While he warmed himself by a little fire, a servant girl said to him, "You were with Jesus!" Peter replied, "I <u>don't know</u> what you're talking about!"

3. Don't know: Fingers of right hand on forehead; move hand away, flipping palm out.

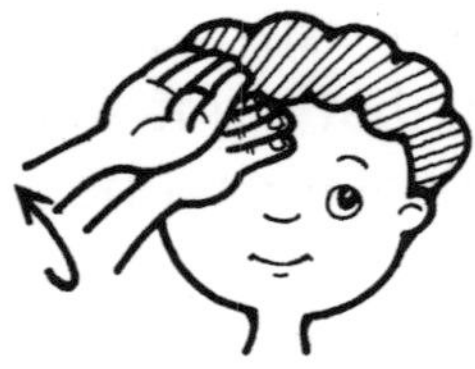

4. Then another girl said to someone else, "He's one of Jesus' friends." Peter answered, "I am <u>NOT</u>!" In a little while someone else said, "I'm sure you're one of Jesus' friends. You're from Galilee!" Peter cursed and said, "I <u>don't KNOW</u> this man you're talking about!"

4. Not: Move fist sharply away from chin. Don't know: Repeat #3.

5. Just then, a rooster crowed; and Peter remembered Jesus' words: "Before the rooster crows, you will deny three times that you know Me." Peter began to cry. He had told Jesus he would NEVER say he didn't know Him. Now he had done just that—THREE TIMES!

5. Rooster: Place right thumb against forehead with two fingers extended.

6. A few hours later, Jesus was crucified. He died on a cross to pay the price for sin. All of Jesus' friends were VERY sad. And where was Peter? He was hiding out, sorry and so afraid. He had done something so AWFUL! But three days later, Jesus came back to life! He wasn't dead anymore! And one of the first things Jesus said was, "Tell my disciples—and Peter—to meet Me in Galilee!"

6. Cross: Move curved right hand down; then from left to right.

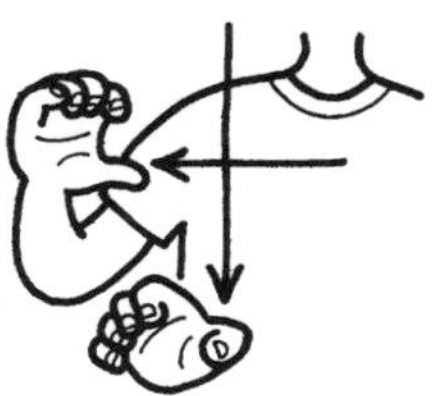

7. WELL! When Peter heard that, he felt better. And when he himself saw Jesus alive again, Peter must have been overjoyed! But in the days after Jesus' resurrection, he still wasn't sure what to do. So one day he told the other disciples, "I'm going fishing." They said, "We're going, too." They went to Galilee and fished all night. They caught NOTHING. But at dawn, someone on shore said, "Throw out your net on the other side!" They did, and they caught LOTS of fish!

7. Fishing: Left fist over right; move hands as though holding fishing pole.

8. "It is the LORD!" John shouted. When Peter heard these words, he jumped in the water and swam to shore to be with Jesus. Jesus wanted Peter to know he was forgiven. Jesus said to Peter, "Feed My sheep. Feed My lambs." Jesus meant that He wanted Peter to tell others about God's love. Jesus hadn't given up on him! Jesus had given Peter important work to do. But best of all, Peter knew that Jesus had FORGIVEN him and that he could make a brand new start with Jesus!

8. Forgive: Stroke edge of left palm with right fingertips.

## Conclude the Story

**Why did Peter need to be forgiven?** (Broke his promise to Jesus and said three times he didn't know Jesus.) **How did Jesus show Peter he was forgiven?** (Helped him catch fish. Asked him to tell others about God. Didn't give up on Peter.)

**God doesn't give up on us, either. He loves us and wants to forgive us. And every time we ask God to forgive us, He will help us make a new start!**

## Matthew 28:16-20; Acts 1:1-11

# The Great Commission

## Materials

Drawing materials/equipment for teacher and each student.

## Tell the Story

As you tell each part of the story, draw each sketch. Students copy your sketches.

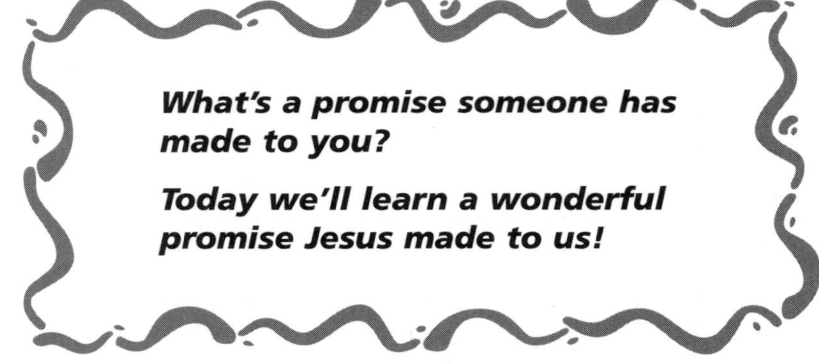


1. After Jesus died and came back to life, He visited His friends many times. Once, Jesus surprised two of His friends by walking with them along a road. Each time Jesus talked with His friends, He helped them understand more about God's good plans for them.

1. Draw road from two "S"s. Add stick figures.

2. Once when He was eating with His disciples, Jesus said, "Wait in Jerusalem for the gift My Father promised. In a few days, you will receive this IMPORTANT gift." God would send His Holy Spirit to help Jesus' followers know He was with them and to help them live as God wanted them to.

2. Gift box from lines and "3"s.

3. On another day, Jesus gave His friends more important instructions. "I want you to tell all the people in the world about My love for them," Jesus said. "Teach people EVERYWHERE how to obey My instructions about how to live." Jesus' friends may have thought, *How could we do a big job like that?* But then Jesus promised that He would be with His friends all the time, everywhere they went, always!

3. Megaphone: "O," lines and "C"s. Add "TELL EVERYONE!"

4. When it was time for Jesus to go back to heaven, His friends walked up the Mount of Olives to meet Him. (The Mount of Olives is a hill outside the city of Jerusalem where many olive trees grow.)

4. Ridge from "C"; trees from "3"s and lines.

5. When they were all together, Jesus said, "I want you to be witnesses of Me to people all over the world." Jesus wanted the disciples to tell others all the things they had seen Jesus do and all the words they had heard Him say.

"The Holy Spirit will help you," Jesus said. "Start in the city of Jerusalem. Then tell about Me outside the city. Don't forget the people in Judea and Samaria. Go all over the earth telling about Me!"

5. Draw 4 circles; add labels.

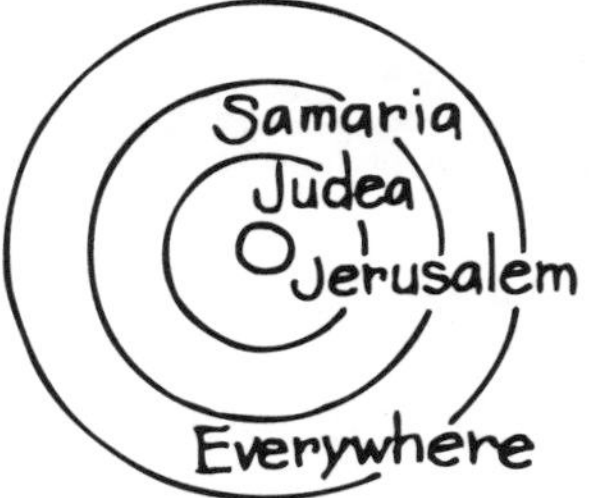


6. After Jesus said this, He began to rise from the ground, higher and higher until a cloud hid Him. The disciples were still looking up into the sky when, suddenly, two angels appeared! "Why do you stand here looking into the sky?" the angels asked. "Jesus has gone to heaven! Someday He will come back the same way He left."

6. Heads from "C"s; cloud from "3"s.

7. Jesus' friends walked back down the hill. They must have been VERY excited to know that Jesus would come back again. They may also have felt a little sad that Jesus was not with them anymore. But then they remembered the promise Jesus made: "I AM with you ALWAYS." Even though they could no longer see Him, He was still with them!

7. Add "I am with you always" to cloud.

8. Those first friends of Jesus obeyed His instructions. They waited in Jerusalem until God sent His Spirit to be with them and help them. Then the disciples went to MANY places, telling people about Him. Soon people EVERYWHERE were talking about the good news about Jesus!

8. Add arrows to circles in #5, beginning at Jerusalem.

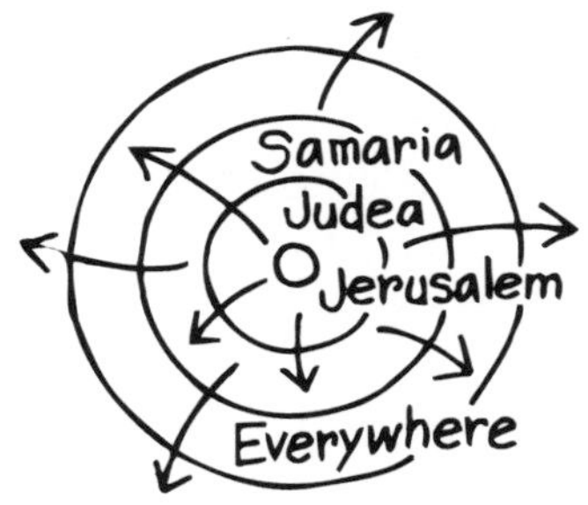


## Conclude the Story

**What promise did Jesus make to His disciples?** (To always be with them.) **What things do you think the disciples told others about Jesus?** (Jesus is alive. Jesus died for you.)

**Jesus came to earth and died on the cross to take the punishment for our sins. That was an important part of God's big plan. But Jesus came back to life! And because He is alive, we know He will keep His promise to be with us, the people in God's family, now and forever!** Talk with students about becoming Christians (see "Leading a Child to Christ" on p. 13).

**Acts 2**

# God Sends the Holy Spirit

## Materials

Drawing materials/equipment for teacher and each student.

## Tell the Story

As you tell each part of the story, draw each sketch. Students copy your sketches.

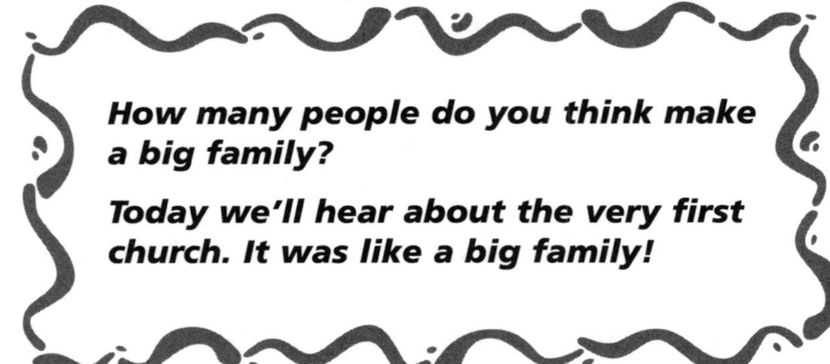


1. After God raised Jesus from the dead, Jesus talked with His friends many times. But one day, Jesus went back to heaven. *What's going to happen now?* the friends wondered.

1. Draw question mark; add face details.

2. Some of Jesus' friends may have thought about going back to their old jobs as fishermen or tax collectors. But they remembered Jesus' words before He left.

"Do not leave Jerusalem," Jesus had said. "Wait for the gift My Father promised you—the Holy Spirit. When the Holy Spirit comes, you will receive power and you will tell people everywhere about Me." So Jesus' friends stayed in Jerusalem together. They prayed and waited.

2. Draw fish and coins.

3. Ten days later on a special holiday called Pentecost, the waiting was OVER. While Jesus' friends were all together praying, they heard a sound like a rushing, powerful wind. They looked up from their praying to see what was happening. *What was THIS?* It looked like little flames of fire were burning above each of their heads! And when they began to talk, they were speaking other LANGUAGES! God had sent His Holy Spirit, just as Jesus had said He would!

3. Lines for wind; flame from "C"s.

4. This was too EXCITING to stay indoors! As Jesus' friends came outside, they saw a HUGE crowd of people coming toward them. These people had all heard the sound of the rushing wind, too. They came hurrying up to where Jesus' friends were.

4. House from "U"s, lines. Add "C"s for crowd.

5. As these people came near and listened, they heard the different languages Jesus' friends were speaking. Many of the people in that crowd were visiting Jerusalem from other places in the world. They were amazed to hear Jesus' friends speaking in their own languages!

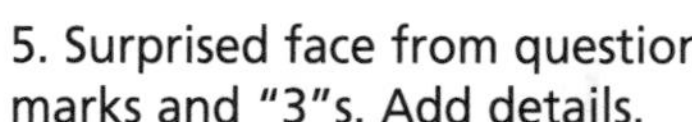

5. Surprised face from question marks and "3"s. Add details.

6. Then Peter began to explain the amazing things that were happening. Peter told them about Jesus and how He died on a cross. Peter said that Jesus came back to life to show that He truly was from God. The people asked Jesus' friends, "What shall we do?"

6. Exclamation point; draw lines to make cross.

7. Peter told them, "You must stop doing wrong and start obeying God. Believe in Jesus and be baptized. God will give you His gift of the Holy Spirit, too." And that day, about 3,000 people became part of God's family! This big family met every day. They sang and praised God and talked to each other about Jesus.

7. Print "3,000." Add faces.

8. This big family loved each other in a BIG way! They shared all the things they had. People sold things they owned so that they would have money to give to others who needed food or clothes. Their love came from God; His Holy Spirit helped them love each other. And every day, more and more people became part of God's family as the good news about Jesus spread throughout the city of Jerusalem.

8. Add a heart around faces.

## Conclude the Story

**What are some things Jesus' friends did to obey Jesus?** (They waited for the Holy Spirit. They told others about Him.) **to show God's love to each other?** (They shared with each other. They prayed together.)

**God's family still shows lots of love. That's the way Jesus said other people would know who was in His family: by the love we show each other.**

## Acts 2:42-47; 4:32-35; 5:12-16

# God's Family Shares

## Before the Story

Guide students to briefly practice signs for underlined words.

***How many people are in your family? How many people would it take to have a BIG family?***

***The people who loved Jesus when He lived on earth were like a family. Listen to find out what the people in that family did.***

## Tell the Story

As you tell the story, lead students in responding as shown when you say the underlined words.

1. After Jesus returned to heaven, God sent His Holy Spirit to Jesus' followers. Because of that gift, 3,000 people became part of God's <u>family</u> in just one day. What a BIG <u>family</u>! All the members of God's <u>family</u> listened carefully to the teachings of Jesus' followers, now called apostles. As God's <u>family</u> learned more and more about Jesus, they continued to grow! Let's discover how they helped each other grow as God's children.

1. Family: With thumbs and index fingers touching, make outward circle until hands touch.

2. First, whenever they <u>worshiped</u> together, whether at the Temple or in each other's homes, the members of God's family sang praises, prayed and read and talked about God's Word. They <u>worshiped</u> God with all their hearts. They were glad to be together!

2. Worship: Left hand over right fist; move hands to body and bow head.

3. A second way they helped each other was by inviting each other over to their homes to <u>eat</u> their <u>meals</u> together. God's family also celebrated a special <u>meal</u> together, called the Lord's Supper, in order to remember that Jesus died on the cross in order to forgive their sins.

3. Eat, meal: Fingertips touching, move right hand to mouth a few times.

4. But this family did even more! Every day, members of God's family met together to worship God at the <u>Temple</u> in Jerusalem and to hear more about Jesus. That was the third way they helped each other grow as God's children. Many people who didn't believe in Jesus came to the <u>Temple</u> as well. When these people heard the teachings of God's followers, many of them believed in Jesus and became members of God's family, too!

4. Temple: Place heel of right fist on back of left fist.

5. God's family helped each other in a fourth way: The apostles showed love and care for others in ways that helped people see God's power. People with sick relatives and friends gathered from the towns around Jerusalem. All of those who were sick were healed! What an exciting time it was for God's family!

5. Sick: Right middle finger on head, left middle finger on stomach.

6. These people in God's family loved God and each other so much, they shared everything they had with each other. This sharing was the fifth way they kept growing as a family of believers in Jesus. Nobody said "That's MINE!" about anything. Everything they had they shared. They took good care of each other and made sure that no one in God's family was hungry or needy. They followed Jesus' example to love and obey God.

6. Shared: Move right hand back and forth on left.

7. In order to take care of the members of God's family who were poor, some of the wealthy people would sell their land or other belongings. Then they would bring the money to the apostles and hand it ALL over to them! The apostles would then give the money to anyone in God's family who needed it. They wanted to please God by loving and caring for each other.

7. Money: Touching, right fingertips strike left palm a few times.

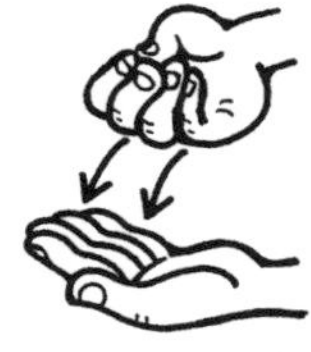

8. It was a BIG family, and they loved each other in five BIG ways! That love came from God's gift, the Holy Spirit. His Holy Spirit helped them love each other. Every day, more and more people became part of God's family as the good news about Jesus spread throughout Jerusalem.

God's family still shows lots of love. That's the way Jesus said other people would know who was in His family: by the love we show each other.

8. Love: Cross fists over heart.

## Conclude the Story

**What are some of the ways the people in God's family helped each other?** (Worshiped and ate together. Shared belongings. Gave money for poor people.) **What did the actions of God's family show?** (How much they loved God and wanted to obey Him.)

**When we become members of God's family, God gives us everything we need in order to love and obey Him. As we worship God for His gifts to us, other people come to believe in Jesus and celebrate with us!**

## Acts 3:1-16

# A Lame Man Walks Again

### Materials

Drawing materials/equipment for teacher and each student.

***What are some things you can do with your feet and legs?***

***Today we'll hear what happened to a man who couldn't use his legs.***

### Tell the Story

As you tell each part of the story, draw each sketch. Students copy your sketches.

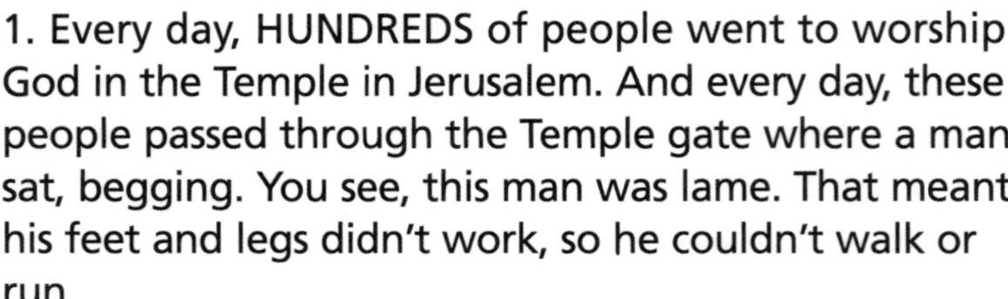

1. Every day, HUNDREDS of people went to worship God in the Temple in Jerusalem. And every day, these people passed through the Temple gate where a man sat, begging. You see, this man was lame. That meant his feet and legs didn't work, so he couldn't walk or run.

1. Draw "X" for legs; add stick figure.

2. In his hands, the lame man held a bowl. Every day, as people went into the Temple, he asked them to give him money. He needed help! But the only help he got was coins in his beggar's bowl.

2. Draw bowl from "O" and "U."

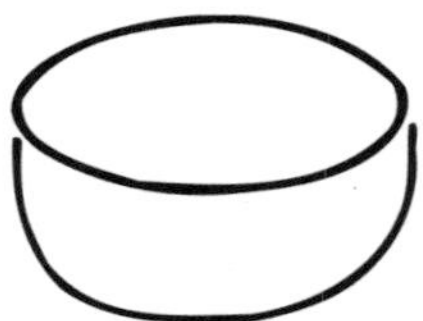

3. One day, when Peter and John were on their way into the Temple, the lame man called, "Do you have some money for a poor lame man?" But Peter knew the lame man needed something else besides money. Peter said, "I have no silver or gold to give you. But I WILL give you what I have."

3. Make faces from "P" and "J."

4. Peter took the lame man by the hand and helped him to his feet, saying, "In the name of Jesus, walk!" And the man DID! His feet and legs were suddenly STRONG! He walked. He leaped!

4. Leaping figure from "N."

5. The man was so excited and happy, he went into the Temple with Peter and John, jumping up and down and praising God!

5. Draw man's face near Peter's and John's.

6. The people in the Temple were amazed. "That's the same man who's been sitting and begging by the Temple gate for years!" someone said. Everyone wondered how this man could be jumping and walking! Soon a crowd had gathered!

6. Add "C"s for crowd around Peter, John and man.

7. Peter said, "Why does it surprise you that this man can walk? WE haven't made this man walk by our own goodness or power! It is the power of God—the power of the same God who sent Jesus to you, even though you killed Him—it is HIS power that has healed this man. By trusting in the name of Jesus, this man is completely well!"

7. Print "GOD"; add burst from "V"s.

8. The people listened as Peter told all about God's power. And THOUSANDS more people believed in Jesus and became part of God's big family, the Church!

8. Add smiling faces to crowd.

## Conclude the Story

**What did the lame man usually get when he begged?** (Money.) **What did he need most?** (To be able to walk again.) **What did Peter give him to help him?** (He healed Him with God's power.)

**When we give to others, we don't have to give money, either. We can give to others by being friendly, kind or patient. Jesus helps us give to other people in more ways than just giving money!**

### Acts 4:32—5:11

# God's Family Learns to Give

## Materials

Play dough (¼ cup, or 2 oz.) and plastic knife for each student.

## Tell the Story

**Follow along with me as we use our dough to tell today's story.**

***What is something that is really hard for a kid your age to share?***

***Today we'll hear about some people who shared—but only to try to impress people.***

1. **Flatten your dough and cut out a coat shape.** At the time when the first Christians in Jerusalem began to meet together, there were no hospitals or places for homeless people to stay. There were no food pantries where hungry people could get food. Instead, God's family shared everything they had with each other. A man who had two coats gave one to a man who had no coat. A woman who had extra grain shared it with a hungry neighbor. The first Christians were glad to share!

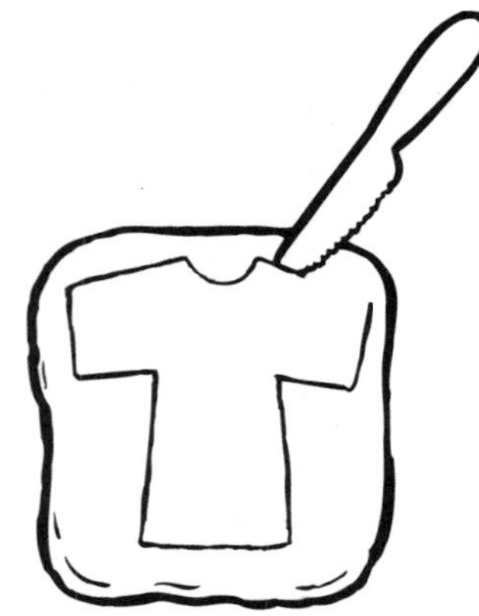

The Bible says that there were NO poor people in this church, simply because everyone shared. Whenever people who owned land sold their land, they brought the money they made to the church leaders. The church leaders gave the money to whomever needed it.

2. **Make the letter B.** One member of God's family in Jerusalem was named Joseph. The church leaders nicknamed him "Barnabas," which means "son of encouragement." They called him this because his joyful giving encouraged everyone else! One day Barnabas brought the apostles a large amount of money.

"I sold my field. Here is all the money I got for it. Please, use it to help the others," he may have said.

Everyone must have been quite impressed with such a generous gift. But Barnabas hadn't given the money to impress anyone. He gave it simply because he wanted to show his love for Jesus and help God's family.

3. **Divide your dough in half and flatten one half. Cut 10 flat circles for coins.** Now a husband and wife named Ananias (an-uh-NI-uhs) and Sapphira (suh-FI-ruh) were part of the Jerusalem church, too. Surely they had noticed that Barnabas was very well respected. It might be that Ananias and Sapphira wanted to be as well liked

and respected as Barnabas. Maybe they were a little jealous of all those thank-yous that Barnabas had gotten. Whatever it was they felt, they decided to copy Barnabas.

Soon Ananias and Sapphira sold a field, too. But instead of giving all the money they had made to the church, they agreed that they'd keep part of the money.

4. **From the other half of your dough, make an open bag. Then put eight coins into the bag and close it to make a money bag.** When Ananias brought the rest of the money to Peter, one of the church leaders, Ananias acted like he was giving ALL the money he had made. He probably thought Peter would be very impressed. But instead Peter shook his head sadly.

Peter looked at Ananias. "Why did you lie?" he asked. "You could have KEPT all of the money if you wanted. You haven't lied to me. You have lied to GOD!"

When Ananias heard these words, he died right there on the spot! Some young men of the church buried him.

Meanwhile, Sapphira waited and waited for Ananias to return. She finally came looking for her husband.

When Peter saw Sapphira, he asked her if what he'd been given was the full price for the land. Peter wondered, *Would she tell the truth?*

"Oh, yes," Sapphira answered. "That was the price!"

Peter asked. "Why would you agree to lie to God?"

*Lie to God?* Sapphira must have thought. Then she realized what she had done. Like her husband, she died instantly.

Barnabas gave his generous gift out of love. Ananias and Sapphira gave their money for a selfish reason. It wasn't wrong for them to give only part of the money they made. But it was wrong for them to lie to God and God's family about what they were doing.

## Conclude the Story

**Why were there no poor people in God's family at Jerusalem?** (Everyone shared what they had.) **What did Barnabas do? Why?** (Sold land and gave all the money to the church. Gave out of love.) **What was wrong with Ananias and Sapphira's actions?** (They said one thing, but they did something else.)

**We can all think of ways to show goodness in our lives. But goodness is more than just talking about doing good things. This story helps us know that a big part of goodness is living with God's help so that our actions match our words.**

## Acts 6:1-7

# The Hungry Widows

### Materials

Play dough (¼ cup, or 2 oz.) for each student.

### Tell the Story

**Follow along with me as we use our dough to tell today's story.**

***When has a friend had a problem? How did that friend solve the problem?***

***Today we're going to find out how some people in God's family solved a problem together.***

1. **From part of your dough, make many small balls for people.** All over Jerusalem, many people heard the good news about Jesus. People believed Jesus is the Son of God and asked God to forgive their sins. THOUSANDS of people became part of God's family!

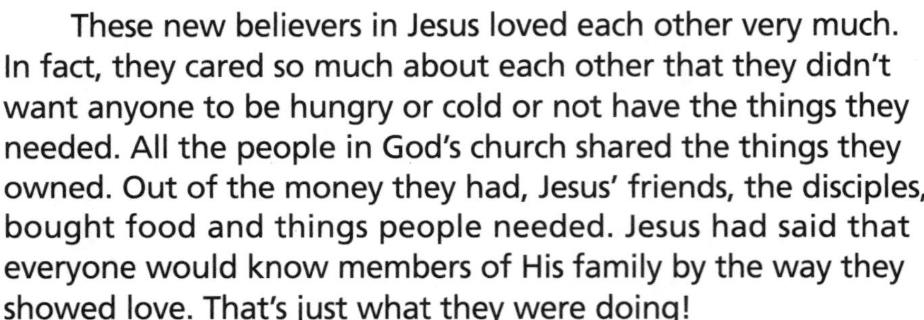

These new believers in Jesus loved each other very much. In fact, they cared so much about each other that they didn't want anyone to be hungry or cold or not have the things they needed. All the people in God's church shared the things they owned. Out of the money they had, Jesus' friends, the disciples, bought food and things people needed. Jesus had said that everyone would know members of His family by the way they showed love. That's just what they were doing!

2. **Divide your people into two groups. From the rest of your dough, make some VERY small balls for food.** But in this growing family of God, there were some widows who had a need. (A widow is a woman whose husband has died. In Bible times, widows often had no way to earn money.) These widows needed help to get enough food. They were not from Jerusalem, however; they were from countries where the people spoke Greek.

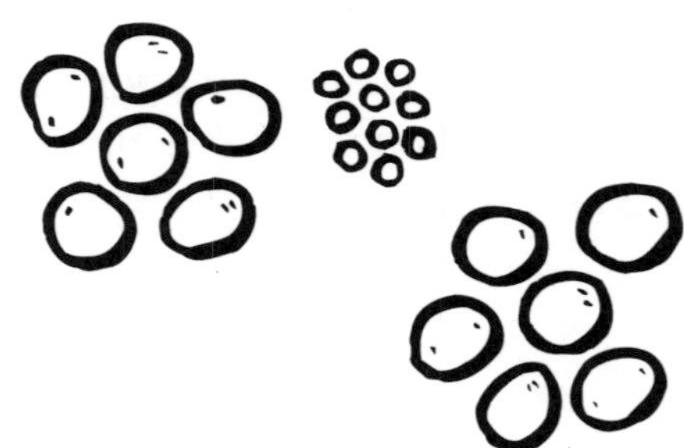

Now the people in the church were already generously giving food and money to anyone who had a need, these widows included. But the problem was this: The Greek widows were not getting as MUCH food as the Hebrew widows—the widows who had always lived in Jerusalem. Maybe it was just because someone forgot. But the Greek widows might have felt it was because they were different. Maybe they felt as if the members of God's family didn't care as MUCH about them as they did about the Hebrew widows.

These Greek widows could have gotten angry. They could have quit meeting with others in their church family. But instead they talked to Jesus' friends about their need.

3. **Divide your very small balls, giving more of them to one group of people than what you give to the other group.** "We're not getting as much food as the other widows," the Greek widows said. "We're not being treated fairly."

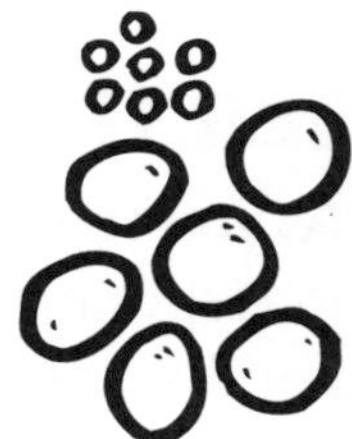

Jesus' disciples carefully listened to the women. They talked about this problem and then called everyone together to talk about how to solve the problem.

Jesus' disciples said, "We need to make sure no one goes hungry. We need to be sure everyone is treated fairly. Because we spend a lot of our time preaching and telling others about Jesus, we need helpers. So let's choose some other people who can take over the work of making sure everyone gets enough food."

4. **Collect your very small balls and divide them in half. Give half to each group of people.** Everyone listened carefully. They thought about what the disciples had said. They agreed that having more people to help with the sharing of food was a good way to take care of the problem. They chose seven men for this special job and prayed for them, asking God to help them do this work in a good way.

After that, we never hear again about ANYONE in the first church family who didn't have enough or who felt treated unfairly! God's family listened carefully and cared about the problem of the Greek widows. That's one way they showed they loved Jesus. And it's also a way they showed goodness in their lives!

## Conclude the Story

**What was the problem in this story?** (Some widows were not getting as much food as some of the others.) **What was done to solve the problem?** (Widows told disciples. Disciples listened carefully and thought of a way to solve the problem.) **What good thing did the disciples do?** (Chose seven men to help distribute the food evenly.)

**When we listen carefully to others, it helps us know good and right things to do. Then we know that God's Holy Spirit is helping us show goodness!**

**Acts 6—8:1**

# Stephen Obeys God

## Before the Story

Guide students to briefly practice signs for underlined words.

*Who is someone you think of as a hero? Why? What is that person like?*

*Today we're going to find out who Stephen, a man in Bible times, said his heroes were and why.*

## Tell the Story

As you tell the story, lead students in responding as shown when you say the underlined words.

1. After Jesus died and rose again, more and more people became part of God's family. These people became the first church. In that church, everyone <u>shared</u> what they had. But because some needy widows had been overlooked, Jesus' disciples called everyone together and asked them to choose seven men whose job would be to take care of the everyday needs of the church, like <u>sharing</u> food and clothes.

1. Share: Move right hand back and forth on left.

2. One of the men they chose was named Stephen. Everyone knew that Stephen loved and obeyed God with his whole heart and had great faith in Him. Stephen not only made sure people had food and clothes, but he also began to tell about Jesus. Some men who didn't believe in Jesus began to <u>argue</u> with Stephen. They got very angry at things he said about Jesus, and they dragged Stephen to the religious leaders and <u>argued</u> against him, telling lies about him.

2. Argue: Index fingers move up and down alternately.

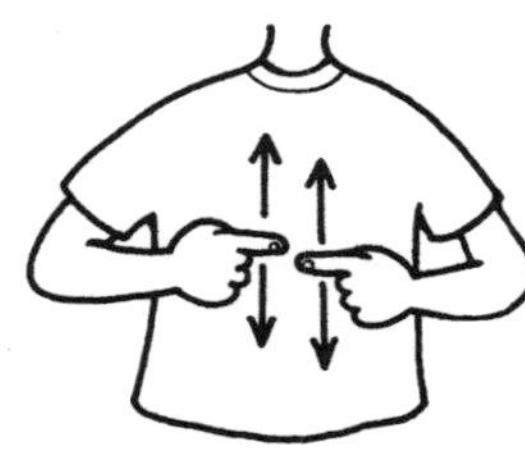

3. The leaders wanted to know if the arguments they had heard about Stephen's words were true. Stephen answered their question by telling a story—the story of God's people. He told how God had first chosen Abraham. He told how Abraham believed God and showed his faith in God by <u>traveling</u> from Ur to Canaan as God showed him where to go. No one could argue with that.

3. Traveling: Two bent fingers of right hand move in wavy forward path.

4. Stephen went on to tell how Joseph, Abraham's great-grandson, had faith in God and obeyed. Joseph had been taken from Canaan to Egypt, but he trusted God through many hard times and then saved his <u>family</u>. Joseph invited his entire <u>family</u> and all his relatives to come to live in Egypt.

4. Family: With thumbs and index fingers touching, make outward circle until hands touch.

5. Stephen told how Moses had shown faith in God when he led the very same family out of Egypt and back to Canaan again. And now that family had grown into a nation! Stephen described how God's law guided His people and how the Israelites had disobeyed God's law by making idols and worshiping them. But even when they disobeyed, God did not forget His people. He gave them judges to rule them, and the Tabernacle, a place to worship Him.

5. Law: Extend right thumb and index finger, move down left palm.

6. Stephen kept preaching, telling how God gave the people of Israel kings to rule them. Stephen told how God loved King David who wanted to build a Temple to honor God. He told how David's son King Solomon had built that Temple. But Stephen reminded the people who were listening that Solomon himself, and the prophet Isaiah, had said that God doesn't live in a building. He is far bigger and stronger and more wonderful than anything people can imagine!

6. Build: Move fingers on top of each other a few times.

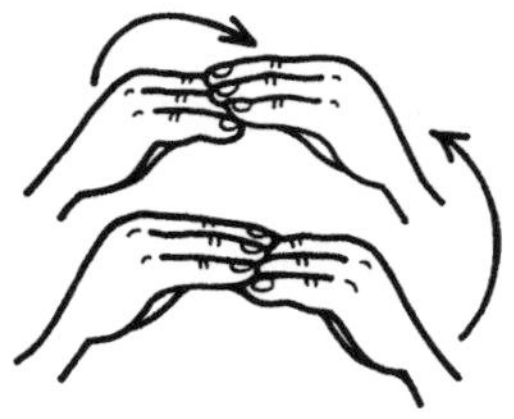

7. Next, Stephen told how God had sent prophets with His messages to warn the people to remember to obey God. The prophets had also told the people that God would send a Savior. Stephen reminded them how these prophets had often been badly treated and even killed because the people did not want to be reminded of God's laws and promises. Then Stephen said, "Just like your ancestors killed the prophets who told about the coming of the Righteous One—Jesus—you have betrayed and murdered Him!"

7. Prophet: Under left hand, two fingers of right hand move away from eyes and point forward; hands move down sides at same time.

8. WELL! The council and the others who heard Stephen became SO angry that they grabbed him and dragged Stephen out of the city. Leaving their cloaks with a young man named Saul, they picked up stones and threw them at Stephen. Stephen fell to his knees and prayed. Then he died from the stones that hit him. At the time, Saul thought this was good. But later, Saul met Jesus. He became Paul, who wrote a lot of what is now our New Testament! And Paul wrote in our Bible how Stephen's obedient actions encouraged him and helped him be brave for God, too.

8. Wrote: Touch thumb and right index finger; make wavy line across left palm.

## Conclude the Story

**What kind of person was Stephen?** (Loved God. Had great faith in God.) **What story did Stephen tell?** (The story of men who led God's people to obey God.)

**Stephen told people about Jesus, even when it was hard to do. Stephen's act of faith later helped Saul, who became Paul, believe in God. Stephen's faith and the faith of many thousands of other people who obeyed God help us remember to show our faith in God, too.**

**Acts 8:26-40**

# Philip and the Ethiopian

## Before the Story

Guide students to briefly practice signs for underlined words.

## Tell the Story

As you tell the story, lead students in responding as shown when you say the underlined words.

***When have you read something that was hard to understand?***

***Today we'll find out about a time a man was reading something in the Bible he didn't understand.***

1. Philip was a part of the first church family. He had been chosen to help make sure people's needs were taken care of. Philip's job had a special title: deacon. "Deacon" means servant. And Philip did a fine job of serving people who needed food. But helping to make sure people got enough food was not the only thing Philip did! He also told many people about Jesus.

1. Food: Fingertips touching, move right hand to mouth a few times.

2. One time, God sent an ANGEL to Philip with an important message. The angel told Philip, "Go south on the desert road that leads from Jerusalem to Gaza." Traveling to Gaza wasn't what Philip had been planning to do that day, but Philip changed his plans! He obeyed the angel and began to walk south down the desert road.

2. Angel: Fingertips on shoulders; draw away and out, waving up and down.

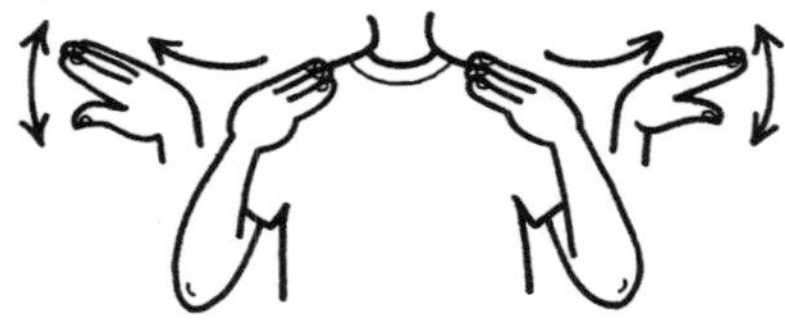

3. As he walked, Philip heard the rumbling sound of a chariot on the road. A chariot is a kind of cart pulled by horses. Important people rode in chariots. Philip saw that it was a fancy chariot, and the man inside was an important leader in a country called Ethiopia. He was in charge of all of the country's money.

3. Horse: Touch forehead with right thumb; bend and unbend first two fingers a few times.

4. Philip could see that this important Ethiopian man was reading from God's Word. God's Spirit said to Philip, "Get close to that chariot!"

Philip began to RUN! Philip kept on running, and soon he was running next to the chariot. He could hear the man in the chariot reading out loud from God's Word.

4. Run: Hook right index finger to left thumb; move forward and repeatedly bend fingers.

5. Philip realized the Ethiopian man was reading from one of the prophet's messages in God's Word. As he ran next to the chariot, Philip panted, "Do you understand what you're reading?"

The Ethiopian man looked up to see Philip jogging along beside him. He said, "How can I understand, unless someone explains it to me? Please, come up and sit with me!"

5. Reading: Move index and middle fingers down left palm.

6. The chariot slowed down and Philip jumped in. He could see that the man was reading in the Old Testament book of Isaiah. The man asked Philip a question. "Who do these words tell about?" Well, Philip knew the answer to THAT question! He began to tell the man about Jesus and how Jesus had been treated just as God's Word had said He would be. Then Philip went on to tell the man ALL about the good news of Jesus!

6. Question: Outline a question mark with right index finger.

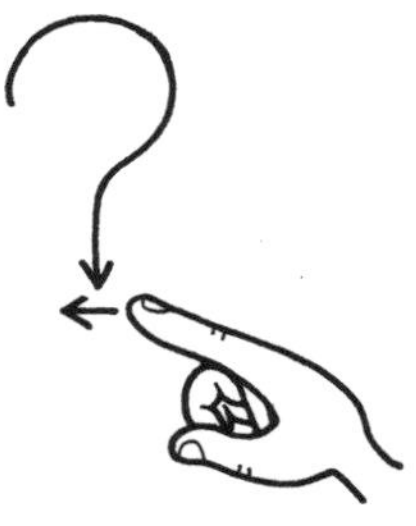

7. As they rode along in the chariot, the Ethiopian man believed what Philip told him about Jesus. Then the chariot rolled past a place where there was water. The Ethiopian man said, "Look! Here is some water. Why shouldn't I be baptized?" (Being baptized is a way of using water to show that a person trusts in Jesus to forgive his or her sins.)

7. Water: Extend three fingers of right hand; touch mouth a few times.

8. Philip agreed. The man called to his driver, "Stop the chariot!" Philip and the Ethiopian man got out and went down into the water, where Philip baptized the man. Then God took Philip and set him in a town called Azotus, where Philip told MORE people about Jesus!

Meanwhile, the Ethiopian man got back into his chariot. He went on his way back to his country, praising and thanking Jesus for making him part of God's family!

8. God: Point right index finger; lower and open hand at chest.

## Conclude the Story

**Who was Philip?** (A deacon. A man who helped others.) **What did God send an angel to tell him? Who was on that road?** (To go down a certain road. An Ethiopian official.) **What did Philip tell the man?** (Told him about the scroll he was reading. Told him about Jesus.) **What did the man ask Philip to do?** (To baptize him.)

**God helps us learn about Jesus and guides our actions through His Word. God's Word is one of God's gifts to us.**

Acts 9:1-31

# Saul's Conversion

## Materials

Drawing materials/equipment for teacher and each student.

## Tell the Story

As you tell each part of the story, draw each sketch. Students copy your sketches.

***What is something you might do to get another person's attention?***

***Today we'll hear how God got one man's attention!***

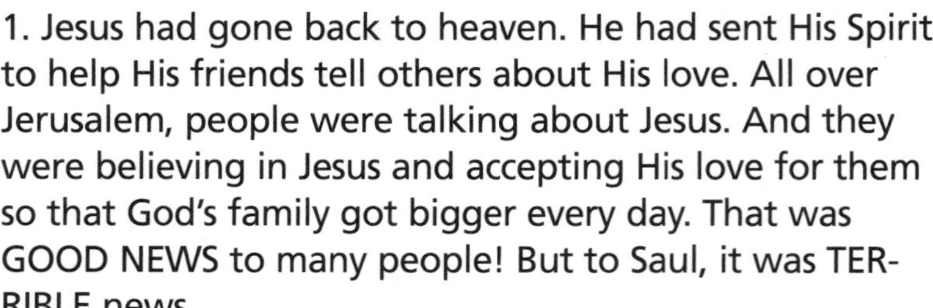

1. Jesus had gone back to heaven. He had sent His Spirit to help His friends tell others about His love. All over Jerusalem, people were talking about Jesus. And they were believing in Jesus and accepting His love for them so that God's family got bigger every day. That was GOOD NEWS to many people! But to Saul, it was TERRIBLE news.

1. Draw large heart. Print "GOD'S FAMILY" inside.

2. Saul was an important religious leader in Jerusalem. But he didn't believe Jesus was God's Son. And he was angry that so many people DID believe that Jesus was sent from God. He was so angry, he wanted to punish people who loved Jesus!

2. Draw "no" slash over heart

3. First, Saul got permission from the religious leaders to throw the people who loved Jesus into JAIL. Then Saul left for Damascus (duh-MAS-kuhs). People came to Damascus from all over the world. Saul thought that if he could keep people there from telling about Jesus by putting them into jail, maybe he could stop this talk about Jesus from spreading.

3. Write "jail." Add face to "a," bars from other letters.

4. As Saul and the men traveling with him got close to Damascus, a bright light from heaven suddenly flashed like lightning around Saul! WOW! Saul fell to the ground. "Saul, Saul!" a voice said. "Why are you fighting against Me?"

4. Flash of light from "V"s.

5. Saul gasped, "Who . . . who are You, Lord?"

"I am Jesus, the One you are trying to hurt." UH-OH! Saul had been so certain that Jesus was NOT God's Son. But now he heard Jesus speaking to him! "Go into the city," Jesus told Saul. "You will be told what to do next."

5. Scared face from "O"s, "C" and "3"s.

6. When Saul got up, he couldn't see anything. The people with him took him by the hand and led him to a place to stay. For three days, Saul didn't eat or drink; he just prayed.

6. Kneeling figure from circle, line and "V"s.

7. Soon, God sent a man named Ananias to help Saul. Ananias prayed for Saul, and Saul could SEE again! Saul finally understood that Jesus is God's Son and that He is alive. Now Saul himself wanted to be Jesus' friend! Ananias baptized Saul and brought him to meet Jesus' friends in Damascus—the same people Saul had wanted to arrest three days before!

7. River from "S"s; add stick figures.

8. Jesus' friends were afraid of Saul at first. But they soon saw that Saul was truly a changed man. So Jesus' friends helped him and after a few days, Saul began to tell people all over Damascus the good news about Jesus! When people heard Saul (later called Paul), they were AMAZED.

8. Scared face to smiling face.

## Conclude the Story

**What was Saul like before he met Jesus on the road to Damascus?** (He wanted to hurt people who believed in Jesus.) **What difference did meeting Jesus make in Saul's life?** (He stopped being angry at the people who loved Jesus. He believed that Jesus is God's Son. He told others about Jesus.)

**God invites each of us to choose to believe that Jesus is His Son and that He died to take the punishment for our sins. When we accept Jesus' love for us, we become members of God's family.**

**Acts 10**

# God's Message for Peter

## Materials

Drawing materials/equipment for teacher and each student.

## Tell the Story

As you tell each part of the story, draw each sketch. Students copy your sketches.

***Who are some kinds of people a kid your age might have trouble accepting?***

***Today we'll hear how Peter learned to accept people different from him.***

1. In God's growing family, most of the people were Jews. Jesus was a Jew and so were His disciples. But Peter, one of Jesus' disciples, learned in a very strange way that God's love is for everyone—even for people who aren't Jews. (People who aren't Jews are called Gentiles.) Here's what happened.

1. Draw stick figures; add "Jews" and "Gentiles."

2. A man who was a Gentile, named Cornelius, loved God. One day while Cornelius was praying, God sent an angel to him. "Cornelius," the angel said, "God hears your prayers. Send for a man named Peter in the city of Joppa."

2. Angel from "V"s and "O"; add details.

3. Right away Cornelius sent three men to Joppa so that they could invite Peter to his house. These three men arrived in Joppa the next day.

3. Print "Joppa" and add 3 faces.

4. When they arrived, Peter was up on the flat roof of the house. Peter was praying while he waited for lunch to be ready. While Peter prayed, God showed him a strange dream: a big sheet with all KINDS of animals in it, from frogs and lizards to pigs and horses!

4. Sheet from "C"; snake from 2 "S"s; pig from "O"s and "V"s; horse from "U", "V"s and lines.

5. God said to Peter, "Peter, you can eat any of these kinds of meat for your lunch!" Well, Peter knew that Jews were not allowed to eat these kinds of meat, so he said to God, "Certainly NOT! Nothing unclean has EVER been in MY mouth."

"Don't call anything unclean that I have made CLEAN!" God said.

5. Add "no" slash.

6. God showed Peter this same strange dream TWO more times! While Peter thought about this dream, God said, "Three men are at your house. Go with them!"

6. Draw thought balloon.

7. Peter went downstairs. Sure enough, three men were at the gate wanting to see him! And they were Gentiles, people that Jews were supposed to stay away from. But God had said to go WITH them. Then Peter must have understood: ALL kinds of people can be part of God's family. So the next day, they all set out for Cornelius's house.

7. Draw "1,2,3" and add details to make 3 different faces.

8. When Peter and his new friends got to Cornelius's house, they found that the house was full of people. Peter said to all the people, "I know now that God loves EVERY person. He has sent me to tell you the good news about Jesus."

8. House from 2 triangles and lines. "C"s for crowd; add faces.

9. The people believed the things Peter said. Right then and there, they became part of God's family! And right then and there, God's Spirit came to them JUST like He had come to Peter. EVERYONE was the same to God. God LOVED them ALL!

9. Add heart around "Jews" and "Gentiles" in #1.

## Conclude the Story

**What did Peter learn about God's love?** (His love is for everyone—Jews and Gentiles.) **How did Peter show God's love and acceptance?** (He told Cornelius, a Gentile, the good news about Jesus.)

**God's love is for everyone, not just people who are like us. And just as He loves everyone, He wants us to love and accept every person in His family!**

## Acts 11:19-30; 2 Corinthians 8—9

# Giving to God's Family

## Materials

Play dough (¼ cup, or 2 oz.) for each student.

***Who are some people who might have a lot of money? What do you think they use their money for?***

***In our Bible story today, we'll find out how some people used their money.***

## Tell the Story

**Follow along with me as we use our dough to tell today's story.**

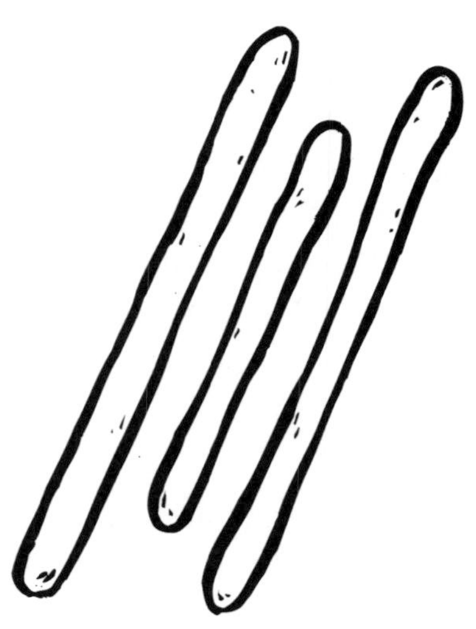

1. **Make several long ropes from your dough. Then use the ropes to make a face with a talking mouth.** It had not been very long since Jesus had died, risen and gone back to heaven. Jesus' followers were busy telling EVERYONE the good news about Jesus! This good news about Jesus was being spread as far away as Antioch, a city hundreds of miles (kilometers) from Jerusalem. And not just Jewish people were becoming members of God's family. Many others were believing, too.

Two of Jesus' followers, Paul and Barnabas, were living and working in Antioch, teaching the believers and telling others about Jesus. Then one day, some men from Jerusalem came to visit them. One of the men, Agabus, said that a severe famine would soon spread through the land. The people in Jerusalem, including all of Jesus' followers who lived there, would not have enough to eat!

The people in Antioch could have said, "Why should we help THOSE people? They're too far away!"

But they DIDN'T say those things. Instead, they were glad to help their Christian brothers and sisters who were going to be having trouble getting food. After all, they were all part of God's family, no matter how far away from each other they lived!

2. **Turn face into a smiling face.** So the believers in Antioch gave as much money as they could to help the believers in Jerusalem. Paul and Barnabas returned to Jerusalem with the gift of money from the believers in Antioch. Later they continued their travels, going to many other cities and telling people about Jesus. Sometimes as he traveled, Paul would stop and stay in a particular city for a while to teach the people more about Jesus.

One place Paul stopped and stayed for a while was the city of Corinth, which was very far away from Jerusalem. He lived there for about a year and a half. Eventually, Paul traveled on, but he sent letters back to the people of Corinth. He wrote letters that helped them know how God wanted them to live.

3. **Make many small coins.** In the first letter that Paul wrote to his friends at Corinth, he asked them to save some money every week for the Christians in the city of Jerusalem. These Christians still needed help from believers in other parts of the world.

Just like the people of Antioch, the Corinthians began to save money to send to the believers in Jerusalem. They knew it pleased God for them to give what they had to help others who were in need.

Because traveling in those days took lots of time, weeks and months went by before the Corinthians got another letter from Paul. "I'm coming to Corinth on my way to Jerusalem," Paul wrote. He was going to take the money they had saved and give it to their brothers and sisters who were in need.

4. **With a friend, make the word "GIVE" from coins.** Paul wrote, "I know you are very willing to take care of your brothers and sisters in God's family. I've told other people about your giving and it's made them want to give, too!"

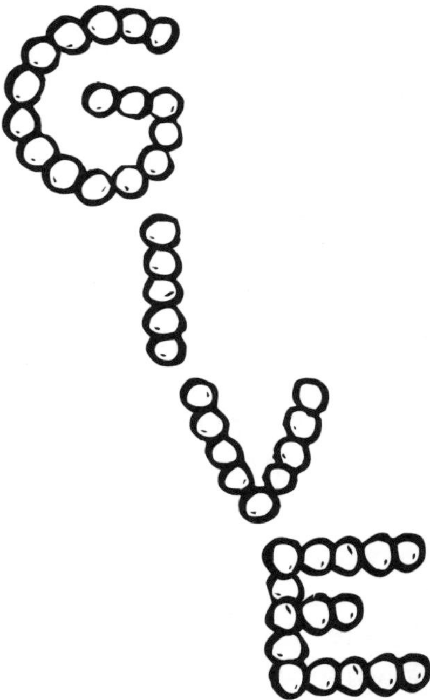


Then Paul wrote an example to help the Corinthians understand more about giving. He wrote, "Giving to help others in God's family is a lot like a farmer planting seeds. If he only plants a few seeds, he'll only grow a few plants. But if the farmer plants a lot of seeds, he grows a lot of plants and has a BIG harvest! God will always give you everything you need, so you can give generously.

"This giving does more than just help to take care of the needs of your brothers and sisters in Jerusalem. It will also make everyone who hears about it glad. They will praise God! And it will show them that you are obeying and trusting God."

## Conclude the Story

**How did people in our Bible story show that they thought giving to others was really important?** (They gave whatever they could to help people they didn't even know.) **Why do you think they wanted to give to others?** (God had been good to them by giving to them, so they wanted to be good to others. They wanted to please God, because they loved Him.)

**Paul took that money to the poor people in Jerusalem a long time ago. But the very same kind of giving still happens today. Helping others by sharing what God gives us is one way to show God's goodness.**

**Acts 12:1-17**

# Peter Escapes from Prison

## Materials

Drawing materials/equipment for teacher and each student.

***When is a time you've been afraid?***

***Today we'll hear how God rescued Peter from a very scary situation!***

## Tell the Story

As you tell each part of the story, draw each sketch. Students copy your sketches.

1. It was time for the Passover, usually a joyful time in Jerusalem. But for God's growing family, it was a SCARY time. You see, Herod, the Roman ruler, had sent soldiers to arrest and KILL James, one of Jesus' followers! Everyone in God's family was very sad. And they were wondering what that cruel ruler Herod would do next!

1. Draw scared faces, sad faces, question marks.

2. It wasn't long before Herod did something else to make them afraid. He sent soldiers to arrest Peter, another one of Jesus' friends. Herod had Peter put into prison. Herod was planning to keep Peter in prison until the Passover holiday was over. Then Herod planned to accuse Peter of doing something wrong and put him on trial, so Herod could kill him, too.

2. Peter from "P" and "3"s; add prison bars.

3. Peter's friends knew that Peter might be killed. So guess what they did. They prayed! They met at the house of a woman named Mary and prayed and prayed with all their might, asking God to protect Peter and to help them.

3. Draw praying hands from "U"s and lines; add face.

4. The night before Herod was going to have Peter killed, God sent an angel to Peter's prison cell. The angel said, "Quick, get up!" And the chains around Peter's arms just fell off! Then Peter and the angel walked right past the guards!

4. Moon from "C"s; add stars.

5. When Peter and the angel got to the huge iron gate leading to the city, the gate opened as if an invisible hand was pushing it! Peter followed the angel to the end of the street, and then the angel simply DISAPPEARED!

5. Gate from "U"; add open side and stick figures.

6. Peter hurried to the house where his friends were praying. He knocked on the door. A servant girl named Rhoda called out, "Who's there?"

"Peter!" he answered. Rhoda was so overjoyed that she ran to the room full of praying people without even opening the door!

"Peter's at the door! Peter's at the door!" she cried.

"WHAT?" they asked."You must be crazy! Peter's in prison. He can't be at the door."

6. Knocking hand and door from "U"s; add details.

7. But Peter kept knocking on the door! When Rhoda finally opened it, Peter's friends were amazed and happy to see him!

7. Draw happy, amazed faces.

8. "God heard your prayers for me," Peter said. "God rescued me! God sent an angel in answer to your prayers!"

Everyone was VERY glad that Peter was safe. They knew now that God had heard and answered their prayers! And so they prayed again—to THANK God for sending Peter safely back to them!

8. Make an acrostic of "PRAYER," "ANSWER" and "SURPRISE!"

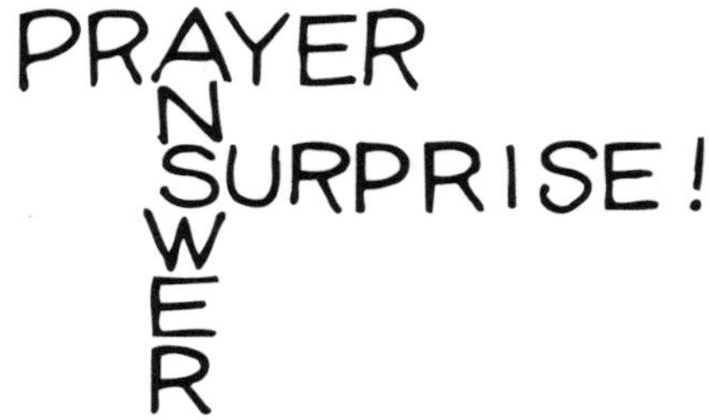


## Conclude the Story

**Where was Peter? What did his friends do? How did God surprise Peter?** (Sent an angel to his prison cell.) **When were Peter's friends surprised?** (When Peter came to their house.)

**Sometimes when we pray, we may think that God doesn't hear us because He doesn't answer us when we expect He will or in the way we expect He will. But God really DOES hear—and He DOES answer our prayers. Sometimes, He answers them in ways that we don't expect! He loves us and He loves to surprise us!**

Acts 14:8-20

# Paul Preaches in Lystra

## Materials

Drawing materials/equipment for teacher and each student.

***What's something great you have heard about?***

***Today we'll find out about the great things Paul told!***

## Tell the Story

As you tell each part of the story, draw each sketch. Students copy your sketches.

1. The good news of Jesus was spreading all over! Paul and his friend Barnabas were telling God's good news from city to city. But some of the religious leaders were FURIOUS at Paul and Barnabas! The leaders wanted Paul and Barnabas to stop teaching about Jesus. The leaders even tried to get people to KILL Paul and Barnabas!

1. Draw 2 cities from rectangles; add walking stick figures.

2. But Paul and Barnabas didn't stop telling about Jesus. They knew God is greater than anyone. They trusted God's power to protect them. One day they traveled to the town of Lystra, where there was a big temple to the false god Zeus. The people of Lystra believed Zeus was the most powerful god. They worshiped him at this temple.

2. Temple from 2 "Z"s and lines.

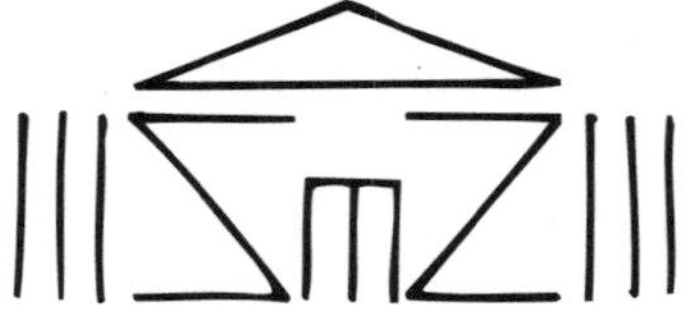

3. Paul and Barnabas began to tell the good news about Jesus. A large crowd gathered to hear them. In the crowd, Paul saw one man who was crippled. He had NEVER been able to walk.

3. Crippled man from "O," "V"s and "W".

4. Paul called out to the lame man, "Stand up on your feet!" The lame man DID. He JUMPED up and started WALKING around! God's power healed the man. The crowd went wild with excitement!

4. Standing man from "O" and "V"s. Add amazed faces.

5. But the people didn't understand what had happened. They thought that Paul and Barnabas were really their false gods Zeus and Hermes. An old story told that Zeus and Hermes had once come to Lystra dressed as men, but no one had welcomed them except an old man and his wife. So the town had been punished!

5. Print "Zeus" and "Hermes"; add "no" slash.

6. Remembering that story, the people didn't want to make the same mistake again! They rushed off to the temple of Zeus to get the priest! Paul and Barnabas soon realized that the people planned to WORSHIP them!

6. Add "C"s for crowd to temple in #2.

7. "Stop!" yelled Paul and Barnabas. "We are just MEN, people like you! We came to tell you about the only living God, the creator of all things!" Paul told how everything good comes from God, not from idols or men.

7. Print "GOD" and "ONLY' as an acrostic.

8. Just then, the same men who had been trying to kill Paul in other cities came into Lystra. "Paul and Barnabas are troublemakers!" they said. Soon everyone in the city was so ANGRY that they began to throw rocks at Paul. When he fell down, they dragged him out of town and left him, thinking he was dead. But Paul's Christian friends found him and helped him back into town. And the very next day, Paul and Barnabas were traveling again!

8. Draw angry and sad faces; add walking stick figure with happy face.

## Conclude the Story

**Who did the people of Lystra think Paul and Barnabas were?** (The false gods Zeus and Hermes.) **What did the people in Lystra want to do? What did Paul tell them?** (He told them to worship only the one true God, the One who has done great things.)

**We know about the great things God has done, too. We can see the beautiful world God has made. And we can read about God's greatness in the Bible. God wants us to tell others about the great things He has done to help people learn about Him!**

What things distract you from God? Focus - binoculars

**Acts 16:6-40**

# Singing in Prison

## Materials

Drawing materials/equipment for teacher and each student.

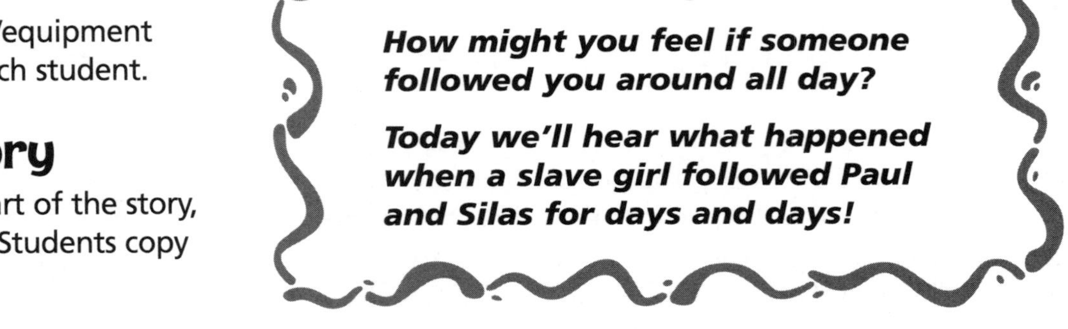

***How might you feel if someone followed you around all day?***

***Today we'll hear what happened when a slave girl followed Paul and Silas for days and days!***

## Tell the Story

As you tell each part of the story, draw each sketch. Students copy your sketches.

1. Paul and Silas had come to Philippi to tell people about Jesus. Many people had listened and had become members of God's family. A new church had been started there and things were great!

1. Draw city gates from 2 "P"s and lines; add cross.

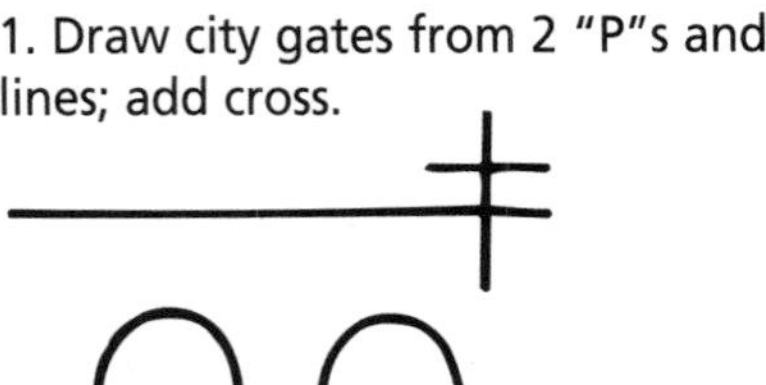

2. One day, a slave girl began to follow Paul and Silas, shouting over and over, "These men are servants of the Most High God, who are telling you the way to be saved!" There was an evil spirit in her that helped her tell people's fortunes. She made a lot of money for her owners. Finally, Paul said to the evil spirit, "Come out of her!" The spirit left. The girl's owners were ANGRY. Now they couldn't make any money from this girl's fortune-telling!

2. Shouting girl's face from "O"s; add hair from "3"s.

3. The angry men took Paul and Silas to the city leaders. They said, "They are teaching things that we think are wrong!" Other people began to shout, too. The leaders ordered the soldiers to beat Paul and Silas. They tore off Paul's and Silas's clothes and beat them with whips that cut their backs open.

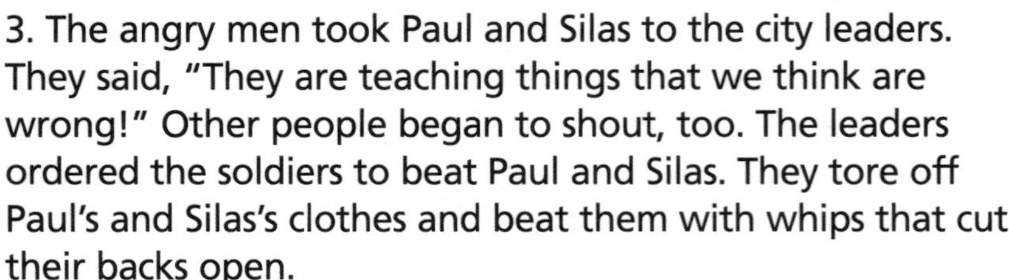

3. Angry face from 2 "V"s and "C."

4. After Paul and Silas were beaten, they were taken to JAIL. The jailer put them in a cell where he was sure they could NEVER get out! Their feet were clamped into stocks—two huge blocks of wood hinged together and locked down, with holes cut for a man's legs to go through. Paul and Silas were locked in a dirty, cold jail!

4. Print "Jail"; add lines and two faces.

5. Now, they could have complained. But what do you think they did instead? They SANG! They PRAYED! They PRAISED GOD! Even though their backs and legs must have been hurting terribly, Paul and Silas knew God was with them. And He would take care of them!

5. Make singing mouths; add music notes to jail.

6. Around midnight, the ground began to tremble and shake. God sent an EARTHQUAKE! The prison doors flew open. The chains fell off. The stocks broke apart! The jailer woke up and RAN to see what had happened. When he saw that the prison doors were open, he was going to kill himself! He was sure his prisoners had escaped. And he'd be KILLED if his prisoners got away! But Paul shouted, "DON'T HURT YOURSELF! WE'RE HERE!"

6. Earthquake from small "W"s that get larger.

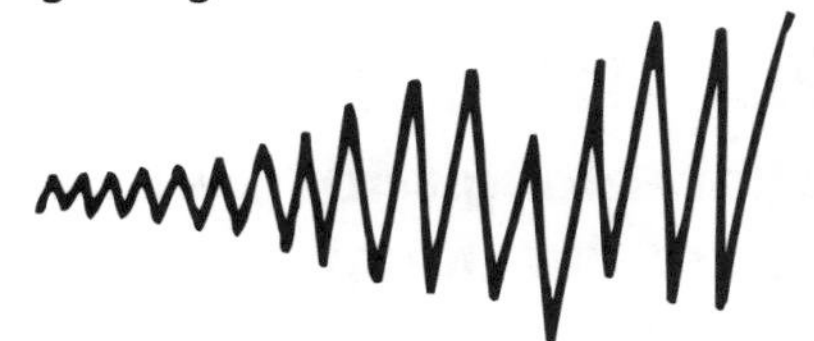

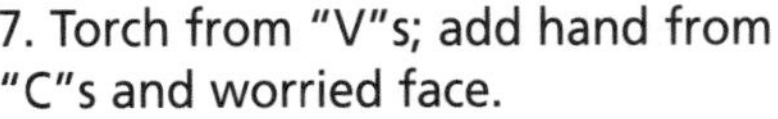

7. The jailer got a torch. He ran into Paul and Silas's cell. "What must I do to be saved?" he asked them. The jailer wanted to know what made them sing when they were in jail. Why didn't they run away when they had the chance? And what made them care about their jailer?

Paul and Silas told the jailer, "Believe in the Lord Jesus Christ, and you will be saved—you and all your household!"

7. Torch from "V"s; add hand from "C"s and worried face.

8. The jailer took Paul and Silas to his home and bandaged their wounds. Then he called his family and servants to listen to Paul and Silas tell about Jesus. They learned how Jesus had died to take the punishment for their sins and had come back to life again. EVERYONE in the house believed in Jesus and was baptized.

The very next morning, the city leaders found out they had made a BIG mistake to arrest and beat Paul and Silas. Paul and Silas were free again to tell people the good news about Jesus.

8. "C"s for gathered household; turn "C"s into happy faces as you finish story.

## Conclude the Story

**Why were Paul and Silas put into jail?** (Angry people told lies about them.) **What did they do in jail?** (Sang. Prayed. Praised God.)

**Sometimes we can be scared or have big problems, too. But we can thank God no matter what happens to us because we know He is always with us.**

## Acts 17:16-34

# Paul Tells About God

## Materials

Play dough (¼ cup, or 2 oz.) for each student.

## Tell the Story

**Follow along with me as we use our dough to tell today's story.**

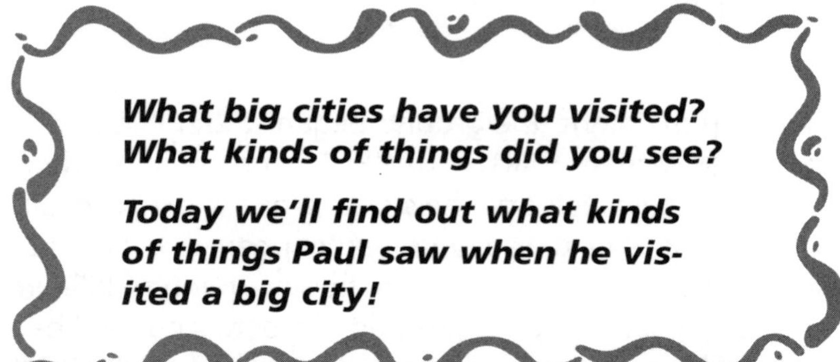
***What big cities have you visited? What kinds of things did you see?***

***Today we'll find out what kinds of things Paul saw when he visited a big city!***

1. **Make six fat cylinders for pillars. Place a rectangle on top.** The city of Athens is a big, important city. It is the capital of the country of Greece. Athens is also a very, VERY old city. Even in Bible times, the city was old! Athens was famous for its big harbor. Many ships came to Athens, bringing things to sell and bringing people, too. It was famous for its many theaters, temples and statues. Athens was also well known as a city where people came together to talk about new ideas.

One day Paul, a follower of Jesus, came to Athens. Paul had never been to this big city before. As he walked through the streets, he saw beautiful buildings. He saw theaters where plays were acted out. He saw marketplaces full of colorful things to buy. But what interested Paul MOST was the fact that there were so many statues. Most of these statues weren't meant to be only beautiful decorations. They were meant for people to PRAY to. These statues were IDOLS—false gods!

Because of all the idols in this city, Paul could see that these people DIDN'T know about the one true God. They worshiped MANY false gods. Paul felt very sad as he walked through the streets of the beautiful city. NO one seemed to have heard about Jesus, who had come to take the punishment for the sins of ALL people—even the people of Athens!

So what do you think Paul did? He started talking to EVERYBODY! Everywhere he went, he told anyone who would listen all about Jesus—about how He is God's Son who died on the cross and how He rose again so that people could be forgiven for their sins and become part of God's family.

2. **Make one or two things God has created.** Pretty soon, the news had spread all over Athens that there was a man in town who had some NEW IDEAS! A group of men who spent most of their time talking about new ideas came and listened to Paul. After they had heard Paul speak, they asked Paul to come to the Areopagus (ahr-ee-AH-puh-guhs) and talk to everyone in their group. The Areopagus was the place where the leaders of Athens met to make important decisions.

Of course, Paul went! He stood up in the meeting of these men who worshiped so many gods. Now Paul COULD have told the people that their beliefs were all wrong. He COULD have made fun of what they believed. But instead, Paul showed his respect for them by speaking kindly.

"I can see that you are very religious people," Paul said. "As I've walked around your city, I have seen statues and places to worship EVERYWHERE. I even found a place where you worship the god you call 'the unknown god.' I can tell you all about this God you don't know!

"This God made the world and everything in it. He made the trees, the mountains, the rocks and sky. He made all of us! Everything belongs to Him—the one true God.

"The one true God has a message for you: He wants you to stop sinning and do right. He has made a way for you to do this. He sent Jesus, the One He had promised to send. This same Jesus died, but God raised Jesus from the dead!"

Some people didn't want to listen to Paul's words. But when Paul left the meeting, others went with him to learn more about Jesus. It wasn't long before these people believed the good news that Jesus is God's Son who died to pay for everyone's sins and that He lives again. They became part of God's family, too! Because Paul had told the good news of Jesus by speaking gently and respectfully, God's family grew and grew in the huge and ancient city of Athens!

## Conclude the Story

**What did Paul see when he came into Athens?** (Places to worship many gods.) **What did Paul do?** (Told many people about the one true God and about Jesus.) **How did Paul act when he told the people of Athens about God?** (Gently. He showed respect for them.)

**Every day we meet people we can treat with gentleness and respect. Even when it's hard to show respect to others, God will help us be kind and show gentleness in our lives.**

**Acts 24—28**

# Paul's Shipwreck

## Materials

Drawing materials/equipment for teacher and each student.

## Tell the Story

As you tell each part of the story, draw each sketch. Students copy your sketches.

***When is a time you have told good news?***

***Today we'll hear about some ways Paul told the good news of Jesus!***

1. Paul was a prisoner now. The leaders in Jerusalem who had wanted to stop him from telling about Jesus had finally gotten him arrested. But because Paul was a Roman citizen, he received permission to sail to Rome to meet with the mighty Roman emperor.

1. Draw hull of ship from "C"s. Add details as shown.

2. At the first stop of their journey, Julius, the centurion who was to take Paul to Rome, let Paul visit friends. When the ship sailed again, the wind nearly blew the small ship off course. At the second stop, Paul and his friends and Julius got on a larger ship sailing for Italy.

2. Add mast from "+" and sails from "7"s to hull.

3. This ship was loaded with cargo and 276 passengers. As they traveled, the weather grew worse and worse! THEN the winds became BIG gusts. Waves tossed the ship from side-to-side! Day after day the storm raged. The sailors threw overboard the cargo and EVERYTHING they didn't need! But the terrible storm kept on. "We're going to die!" cried the sailors.

3. Add lines for wind and "C"s for waves.

4. But Paul had good news! "Don't be afraid," Paul said. "God has promised we'll all be safe." As the ship began to break apart, everyone jumped overboard and swam or floated to land! The ship was gone and the cargo had sunk, but everyone was safe—just as God had promised and Paul had told them.

4. Add stick figures to water.

5. Paul and his shipmates landed on an island. The people of the island kindly built a fire while Paul gathered wood. A very poisonous snake darted out of the pile of wood in Paul's hand and bit him. But the snake's poison didn't hurt Paul at all. Everyone was amazed!

5. Fire from "X" and "V"s. Add snake from "S".

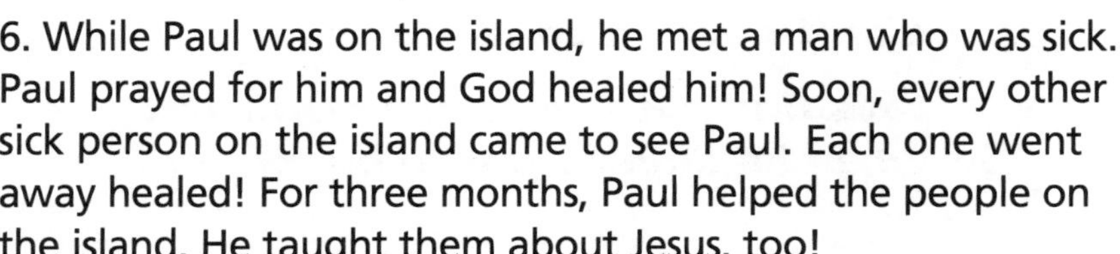

6. While Paul was on the island, he met a man who was sick. Paul prayed for him and God healed him! Soon, every other sick person on the island came to see Paul. Each one went away healed! For three months, Paul helped the people on the island. He taught them about Jesus, too!

6. Praying hands from "U"s and "I"; add face.

7. When spring came, it was time to sail for Rome. After several stops, Paul and his traveling companions arrived in Rome. Even though he was still a prisoner, Paul was not thrown into a dungeon or put into stocks. He was allowed to rent a house and a soldier was left to guard him. Paul must have told that soldier about the Lord Jesus!

7. House from rectangles, "U"s; add soldier.

8. For the next two years, Paul lived in his house and gladly welcomed everyone who came to see him. He preached and taught about Jesus, and many people believed the good news about Jesus. Paul's enemies in Jerusalem thought that by arresting Paul they were going to stop his preaching, but Paul didn't let anything stop him from sharing the good news! Now, in Rome, there were new opportunities to tell even MORE people about Jesus!

8. Add stick figures and conversation balloon to house.

## Conclude the Story

**What were some of the things that happened to Paul?** (Shipwrecked. Bit by a snake. Arrested.) **What did Paul do in each of those situations?** (Showed love for God and others. Told others about Jesus.)

**No matter what happened to him, Paul kept on telling people about Jesus. We can keep on telling about Jesus our whole lives, too, always looking for ways to share God's love with others.**

## Philemon

# Paul Helps Onesimus

## Materials

Play dough (¼ cup, or 2 oz.) for each student.

## Tell the Story

**Follow along with me as we use our dough to tell today's story.**

***Have you ever wanted to hide? Why? Where would you go if you didn't want to be found?***

***Let's find out where one man went when he didn't want to be found.***

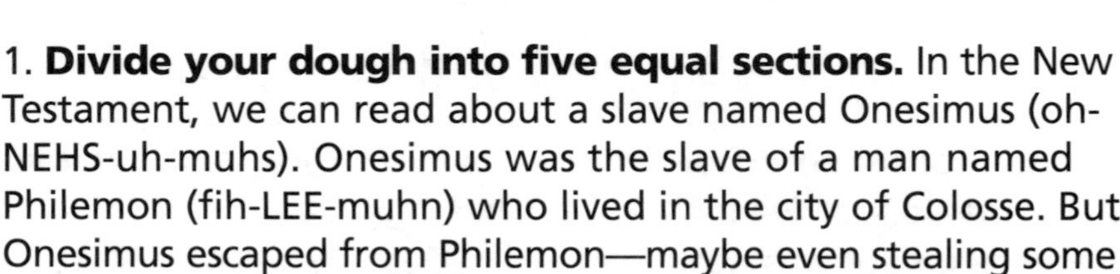

1. **Divide your dough into five equal sections.** In the New Testament, we can read about a slave named Onesimus (oh-NEHS-uh-muhs). Onesimus was the slave of a man named Philemon (fih-LEE-muhn) who lived in the city of Colosse. But Onesimus escaped from Philemon—maybe even stealing some of Philemon's money—and ran away to the big city of Rome!

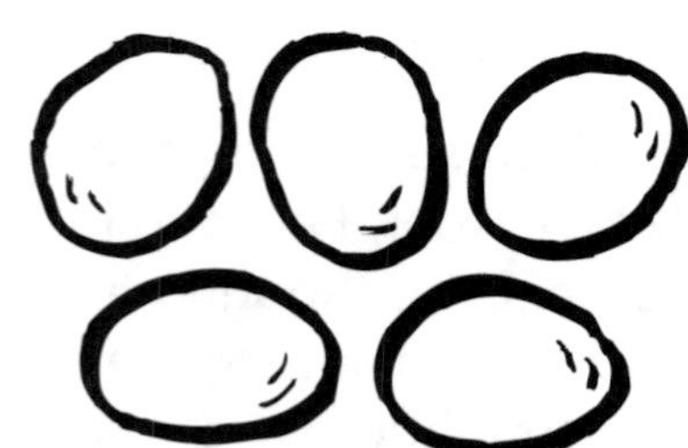

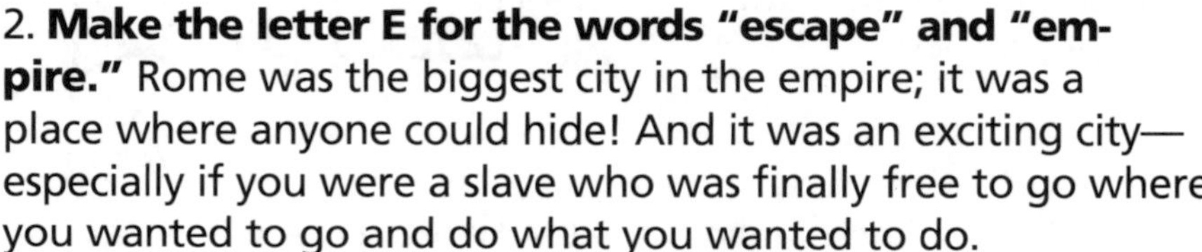

2. **Make the letter E for the words "escape" and "empire."** Rome was the biggest city in the empire; it was a place where anyone could hide! And it was an exciting city—especially if you were a slave who was finally free to go where you wanted to go and do what you wanted to do.

But Onesimus must have felt scared. He probably didn't know anyone in the city. And if he DID see someone he knew, Onesimus would have hidden! If anyone who knew Onesimus saw him, that person might tell the soldiers that they'd seen a runaway slave! Then Onesimus would be captured and sent back to his master, Philemon. Onesimus would have been severely punished. He could be sent to work in a mine, beaten, tortured or even killed!

3. **Make the letter P for the words "Paul" and "Philemon."** Somehow, Onesimus heard that Paul—the man who loved Jesus—was in Rome! Onesimus may have heard his master, Philemon, talk about Paul or Jesus, for Philemon was a follower of Jesus. No one knows exactly how Onesimus and Paul met. We only know that the two men became friends. Eventually, Onesimus told Paul what he had done.

Paul told Onesimus about Jesus. He probably told Onesimus that God loved him so much that He sent His Son, Jesus, to die to take the punishment for the wrong things he had done. Paul must have told Onesimus that if he believed in what Jesus did for him, he could trust God to forgive him.

4. **Make the letter A for the word "ask."** Onesimus asked God to forgive him, and Onesimus became a member of God's family.

The next days were wonderful. Onesimus helped Paul by doing whatever Paul asked. And all the time, Onesimus was learning more and more about God and His Son, Jesus.

Then one day Paul called Onesimus to him. "Onesimus," Paul said, "I have an idea. My friend Tychicus (TIHK-ih-cuhs) is going on a trip. He's taking a letter from me to the Christians at Colosse. And I want you to go with him."

5. **Make the letter C for the word "Colosse."** COLOSSE! Onesimus's heart jumped! A shiver of fear ran through him. Colosse was the town where Philemon, his master, lived. Paul wanted him to go back to his master!

It would be hard for Onesimus to go back to Philemon. So because Paul loved Onesimus as if he were his own son, Paul wrote a letter to Philemon. "My friend, do me a favor," Paul wrote. "Welcome Onesimus back home the same way you would welcome me." Paul even said he was willing to pay back whatever money Onesimus owed Philemon!

6. **Make another letter E for the word "encourage."** When it was time to leave, Paul handed Onesimus the letter he had written. "Don't be frightened," Paul encouraged Onesimus. "In this letter I've asked Philemon to forgive you and treat you kindly as a brother in God's family."

7. **Arrange letters to form the word "peace."** Paul's words and actions made all the difference in Onesimus's life. He helped Onesimus learn that Jesus would forgive his sins, so he could become a member of God's family. And Paul's letter helped Onesimus return home to receive forgiveness from his master, and it encouraged Philemon to forgive Onesimus so that they could live together in peace.

## Conclude the Story

**What did Paul do for Onesimus?** (Told Him about Jesus. Wrote a letter to Philemon.) **How would you describe Paul's actions?** (Paul tried to make peace between Philemon and Onesimus.) **What did Paul do to help Onesimus and Philemon learn to forgive each other?** (Paul offered to pay whatever money Onesimus owed Philemon.)

**Paul reminded Philemon of Jesus' great love and asked Philemon to treat Onesimus as a member of God's family, not as his slave. When we remember Jesus' love for all people, it helps us remember to forgive each other, make peace and encourage others to do the same!**

# James Writes About Self-Control

## Materials

Play dough (¼ cup, or 2 oz.) and paper clip for each student.

## Tell the Story

**Follow along with me as we use our dough to tell today's story.**

***What is a way words can hurt someone's feelings? What is a way words can help someone?***

***Today we'll hear about how God wants us to use our words.***

1. **Make the letter J from your dough.** James was one of the first church leaders, and many people who study the Bible believe he was a younger brother of Jesus. He wrote the book of James in the Bible. This book was written as a letter to Jews who had become Christians.

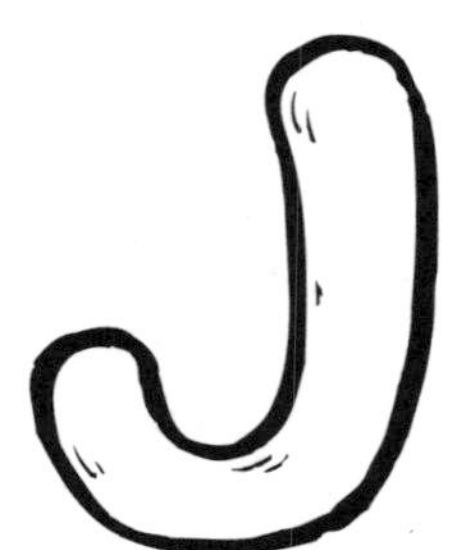

These Jewish Christians lived in many different countries and were often treated unkindly by people who did not love Jesus. They needed lots of help in knowing how to love and obey God in everyday life. James's letter can help us know how God wants us to live, too.

2. **Make a horse.** James tried to help the readers of his letter understand how important it is to control the things we say. He wrote about some things the people were familiar with. The first was a horse's bit. A bit is a small piece of metal about as thick as two pencils. The bit is put into a horse's mouth and attached to the horse's reins. The direction the horse travels is controlled by the way the rider moves the reins and the bit.

3. **Make a ship.** Next, James compares the tongue to the rudder of a ship. A ship moves through the water like a knife slicing the water. The rudder is at the back of the boat. When the rudder is held straight, the boat pushes through the water in a straight line. But when the rudder is turned to one side or the other, the boat moves in a different direction. A very small rudder can change the direction of a very big boat.

The bit and rudder are very small, but the ways in which they are used make a BIG difference! The tongue is just a small part of our bodies, but the things we say with it can make BIG differences, too.

4. **Make a large flame. Use a paper clip to draw details on the flame.** The tongue has so much power that the words we say with it affect the whole body. James compares the tongue to a small spark that can set an entire forest on fire. Just as a little spark can cause a huge, uncontrollable fire, just a few words can cause a lot of trouble! Words can be used to persuade others to do good or bad things. There have been times when people have done some extremely bad things because someone convinced them those things were okay to do. What people have said has led to anger, unfairness, prejudice, murder and even war.

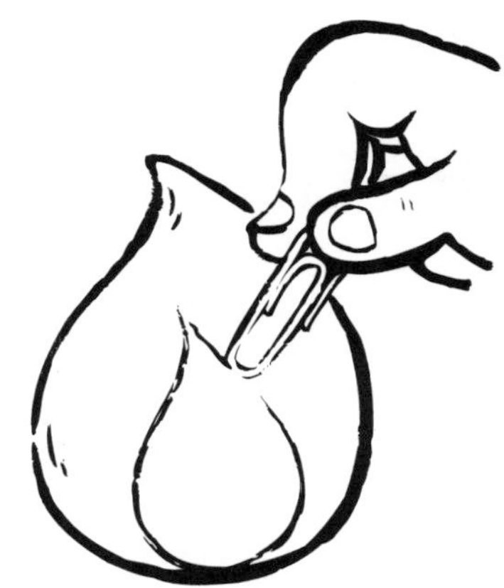

5. **Make the letters of a word God wants us to use.** James tells us that even though all kinds of animals, birds, reptiles and sea creatures can be tamed and controlled by people, we still can't control our own tongues! In fact, James says that we even use the same mouth to praise God and to say bad things to other people.

"This should not be!" says James. "We should use our tongues only to say good things." James wanted us to realize that we need God's power and love to help us control what we say. We can always count on God to help us in controlling our tongues and using our words in good ways.

## Conclude the Story

**What things does James compare the tongue to?** (A horse's bit. A ship's rudder. A spark that can start a forest fire.) **What do we need in order to learn to control our tongues and say things that are pleasing to God?** (We need to become members of God's family and ask for His help.) Be aware of students who may wish to learn more about becoming Christians. Refer to the guidelines given in the "Leading a Child to Christ" article on page 13.

**James was using his words to help others. But after reading James's instructions, it might seem like it's better not to talk at all so that we won't be tempted to say wrong things! But James believed that with God's help we can control what we say and our words can do a lot of good.**

**Matthew 27:11—28; John 18:28—19:16; Revelation 4—5**

# Jesus' Return as King

## Before the Story

Guide students to briefly practice signs for underlined words.

## Tell the Story

As you tell the story, lead students in responding as shown when you say the underlined words.

***Who are some kings you have heard about?***

***Today we're going to talk about the most important king ever!***

1. The people in Jerusalem wanted a king! They wanted a strong, powerful king who would deliver them from their hated Roman rulers. They wanted Jesus to be that king and deliverer. So when Jesus came to the city of Jersualem for the Passover celebration, crowds of people welcomed Him as a king. They waved palm branches and shouted words of praise to Him.

1. King: Right thumb between index and middle fingers; move from shoulder to waist.

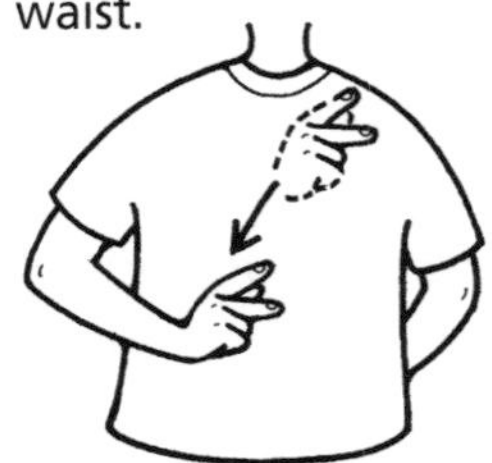

2. *Surely now,* Jesus' friends must have thought, *NOW Jesus will rescue us from the Romans.* But instead, something very different happened. A few nights later, Jesus was in a garden praying to God. With His followers gathered around Him in shock and dismay, soldiers came and arrested Jesus. The soldiers took Him away for a trial—first to the religious leaders and then to the Roman governor.

2. Soldiers: Right fist below left shoulder; left fist several inches below right.

3. Pontius Pilate was the Roman governor, or ruler, who lived in Jerusalem. It was Pilate's job to keep order among all the crowds of Jews in Jerusalem. The religious leaders who were angry at Jesus and jealous of His popularity brought Jesus to Pilate because they wanted Pilate to order Jesus to be killed!

3. Killed: Point right finger; twist and move under left hand.

4. With His hands tied in chains, Jesus stood before Pilate in the magnificent palace where Pilate lived. Pilate had listened to Jesus' accusers saying that Jesus claimed to be the King of the Jews.

"Are You the king of the Jews?" Pilate asked Jesus.

"Is that what you yourself think?" Jesus asked. "Or is that just what you've heard others say about Me?"

4. Asked: Touch palms in front; move hands to body.

5. Pilate decided to ask another question: "What have you done—why were you arrested?" Jesus decided to answer Pilate's question by explaining what it meant to say that He is the King. He said, "My kingdom isn't like the kingdoms on this earth." Jesus wanted Pilate to understand that His kingdom didn't have a palace, or soldiers or laws that people had to obey. Jesus' kingdom was for everyone who believed in the truth about God.

5. Question: Outlne a question mark with right index finger.

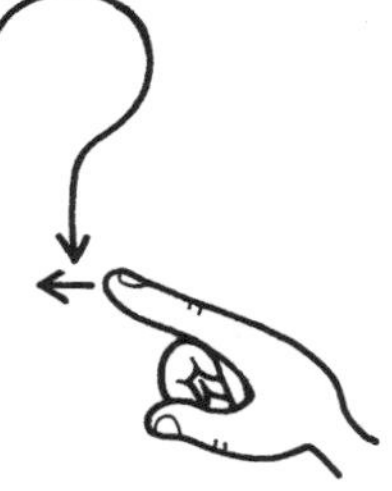

6. Jesus' words confused Pilate! But even though Pilate couldn't find anything wrong with Jesus' actions or words, he still agreed to have Jesus put to death by crucifixion. Jesus was taken by the Roman soldiers, nailed to a cross and died. Pilate probably thought that was the end of Jesus and that His claim to be a king was false!

6. Cross: Move curved right hand down; then from left to right.

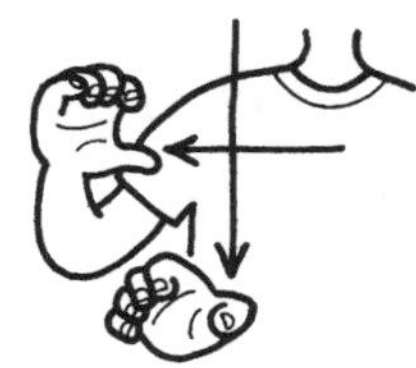

7. But we know that the story of Jesus has a much different ending! On the third day after Jesus died, He came back to life! Jesus visited His friends many times. Jesus' friends may have STILL been hoping that Jesus would free them from the Romans. But Jesus knew that God's plans for Him were much bigger than His friends believed. So Jesus told them more about why He had died and come back to life again and what God wanted His friends to do. Then it was time for Jesus to leave His friends.

7. Jesus: Touch palms with opposite middle fingers.

8. The Bible tells us that right now Jesus is in heaven. He is Ruler and King over all the earth. Some day Jesus will come back and everyone in all creation will kneel down before Jesus and declare that He is Lord. In heaven, people from every nation praise Him in every language there is! Jesus is the King of everything—on earth and in heaven. And because He died to take the punishment for our sins and rose again, we can be part of His family and know Him as our King!

8. King: Right thumb between index and middle fingers; move from shoulder to waist.

## Conclude the Story

**Why did the people in Jerusalem want a king?** (To free them from the Romans.) **What did Pilate ask Jesus?** (If He was really a king.) **How did Jesus show that He was the true King?** (By dying on the cross and coming back to life.)

**The kings on earth we hear or read about may have lots of power. But Jesus is more powerful and mighty than any earthly king. Because Jesus is God's Son sent as the King over all the earth, we can worship Him now and forever!**

# Scripture Index

# Storytelling Technique Index

## Drawing

## Play-Dough Sculpting

## Signing

# Topical Index

## Forgiving Others



## Giving to God



## Giving to Others



## God's Care



## God's Forgiveness



## God's Love

## God's Power



## God's Presence



## God's Promises



## God's Word

## Loving God



## Loving Others



## Obeying God



## Talking to God

## Telling Others About God



## Thanking God



## Worshiping God